Fledgling Days

Fledgling Days

EMMA FORD

THE OVERLOOK PRESS
WOODSTOCK • NEW YORK

First published in the United States in 1999 by
The Overlook Press, Peter Mayer Publishers, Inc.
Lewis Hollow Road
Woodstock, New York 12498

Library of Congress Catalog-in-Publication Data

Ford, Emma.
Fledgling days : memoir of a falconer / Emma Ford
p. cm.
1. Falconry--England--Kent--Anecdotes. 2. Falconers--England--Kent--Biography.
3. Ford, Emma. I. Title.
SK321.F68   1999
99-10818
799.2'32'094223--dc21

Manufactured in the United States of America

Originally published in Great Britain by John Murray Ltd.

ISBN: 0-87951-947-9

1 3 5 7 9 8 6 4 2

Fledgling Days

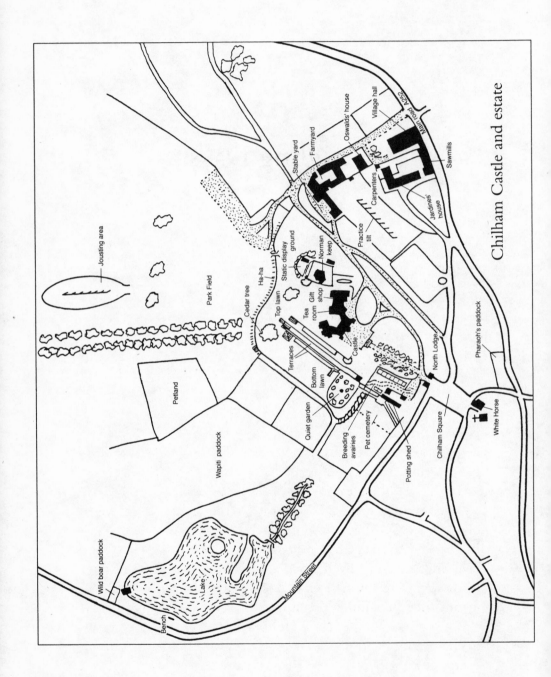

Chilham Castle and estate

1

A WISP OF BLACK wool nestled in the folds of a scarlet mohair shawl. Intrigued, I touched it tentatively with a finger and a tiny black snout emerged. Coal-black eyes regarded me briefly before the head was withdrawn into the cosy depths of the shawl. Disappointment welled up inside me. This wasn't a dog – not a proper dog.

A month ago, my parents had announced their divorce and the world had crashed about my ears. At the age of eight, I was left with only the memories of our family home. Each night as I lay in bed, during those moments between wakefulness and sleep, I saw images of our big, rambling house, of playing with the St Bernard puppies in the garden and hugging my father on the stairs when he came home from the office just before bedtime. In the morning, I woke to the chilly reality of my new home – a small cottage with three unheated bedrooms, on the outskirts of the village of Chilham in Kent.

My mother and I lived alone now. The only vestiges of our former life were my tabby cat, Lucy, six bald-headed tumbler pigeons and a handful of furniture which we had brought with us from Medlar House. My older brother Charlie was away at boarding school and my beloved St Bernard puppies had been sent back to their breeder. The infrequent occasions when I saw my father were now described as 'access'. In the throes of all this upset and upheaval, I had been pinning my hopes on the promise of a puppy. It was a bitter blow to be presented with a poodle.

For as far back as I could remember, I had rescued sick and injured wildlife. My bedroom at Medlar House frequently resembled a cross between a small-animal practice and a children's zoo. Appreciating my passion for animals, my mother desperately hoped that the poodle she had bought for me would compensate for the loss of Porgy and Bess, the St Bernards, whom I missed terribly. However I could see no potential whatsoever in Bella, as she was later christened, as a future companion to accompany me in my rambles around the countryside. I couldn't even imagine her fetching a stick.

'We simply don't have the room for a big dog here,' my mother tried to explain. 'Poodles are very intelligent and loyal. Give her a chance.'

On my return from school each evening over the next couple of weeks, I attempted to form some sort of attachment to Bella, but in those early days she spent most of her time sleeping in her basket, waking only to pick delicately at a bowl of freshly chopped ox-heart, or to shiver miserably in the garden when it was time for her to go out. She seemed totally devoid of the playfulness of the average puppy: even Lucy, who had played endlessly with Porgy and Bess, treated her with disdain.

I had inherited my love of animals from my mother. At the age of thirty-six, tall, slim, dark-haired and elegant, she had a manner which fluctuated between vague and anxious. In the aftermath of a fifteen-year marriage to my father, she had plenty of concerns of her own, yet she understood that more than anything else, animals would help me make the adjustment to our new life. In the evenings, she and I would sit with our supper in front of a roaring fire and she would tell me stories of the animals she had kept over the years since her own childhood.

All her dogs had been very badly behaved. The worst ever was a bull terrier called Buster, whom she had given to my father as a wedding present. Looking at pictures of Buster, as he leered evilly from the pages of the family photo album, bow-legged and four-square to the wind, it was easy to imagine him behaving atrociously.

My favourite photo showed Buster in the garden of Hillside, my parents' first home. Built of mellow brick, it was a three-storied house with a creeper-covered barn to one side and a sheltered walled garden at the rear, with wide herbaceous borders and a pond.

When she chose Buster, my mother was warned by the breeder that he was an unruly puppy, the worst behaved, most independent of the litter. Looking at him, though, she hadn't been able to resist him. He had long white stockings stretching up his front legs, brindle patches over both eyes and a brindle body with a small white tip to his tail. His ears flopped over at the corners, creating an impression of puppyish innocence belied only by his smug grin. It was love at first sight and my mother took him home with a large red bow knotted around his neck.

Installed in a warm basket next door to the stove in the large, flag-stoned kitchen at Hillside, Buster settled in straight away. At this stage he was too small to climb the big steps which led up to the back door, but he rambled cheerfully round the kitchen, mouthing the legs of the old wooden table and shaking his blanket in a display of mock viciousness. My father was enchanted with him.

As Buster grew, so his capacity to cause trouble grew with him. He learned to use his paws to open all the internal doors, which had no locks, and this gave him unchaperoned access to the entire house. He chewed indiscriminately: clothes, shoes, furniture and curtains all fell victim to his strong jaws. Even in the garden he managed to seek out trouble. Eyeing up washing on the clothes-line from a distance, he would back off into the furthest flower bed. Then, emerging from the foliage like an

3

express train, he would charge down the garden and take a flying leap at the clothes on the line. Latching on to a garment, he would swing by his teeth, his jaws set in a grotesque grin of pleasure, until he could hold on no longer. As his teeth developed, he was also able to chew the bottoms off the clothes and would go down the line like a circular saw, decimating garment after garment.

One morning my mother saw him flash past the large drawing-room window completely shrouded in a lacy pink négligé. The négligé had been her first wedding anniversary present from my father and she was livid to see Buster parading around the garden with it, towing it through the mud. She rushed outside and gave chase. She pursued him for twenty minutes before she managed to retrieve it, tattered and filthy.

Over the years, although they both doted on him, my parents were forced to admit that the breeder had been right, Buster really was a handful. When scolded, he would slink into the back of an armchair and put his head backwards through his front paws, kicking his hind legs straight up the back of the chair, so that his tummy was facing outwards. He would then roll his eyes in opposite directions. My mother said the effect was so comical that they simply couldn't stay cross with him for long.

Buster was lethal with cats and with other dogs but, with a few exceptions, he loved people and welcomed visitors to the house with enthusiasm. One morning he was outside sunning himself in the garden, lying with his back legs stretched straight out behind him, when he saw guests arrive in the drawing-room. Eager to introduce himself, he raced down the garden, leaped into the air and crashed straight through the drawing-room window in a shower of glass. Incredibly, he suffered only a single tiny cut on the end of his nose.

There was the odd person he didn't like. A state of mutual antipathy existed between Buster and my mother's plump daily woman, Mrs Branch. She arrived each day around noon, puffing up the hill on her old Raleigh bicycle. Buster greeted her with much barking and bluster and she wheeled her bicycle straight at him, cursing and forcing a passage to the kitchen door.

Once she was in the house, Buster would change tactics. He followed her around, watching her every move. When he got too close, she would flick her duster at him, which he hated. While she washed the kitchen floor, he disappeared into the garden, invariably returning just as she had finished, his paws covered in mud. As she completed cleaning each room, he galloped around it, raising dust and scattering books and papers in his wake.

'Its that dawg or me!' Mrs Branch threatened, in her broad Kentish accent.

My mother defended him stoutly, but it wasn't only Mrs Branch who disliked Buster. My great-aunt Pauline used to refer to him as 'that damn dog'. She visited rarely, but when she did, she was woundingly critical of the household in general and of Buster in particular.

On her first visit to Hillside, Aunt Pauline inspected the whole house and was scathing about the quality of the furniture, the majority of which my mother had picked up in local auctions. The only item which she admired was a *petit point* footstool. One day, in the hopes that she would find less to criticize in the countryside, my mother decided to take her out for a picnic. To keep the peace, Buster was left behind in the kitchen.

On their return several hours later, my mother, knowing that Buster normally saved his most spectacular party-pieces for the people who disapproved of him most, entered the house nervously. They went into the drawing-room to find it covered in straw. In the centre of the room lay Buster, grinning manically, with the last vestiges of shredded *petit point* dangling damply from his jaws.

Nothing was sacred. Just when they thought that he couldn't possibly dream up anything new, Buster came up with another stunt. As my mother arrived home from shopping one day, he greeted her at the gate. She only had to look at his face to know that this time, he had done something really wicked. He was grinning from ear to ear.

She had been out all morning. It was a hot day and the back door had been left open so that Buster could either sun himself in the garden, or seek shade in the cool of the kitchen. In her absence, Buster had become bored. Roaming around the garden, he discovered a hose pipe, which had been left running into the fish pond. He plucked the hose out of the pond and with his teeth he pulled it across the garden towards the house.

By tugging the hose, without a single kink, Buster managed to pull it round three corners and tuck the last couple of inches over the lip of the kitchen door, allowing the water to cascade down the steps into the kitchen. My mother arrived at the back door and gazed in horror at the foot or so of water which was by then lapping the second step. Buster launched himself cheerfully into the middle of it, splashing about and wagging his tail vigorously. At that moment Mrs Branch arrived and peered over my mother's shoulder.

'That dawg's a bleeding menace!' she announced sourly.

For once, my mother had been forced to agree with her.

As memories of Medlar House faded to a series of disparate snapshots, my days at Chilham began to fall into a routine. In the mornings, my mother drove me to school in nearby Ashford. After she picked me up at the end of the day, I used to rush through my homework and head outdoors to explore.

Endowed with a picture-postcard charm, Chilham sat astride a hill, with a square at the apex and four roads, one from each corner, sloping gently downwards, clustered with attractive houses and terraced cottages. The main gates leading to Chilham Castle stood at one end of the square, flanked by their gate houses, and opposite them lay the parish church and the White Horse pub. In the square, where residents jostled for parking space with the summer influx of sightseers and day-trippers, there were a couple of antique shops and the Copper Kettle tearooms. Two old fashioned butchers, the village shop, a tiny post office and Baldock's the garage made up the remainder of the village.

Our cottage, Carpenters, nestled at the foot of the hill. Half-timbered like the majority of the village, it had taken its name from the estate carpenter, by whom it had originally been built. Inside, it smelled of polish and old oak. It featured some beautiful wood, including an oak staircase and a little gallery with a window seat that overlooked the castle stable block and paddocks beyond. Outside, it was surrounded by a fine old-fashioned cottage garden, with borders which became a blaze of colour in the spring and summer months. A small rockery sprouted wild strawberries and a large bed of richly scented catmint, which was flattened regularly by Lucy, who rolled in it luxuriously when it was in flower.

The garden housed a small brick potting-shed, with a dovecote in the roof. A stone wall ran from this shed down one side of the garden. On the opposite side, a wooden fence divided us from the grounds of a large empty house and the old estate sawmills. A short distance away there was another unoccupied farmhouse. The three houses stood alone, backing on to the castle estate and screened from the road by the village hall, a rambling Elizabethan building which came alive at weekends, when it hosted a variety of activities ranging from scout camps to church youth club discos.

The sawmills on the edge of the estate were partially derelict. Each evening I disappeared into these old buildings to explore, with Lucy trotting behind, tail erect and whiskers bristling with curiosity. There were no other children of my own age to play with, but I was happy in my own company, climbing over fallen rafters and picking my way through broken glass. A section of roof had collapsed and from this Kent peg tiles spilled on to the ground in untidy heaps. In the areas under cover, the earth had a strange texture, it was soft, dry and fine, like grey flour. In damp areas, mushrooms and toadstools thrived: red, spotty ones, cone-shaped ones with blue-black shaggy edges and huge puff-balls, which, when dried out, collapsed when I stamped on them, in an explosion of brilliant yellow smoke.

Fireweed, with its shocking pink flower, covered most of the site and a profusion of wildlife inhabited the nooks and crannies. Feral cats, which had left behind a life of domesticity in the village, stalked the ruins. When we encountered one, rather to my disappointment, Lucy showed no signs of wanting to make its acquaintance. Instead, she turned up her little pink nose and ignored it; but, I noticed, she stuck close by my side until it had made itself scarce. By turning over tiles and rooting through the debris I unearthed frogs, toads and slow worms, which Lucy variously batted with a paw or hissed at. I returned from these adventures dirty but happy, with a handful of wild flowers or some dodgy-looking mushrooms, which were relegated to the bin.

As Bella grew, I began to realize that my initial thoughts about her had been unjust. She was a game little dog who, contrary to my early fears, accompanied me enthusiastically on my outdoor adventures. When I cycled, she travelled in my bicycle basket, front paws propped on the lip of the basket and ears trailing back in the wind. She was obedient and I trained her to a reasonable standard. To my surprise, she could jump like a stag and was soon able to clear the three-and-a-half-foot garden wall with inches to spare. She chased every cat in the district with the exception of Lucy and a huge black tomcat which lived in the sawmills. This victim refused to run, despite Bella's best efforts to the contrary. As she tore up to it, the cat merely sat and looked at her and she was forced to screech to a halt in front of it. There was a brief moment of Mexican stand-off, before Bella sloped ignominiously away. When bad weather prevented Bella and me from venturing outside, I occupied my time by building a course of 'jumps' indoors, blocking every doorway with a fireguard, a deck chair on its side or some similar barrier. The construction completed, I tore through the cottage hurdling the jumps with Bella keeping pace at my heels.

8

During Bella's first six months in the household, Lucy had a litter of kittens. A box was arranged for her in the bathroom, next to the airing-cupboard. Although she was still a puppy herself, Bella took a curiously maternal interest in the kittens. She spent hours on her hind legs, her front paws propped on the edge of the box, peering in at Lucy and her family. In due course, she started to chew the cardboard, and in a few days had managed to eat away the front of the box so that she could stand on all four paws and rest her chin on the chewed edge.

Like all mothers, Lucy periodically needed a break from her charges. Rising to her feet and stretching, she left the box and strolled downstairs to spend an indulgent five minutes on her own. On her return, she was not at all happy to find Bella inside the box, curled up with the kittens. Bella was ejected unceremoniously and, with a small red cut on the end of her nose, she resumed her vigil at the edge of the box.

The next time Lucy left the box, she returned to find one of her kittens missing. Bella had picked it up gently in her mouth and made off with it on to the landing, where she lay, cradling the kitten between her front paws, clearly entranced with it. Not wishing to be on the receiving end of another swipe from Lucy's claws, she backed off as Lucy approached to retrieve the kitten. Thereafter kitten-napping became Bella's chief occupation and the long-suffering Lucy would constantly have to follow her around the house in order to recover her family.

On a wet afternoon in May, two months after we had arrived at Carpenters, I walked home from the bus, which dropped me off from school on the far side of the village square. My mother had gone to visit my aunt in Suffolk the previous day and was due home that evening. I had spent the intervening night with a school friend. Recently, I had taken the bus to and from school quite often, as our ancient Morris Minor was becoming increasingly unreliable. In an attempt to encourage it to start in the mornings, my mother ran a cable with a sixty-watt light bulb out of the dining-room window, across the garden and under the bonnet. This Heath Robinson contraption was switched on every night, in the hope that it would provide the warmth necessary to encourage the engine to fire up the next morning.

It was through this curious device that my mother had come to exchange her first words with Lord Massereene and Ferrard, who owned Chilham Castle and the surrounding estate. We had already heard quite a lot about him, apparently he was the most titled peer in Britain. He was widely known as 'Lord Masserati and Fast Car' due to the fact that he had raced at Le Mans in 1937.

We had been eagerly awaiting our first sighting of him and our patience was rewarded when he passed by Carpenters late one afternoon and stopped to look at the Morris with its trailing cable.

'Are you afraid it's going to run away?' he called across the wall to my mother, who was gardening, hindered by me and Bella.

We were more amused by his appearance than his sense of humour. He was the archetypal personification of the British aristocracy, tall, thin and distinguished-looking, but slightly dishevelled. He sported a pair of cavalry twill jodhpurs with a split in the knee, and a shapeless tweed jacket covered in dog hair. Sticking to his chin there was a smidgen of bloodstained loo paper. In the years which followed, we came to realize that although its precise position varied, this adornment more or less amounted to a permanent fixture. Barra, his overweight yellow labrador, walked at heel. Lord Massereene rarely started or finished a sentence, instead he had an annoying habit of delivering the middle part whilst staring vacantly into the distance, so you were never quite certain if he was talking to you or addressing somebody who had appeared behind you.

I was thinking about Lord Massereene as I hurried through the rain that evening. I wanted to get his permission to birdwatch on the estate and to look for badgers. So far, my knowledge of Chilham and its environs was limited to the space between home turf and the bus stop at the far side of the village.

I was anxious to expand my horizons. The castle estate beckoned, but I didn't know how to approach Lord Massereene to gain his permission. To my disappointment, my association with Chilham's wildlife to date had been limited to the inhabitants of the sawmills and so far nothing sick or injured had required my ministrations.

It was ironic, therefore, that I should arrive home that evening to find a large cardboard box, liberally punctured with air holes, waiting for me on the kitchen table. Cautiously, I lifted the lid and peered inside. A pair of huge, liquid eyes, fringed with eyelashes which would have done justice to a supermodel, peered up at me. The owner of the eyes snapped its beak several times in quick succession. With delight, I recognized it as a young tawny owl.

Whilst my mother was in Suffolk, a tree adjacent to my aunt's garden, containing a tawny owl nest hole, had been felled. My mother had rescued the diminutive owlet and brought it home for me. We dubbed him 'Whitney', after his home village of Whitnesham. He could only have been a couple of weeks old. He amounted to no more than a tiny ball of thistledown, armed with two sets of needle-sharp talons, which peeked from beneath his fluffy bloomers.

We quickly discovered that Whitney's innocent appearance belied an enormous capacity for causing trouble. He couldn't stay loose in the house while I was at school, so with amateurish carpentry skills, we turned a rustic children's playhouse, left behind in the garden by the previous occupants of Carpenters, into suitable quarters for a small owl. With mesh over the window and the top half of the stable door and a couple of perches, it kept him out of harm's way until I returned from school and brought him into the kitchen.

Each evening as I attempted to do my homework, Whitney would explore his new surroundings with a glint of mischief in his seductive brown eyes. He was not yet able to fly, but he could shin up the curtains, using a combination of beak and talons.

Once he reached the worktops he stood, head swaying from side to side, until he focused on some object which he deemed worthy of closer inspection. Stalking the object, he would pounce on it with glee. Whatever it was – some item of cutlery or a kitchen utensil – would inevitably crash to the ground.

When Whitney got bored with this game, he came over to where I was working and tugged at my hair with his beak, clambering up my arm and on to my shoulder. From this vantage point, he peered short-sightedly at my homework, before leaping off into the middle of my books, leaving little shards of feather sheath and fluff in his wake.

Shortly after Whitney's arrival, I was unwise enough to leave him alone in the kitchen for a short time. In my absence, he came across a bag of mushrooms. I was only gone for about five minutes, but when I came back I found Whitney with his head inside the brown paper bag. He had eaten at least half the contents.

I was horrified. Tawny owls are purely meat eaters and I was sure that consuming a quarter of a pound of mushrooms would do him no good at all. I called my mother, who was equally aghast and we decided that we needed to rid his system of the mushrooms as rapidly as possible. We wrapped him, protesting loudly, in a tea towel and with the aid of an eye dropper, syringed a healthy dose of liquid paraffin down his throat.

That night, we decided that Whitney had better stay indoors. We carefully cleared away anything remotely breakable in the kitchen and retired to bed, knowing that we could do no more for him. In bed, I tossed and turned uneasily. It was suspiciously quiet downstairs – no crashes or bangs – and I began to fear that the mushrooms had been his undoing and that I would find him dead in the morning.

In the small hours, I could stand it no longer. I crept downstairs and peered anxiously round the kitchen door. It was still too dark to see clearly, but I was instantly struck by a revolting smell. I switched on the light and was relieved to see Whitney,

rudely awakened from a doze, with one eye half open, perched on a pelmet.

Delight at finding Whitney alive was tempered with horror at the carnage which surrounded him. The entire kitchen and every appliance therein was plastered in owl droppings. Smelly at the best of times, these droppings, laced with large quantities of partially digested mushrooms and expelled forcibly with the aid of liquid paraffin, plumbed new depths of vileness. Everywhere – the curtains, the cooker, even the radio – was decorated with a slimy, foul-smelling little pile. Recoiling in horror, I turned off the light and crept back to bed where I remained until I was awakened to my mother's grief at the state of her kitchen and the singularly unpleasant task of cleaning up the mess before school.

I had a few friends at Ashford School whom I saw at weekends and occasionally during weekday evenings, but I didn't have a particularly close friend in whom I confided. Tall for my age, and quiet, like my mother, I worked hard at my studies, but lived for the evenings and weekends when I was reunited with my small menagerie. All of my school essays were about Whitney, Bella and Lucy, regardless of the subject set, and as word got around that I had an unusual pet, I received a request from a family of four girls who lived locally, asking if they could come and see Whitney one evening after school. Our mothers duly spoke on the telephone and arranged for the girls to come to tea the following day.

Thrilled to have a chance to show Whitney off, I waited impatiently for school to end that day. The girls' mother collected us from school and in the car on the way home, I told them all about Whitney, promising that they could stroke him and even try to hold him, if he'd sit still. Arriving home, I collected my glove, ran down the garden with the four girls following behind, and picked Whitney up from his perch in the playhouse.

To my amazement and disgust, they were frightened of him. Even Jane, the eldest, who was eleven and rather superior, didn't want to hold him. I simply could not understand why they were so nervous. Whitney gave them the benefit of his full repertoire, weaving and bobbing his head and walking crab-like up my arm and on to my shoulder, but they didn't even want to stroke him.

'He won't bite,' I told them. 'Look, he's really sweet.'

'He might have fleas,' Jane warned the others, hanging back.

I was deeply insulted. To my mother's annoyance, I lapsed into silence over tea, while they stuffed themselves with jam scones and chocolate biscuits. When they left, I got into terrible trouble for being rude. I decided I didn't want anyone else to see Whitney. In future, I vowed to keep my friends separate from my animals.

I was still smarting from this incident when, a week later, a removal van arrived at the farmhouse next door and the old house suddenly became a hive of activity. Burning with curiosity, I crept through the undergrowth and peered cautiously over the wall. To my astonishment, I came eyeball to eyeball with a falcon.

2

I KNEW IT WAS a falcon from its streamlined shape and the characteristic dark stripe beneath its eyes, but I didn't have a clue
what species it was. It had a blue-grey back, a cream chest finely
streaked with dark brown and a striking chestnut-pink crown to
its head. Dark eyes returned my stare unwaveringly.

For quite some time I was transfixed. Then, as if drawn by a
magnet, I climbed over the wall and sat cautiously in the grass
beside it. It didn't seem overly perturbed by my presence. I
hadn't been there very long before a short, sandy-haired man
approached me. He introduced himself as Allan Oswald.

'I'm a falconer,' Allan told me. 'I'm taking up the position as
falconer here on the estate for Lord Massereene.'

'What sort of falcon is this?' I asked, overawed by the news
that we were getting a falconer as a neighbour.

'She's a lanner falcon called Cindy,' he informed me. 'As you're
a neighbour you'd better come and meet the rest of the family.'

The rest of the family consisted of Allan's wife, Ann, and their
two sons, Simon, who was six years old and Michael, who was
eleven, plus an Afghan hound called Gelert, a tabby cat called
Tatty Mog and – to my delight – a tawny owl called Fred and a
huge Imperial Eagle called Bugsy. Bursting with all this news, I

left the family to settle in and rushed home to update my mother.

Thereafter I spent all my spare time next door. Allan started to build up his collection of birds in preparation for displaying them in the grounds of the castle. Two young kestrels arrived in a box from Scotland, as tiny grey balls of down. They were closely followed by an American Redtailed Buzzard and a goshawk. The Redtail was a cream-chested bird, with a four-foot wingspan, powerful feet and a vivid chestnut tail. The goshawk was the most menacing of all the hawks, with a grey back, a white chest tightly barred with dark grey and fiery orange eyes, which blazed in annoyance at my timid approach. I helped out as much as I was allowed to – scrubbing the mews where the hawks were kept, gutting game to feed to them and helping to clear junk from the outbuildings adjacent to the house, to make room for a workshop.

When it was completed, the workshop contained a lot of complicated-looking machinery, which Allan told me was for making perches for the hawks to sit on. The walls of the workshop were adorned with colourful lengths of rope, gloves and other curious items of equipment made from leather and what appeared to be bundles of feathers. Allan spent a lot of time in the workshop, making bits and pieces, and I joined him whenever I could, full of questions.

'What are these?' I asked, pointing to the feathers.

'They're called lures,' Allan told me. 'They're used to train hawks how to hunt – they're made from the wings of their prey.'

'Don't hawks know how to hunt already?' I was puzzled.

'It's not that simple,' Allan tried to explain. 'Some hawks I get have never hunted in the wild, and even if you do get a hawk which knows how to hunt, you have to teach it what sort of game you want it to catch for you. That's where the lure comes in: if you want your hawk to catch a pheasant, you use pheasant wings on the lure.'

I was still confused. Allan lent me a book called *Falconry for You* which only sparked more questions. I seemed to be much more enthusiastic about the hawks than were either of Allan's sons and he responded to my endless questions with kindness and patience.

In my eagerness to learn, I swept up the piles of wood shavings from the stone floor of the workshop and generally performed any task which would bring me a step closer to the birds themselves. I got up early to help before school in the mornings and rushed home each evening, gobbled my tea and disappeared next door to spend an hour or so with Allan and the hawks, before reluctantly returning home to do my homework. My enthusiasm was rewarded beyond my wildest dreams when a new eagle arrived next door and Allan asked me if I would like to train it.

The bird was a Wahlburgs Eagle called Wally. He was the colour of plain chocolate all over, with lighter brown eyes, legs feathered to the ankle and powerful yellow feet, the span of my hand. With the exception of Bugsy, he was the largest bird in the collection, standing about two feet high from foot to crown.

I was totally in awe of Wally. I simply couldn't believe that I was to train an eagle, I'd have been happy with a kestrel. Despite his size, I wasn't at all nervous of him. At first, he seemed very nervous of me, so I sat by his perch for hours at a time, trying to win his confidence. His flecked brown eyes betrayed anxiety and fear, he had a hunted look. More than anything else I wanted to see that look replaced by one of trust. I felt I was privileged to be close to him and this feeling inspired endless patience. As I sat in the grass beside him, we stared at each other and, almost imperceptibly, a relationship started to form between us.

After a while, Allan allowed me to pick Wally up on to my glove. Although I was tall for an eight year old, Wally dwarfed me. Perched on my gloved hand, his eyes were level with mine. His sheer bulk was overwhelming. He felt dauntingly heavy, but I was determined not complain lest he was taken away from me. For the main part, he would sit stock still, staring fixedly into my eyes, sensitive to my slightest movement. If I moved a muscle, he bated, launching himself off the glove in a panic, only to be pulled up short by the restraining jesses.

Despite Wally's size, I instinctively felt that he wouldn't harm me. Handling him made me feel protective towards him and I experienced the first prickings of an intense passion for this beautiful brown bird I had been entrusted with.

After a few short sessions of handling Wally in the garden, Allan allowed us to broaden our horizons by going for walks. The aim, Allan said, was to get Wally to the stage where he felt safe on my glove, regardless of our surroundings. To my delight, I was suddenly at liberty to walk across the castle estate. Early each morning before school, I collected Wally from the mews and headed up the back drive to the castle, past the stable block, across the lawns and down through the terraces towards the lake, which lay within in its own walled gardens.

The gardens at Chilham Castle had been designed by Capability Brown. The formal areas were laid out with the precision of a chess set, with three terraces, punctuated by manicured topiaries, leading down to the lake. Here there were trickling water gardens and a mixture of specimen trees, rhododendrons and wild flowers; it was my favourite part of the grounds. A bridge, with brick archways under which the water flowed, formed a narrow causeway on to an island in the middle of the lake. The island was wild and unkempt, with thick areas of vegetation which provided a nesting haven for wild duck.

Round the edge of the lake lay a path. With Wally on my glove, I followed this path every morning, past the old wooden boathouse to a rustic bench, positioned midway round the lake at the furthest point from the castle. Here, I could prop my arm on the arm of the bench and rest the aching muscles in my left hand.

Ensconced here, I watched the wildlife. As Wally relaxed, so his attempts to fly off the glove became less frequent and his gaze too was drawn by the activity on the lake. As the early morning mist cleared, a profusion of brightly coloured waterlilies and water irises came into focus. Mallard, moorhens and coots upended to feed on the weed beneath the water's surface. Ripples betrayed the presence of a carp. In a nearby clump of lilies a greater-crested grebe watched over her tiny stripy chicks, as they clambered laboriously over the large flat leaves to join her in the water. Insects droned. Dragonflies zipped over the surface of the water. The peace was punctuated only by the occasional alarm call of a moorhen, as it skidded out of reach of a bossy coot.

These early morning walks coloured my life. Gradually, my future crystallized in front of my eyes and I knew with a burning certainty that I wanted to spend the rest of my life in the countryside, with a hawk on my hand.

Back on the home front, I was running into a problem. The supply from the mousetraps I had set up in the sawmills was beginning to be outpaced by Whitney's demand for food. He was growing in front of my eyes and his appetite was growing with him.

He was large enough now to swallow a mouse in a couple of gulps, pausing briefly for breath midway, before knocking back the tail. As I watched him munching his fourth mouse of the day, the idea struck me that if only I could breed my own mice, Whitney would have an ample, self-perpetuating supply.

The flaw in my plan, my mother pointed out, was that even if we purchased a pair of mice straightaway, they would not produce baby mice the very next day. Whilst we were both a little hazy on the gestation period for mice, this was indeed an obvious snag.

Allan came to the rescue. He suggested telephoning a nearby research laboratory which kept mice. After my mother had over-come the difficulties inherent in explaining to a perplexed lab-oratory manager why she wanted to procure several breeding pairs of mice and a backup supply of dead ones, we set off to collect six pairs of live mice and two hundred freshly killed,

19

which I intended to freeze in packets in order to sustain Whitney until the pairs produced.

During the journey home I considered my plan for Whitney's future. I knew I couldn't keep him forever. He was nearing the time when I would have to release him to lead a natural life in the wild. Allan had told me how to go about this. The technique was to feed Whitney in the same place each day, close to his shed, then eventually to leave him out one night. Thereafter the familiar feeding point would need to be replenished on a daily basis, until such time as Whitney was fending for himself and no longer in need of supplementary rations. In the language of falconry, this process was termed 'hacking back to the wild'.

The minute the car drew up at home, I leaped out. Armed with half a dozen dead mice, I ran down the garden to Whitney's shed. As I neared the shed, my eye lighted in horror on a four-inch gap at the edge of the mesh over the window. Whitney had pushed his way out and escaped. My entire world ground to a halt. I stood with my mouth open, staring at the hole in the mesh, then I started to search the garden frantically. He couldn't fly properly yet so I was sure he wouldn't have gone far.

My mother was exasperated. She had just driven the best part of a hundred miles to collect a carload of mice for an owl which was now AWOL. With a bad grace, she accompanied me as we trudged through the adjacent fields and coppices, searching every bush and tussock. Whitney was nowhere to be seen.

After we had hunted for an hour or so, a neighbour from across the road appeared.

'You wouldn't be looking for an owl, by any chance?' he enquired. 'One flew over my garden a couple of hours ago and now it's sitting in one of the large oaks in the wood beyond.'

We rushed across the road and sure enough, there was Whitney, half-way up a thirty-foot oak tree. Our neighbour was prevailed upon to bring his tallest ladder and prop it against the tree. I started to climb the ladder.

'Get down this instant! I'm not having you break your neck.

I'll do it.' Looking at my mother's face, I decided it was better not to argue.

I watched anxiously as she climbed gingerly upwards. She had never been good at heights, but my sole concern was that she would frighten Whitney. When she was just below him, she extended a shaky hand in his direction. Whitney was unimpressed. He snapped his beak a few times before sailing into the air and alighting in an adjacent tree.

This charade was repeated, at my insistence, several more times before my mother lost her temper and gave up. We returned home owl-less and depressed. Whitney had pre-empted my rehabilitation schedule and I was desperately worried that he wouldn't survive.

Over the next few days Whitney could be heard – and sometimes seen – in the wood over the road. He easily evaded my attempts to recapture him and I reluctantly had to admit that he had rapidly mastered the art of flight, despite the fact that he still had wisps of baby down intermingled with his proper feathers. I left food out for him and it disappeared, but whether Whitney was eating it, or some other inhabitant of the woodland, I didn't know. However, months after I ceased to be able to spot him, I knew he was still alive as my neighbour grumpily reported that he never stopped hooting at night.

Disturbed nights for the neighbours were not the only post-script to Whitney's saga. The redundant pairs of mice were lodged in the potting shed, from whence they escaped and pro-liferated. The house was soon infested with white mice and even my most diligent efforts with mousetraps were no match for them. Eventually a professional firm of 'rodent operatives' had to be engaged to eradicate them and I was gravely unpopular for months to come.

3

WALLY WAS MAKING progress. I had started to reduce his
weight to get him keen for food. Each afternoon, I
weighed him on the old butcher's scales in the mews, where the
acrid smell of Jeyes fluid seemed to permeate every pore. Back
in the garden, I put him down on his perch and, holding his leash
firmly in my right hand, held a piece of meat tantalisingly just
out of his reach, between the thumb and forefinger of my gloved
hand.

Wally had been feeding from my glove for some days now, but
it was time to move on to the next stage. The aim was to get him
to jump to me for food. He craned forward, gripping the perch
tightly with his feet and snapping at the air with his beak. I
wiggled the meat with my thumb. It was a battle of wills, a question of who would give in first. The previous day, after twenty
fruitless minutes of crouching beside him, tempting him to
jump, I had relented and moved my glove closer to the edge of
his perch, allowing him to step up and eat. But today I was determined to get him to jump. Hardening my heart, I decided the
choice was his: jump or go hungry.

Wally leaned forward again, edging along the perch to see if
this would bring him closer to the meat. It didn't. Trembling

slightly from the effort of holding my arm outstretched for so long, I noticed he was drooling from his nostrils. Then, quite suddenly, he crouched, froze for an instant and leapt into the air, landing firmly on my glove. My arm dropped with the impact of his four-pound bulk. I tensed and steadied my glove, worried lest I had made him feel insecure, but he gripped my arm firmly and gulped the meat without hesitation. Lowering his head, he stared into my eyes, imploring me for more.

From then on, it was relatively plain sailing. Having taken the plunge once, Wally jumped six more times that evening, finishing his allotted ration. I had to be careful not to overfeed him, or he would make no progress the next day. The following day, Allan gave me a creance – fifty yards of nylon line tied to a stick – and I tied this to the metal swivel which secured Wally's jesses and started to extend the distance over which I called him. That evening, he jumped six feet. Allan pronounced him ready to be put on display to visitors, along with the other birds.

'You'll soon run out of space here,' he told me. 'If he's on display, you can exercise him on the castle lawns.'

I was so excited that night, I couldn't sleep. The next day was a Saturday, so without school to worry about, I planned to spend the whole day close to Wally, within the roped boundary of the display ground, in case he was frightened by the strange faces of the visitors.

Late each morning, the trained hawks were carried from the Oswalds' garden, up the back drive to the display area at the base of the Norman keep, which lay to one side of the castle. At midday on the day of Wally's first public appearance, I was permitted to carry him up the back drive. When carrying a hawk, Allan had told me always to tie its leash to my glove, lest I should inadvertently let it go. Today, however, I didn't want to appear like an amateur in front of the visitors. I was experienced now, Wally and I knew what we were doing, he rarely even bated off the glove nowadays. I coiled the leash nonchalantly through my fingers.

24

As we walked through the stable yard, with Allan in the lead carrying Bugsy, Wally, for no apparent reason, bated hard towards the tall yew trees beyond the yard wall. Taking me by surprise, he managed to jerk the jesses straight out of my fingers. With his pink leash trailing out behind, I watched in mute horror as he sailed up towards the trees, alighting unsteadily on a branch about twenty feet up.

Turning sharply at the sound of wing beats, Allan realized instantly what I had done. We both knew there was no way Wally would come back down for food: he had never flown anything like that far and had certainly never been into a tree. My heart constricted in my chest and I could scarcely breathe. I had lost Wally and Allan would never trust me again.

'Sit still and watch him!' Allan commanded. 'I'll be straight back.' As he jogged out of the yard to put Bugsy on display, I started to cry. Wally crouched, poised for action, as he scanned the branches above him, looking for a higher perch. Suddenly, he didn't look tame at all. He looked wild. I felt sure he would fly away any second.

Allan reappeared with a tall wooden ladder. 'I'm going to prop this against the tree and see if I can grab the end of the leash. Help me with it, we'll have to do it quietly or we'll spook him.'

Blinded by tears, with my breath coming in rasping gulps, I helped Allan prop the heavy ladder against Wally's tree. Wally poised himself again for flight, looking wildly upwards.

'Now back off and stay quiet,' Allan whispered. He began to climb.

I hardly dared to breathe as Allan crept closer and closer up the ladder. The leash was dangling directly beneath Wally. If Allan could just grasp it in his fingers . . . He stretched out his arm. Wally looked down and exploded off his branch. As he flew, the leash flicked over a thin branch and snagged. Wally was pulled up short, then flipped upside down against the trunk of the tree. He hung, flapping in distress, like a chicken caught by the legs.

I started forward towards the tree, but he was yards out of my

25

reach. Allan clung to the side of the ladder, threw out one arm and, with the ladder wobbling precariously, caught the leash in the tips of his fingers. Painfully slowly, he worked it into his palm. Wrapping it once round his hand, he yanked the leash free from the ensnaring branch. He then made his way awkwardly down the ladder, holding the leash out to one side until he reached terra firma, where he deposited Wally gently on the ground. Picking him up carefully, he tried to get Wally to stand on his glove, but the bird's legs seemed to have gone weak, so he ended up cradled in Allan's arms.

My relief at Wally's recovery was overwhelmed by my mortification at letting him go and the certainty that Allan would never let me touch him again. I had caused this horrible incident through my own cockiness and now Wally was badly frightened, possibly even hurt. I felt physically sick.

'You'd better take him,' Allan said gently. 'Wait here while I get the car.'

To my astonishment, he handed Wally into my arms and

walked out of the stable yard without a backward glance. Wally lay on his back looking up at me. In his eyes I thought I could discern a faint glow of recognition and trust.

Allan arrived with the car, helped us in and we drove back to the house. 'Try to get him up on the glove,' Allan said, once we were back in the garden.

I grasped the jesses with my gloved hand and with my other hand held Wally's chest until he gripped the glove with his feet. I moved my right hand away and he stood properly. He looked a little dishevelled but, incredibly, he seemed none the worse for his adventure.

'Now tie him down to his perch and leave him with his food,' Allan told me. 'He's had enough excitement for one day.'

I left Wally eating and, after apologizing over and over again to Allan, I went home and sobbed out the story to my mother. Looking at my drained, tear-stained face, she wisely sent me to bed for the afternoon where, exhausted by so much crying, I slept soundly. The next day Wally had preened out his dishevelled feathers and Allan told me I could resume his training. I had learned an important lesson: never again would I be tempted to take a risk with a hawk.

Now that Whitney had left and all the kittens had been found homes — except for one tabby and white tom kitten, called Wallis, whom we decided to keep — life at home seemed remarkably normal for a while. Lucy was spayed to prevent further families and, without the kittens to cause a rift, she and Bella settled into an uneasy *détente*. Wallis and Bella, however, were the best of buddies. They played together constantly and even shared Bella's basket. As Wallis grew, this became rather a struggle. He developed into a large, handsome cat, with a charming disposition but, as my mother pointed out, he was something of 'a sprawl' at full stretch. Bella, determined not to be displaced from her own basket, was forced to sleep squashed against one side.

One of the advantages of owning a poodle lies in the fact that they do not drop hair. Unfortunately though, they do need to be clipped at regular intervals. We always put this off for as long as possible, but when Bella began to look like a hearth rug, she had to be taken back to her breeder to be shampooed, blow-dried and shorn. This involved an hour's car journey to the home of Dorothy Reece Webb.

Dorothy was a small, wrinkled woman in her late fifties with gingery-grey hair of the sort of fluffy consistency which could have been the result of a bad perm. A heavy smoker, her fingers were stained a vivid shade of nicotine yellow. She had a sharply pointed nose and a manner to match. Bella's mother, Gigi, was Dorothy's pride and joy. Gigi was a plump, liver-coloured poodle, with a profusion of little pink warts on her muzzle and paws and a snappy nature. To a cynical observer the resemblance between Gigi and her owner was striking.

The first time we went to get Bella clipped, we were invited to lunch. My mother was offered a glass of sherry in the drawing room, in the company of Dorothy's genial, long-suffering husband, Lionel. Poodles of all shapes, sizes and colours sprawled over the furniture. While my mother struggled to find a space to sit down, I was invited to follow Dorothy into the kitchen, to assist her in the task of washing Bella in the kitchen sink.

Poodles were originally bred as gundogs in France, for the purpose of retrieving waterfowl. The name 'poodle' is a bastardized version of their former name 'puddle-hound'. Despite her lineage, Bella hated water. She stood upright on her hind paws in the sink, whinging and cringing as the beastly process got underway.

'For goodness sake, hold her still!' Dorothy admonished, as she poured cup after cup of soapy water over Bella's head. 'Watch what you're doing! She'll get soap in her eyes!'

Her own dark eyes flashed with irritation as I struggled from my perch on a rickety chair to control Bella – who was bordering on hysteria by this stage – and save myself from becoming soaked with the scummy water in the sink. Dorothy lathered and scrubbed the poor little dog energetically until she was finally pronounced clean. I was given a hairdryer and told to dry her off while Dorothy busied herself with preparing lunch. Once Bella was dry, she was scooped up on to the draining board and the clipping commenced. Clouds of black hair drifted around the kitchen as Dorothy, electric shears humming away, mercilessly reduced Bella to a shadow of her former self.

Once the clipping was completed, Bella resembled a different animal. To my dismay, she looked like a lap dog, the type which would be more at home lurking in the folds of an old lady's mink coat. Her appearance notwithstanding, the two of us were vastly relieved that it was over and we were released into the drawing room to await the arrival of lunch. Presently, in came Dorothy, bearing a sizeable plate on which quivered a large chunk of brawn. Adhering to this unappetizing, gelatinous mass were countless tiny wisps of poodle fluff.

A warning glance from my mother confirmed that I would have to eat what I was given and I watched in mute horror as a serving was placed in front of me. Peering at it, I could see poodle hair actually embedded in the brawn itself, glassily preserved alongside cubes of ham and green peas. Nausea welled up inside me as I reached shakily for my fork.

Lionel Reece Webb didn't appear to notice that anything was amiss with the brawn. He launched enthusiastically into tales of his travels with the army. As a colonel in the days when the British Empire was still largely intact, he had travelled widely and now enjoyed nothing more than a captive audience for his stories. Undaunted by disapproving glances from Dorothy, he regaled us with a tale about a Middle Eastern potentate who had served him with sheeps' eyes at a banquet.

'Natives considered 'em a great delicacy, y'know,' he pronounced, 'but I was put off by all the little tubes hanging around the eyeball.'

Dorothy shot him a filthy look, but he pressed on.

'Rather like chewing golf balls,' he continued happily. 'Couldn't risk offence by refusing 'em. Got the hang of the blighters eventually – used to pop 'em in, relax m'throat and swallow 'em whole.'

In desperation, I decided to take a leaf out of his book and try the same technique with the brawn. Carving it into bite-sized pieces with my fork, I popped the first chunk into my mouth, screwed up my face and my courage and swallowed. Shuddering miserably when the cold jelly lodged in my throat, I felt something touch my foot under the table. Looking down I saw Gigi's pink nose poking up towards me from beneath the table cloth.

Greatly relieved by this fortuitous turn of events, I sneaked a piece of brawn off my plate and fed it to her. To my dismay, she promptly disappeared, but twenty seconds later she was back. While we listened to Lionel extolling the virtues of camel-dung fires in the desert, I surreptitiously gave her another piece.

Between us, Gigi and I somehow managed to finish off my plate of brawn and I felt a twinge of sorrow for my mother, who was clearly struggling unaided at her end of the table. After the meal was over, we got to our feet to make our way to the front door. Eager for the off, I followed Bella out into the hall, but froze in my tracks. Down the length of the narrow hallway, at well-spaced intervals, lay little piles of brawn glistening with poodle saliva. I shut my eyes and waited for Dorothy's wrath to descend on my guilty head.

'Lionel, have you been feeding the dogs again?' Dorothy demanded menacingly behind me. 'Just look at the state of the carpet!'

'Well m'dear, I did give Gigi a few bits,' he admitted miserably.

With Dorothy fuming at her unfortunate husband, we made good our escape. I strongly suspected that the vile Gigi had done it on purpose, but miraculously I was off the hook – at least until the next visit.

4

Up close, Pharaoh was much, much bigger than I had expected. I had seen him from the car as we drove past his paddock, but I simply hadn't realized how huge he was.

'You'll need to use the mounting block,' Handley Blakney pointed out, rather unnecessarily. 'I'll lead him up to it. You put your left foot in the stirrup, so that you're facing his tail, take the reins in your left hand, hold the back of the saddle in your right hand and hop up.'

It was a lot to remember. I clambered on to the old green mounting block and reached up for the reins, which were knotted above Pharaoh's neck. Hopping awkwardly on my right leg, I managed to get my left toe into the stirrup and heave myself upwards. As I dropped my right leg over the far side of the saddle, Handley helped my other foot into the right stirrup. I was aboard.

The riding lessons had been Handley's suggestion. My mother played bridge with a small circle of friends in the village, including the Blakneys. One evening, Handley had mentioned that he owned the large grey horse we passed every day on the school run and had enquired if I might like to learn to ride. I was thrilled with the offer and lessons were duly arranged each Saturday morning.

Handley was in his seventies. Silver-haired, with an air of gentlemanly courtesy, he had learned to ride in the army. He habitually wore beige cavalry twill britches, a regimental tie and waistcoat and a dark-brown hairy tweed jacket. Pharaoh – also advanced in years and sharing the same gentlemanly manner and even the same hair colour – had been Handley's mount in the army. When his term of service had ended, the two of them had retired together.

From my point of view, the only snag was that Pharaoh was a seventeen-hand heavyweight hunter. Perched astride him, like a wart on the back of a bear, I peered anxiously at the ground. It was a long way down.

Handley tightened Pharaoh's girth and shortened my stirrups, wrapping the leathers round the irons themselves so that my feet could make firm contact. With the spring sun warming our backs, we set off round the paddock at a leisurely stroll.

'Despite being a heavyweight, he's very responsive,' Handley told me as he led me round. 'If you feel at all unsafe, grab hold of his mane.'

After a couple of circuits, during which Handley told me how to sit correctly, he suddenly announced we were going to trot. As the big horse quickened his stride, I grabbed hold of the mane and bounced awkwardly, convinced that any minute I would come tumbling off. It was exciting, but I was relieved when Handley, puffing like a train, pulled Pharaoh up by the mounting block.

'Next week we'll work on rising to the trot,' Handley pronounced. 'You'll soon get the hang of it.'

Over the next few weeks, my riding slowly improved. After the second lesson I was allowed to go solo, while Handley stood in the middle of the paddock and barked instructions in a military manner. I adored Pharaoh. Despite his age he was, as Handley had promised, very responsive and willing. Soon we ventured out of the paddock into open farmland, where I experienced for the first time the exhilaration of cantering. Most evenings after school, I walked down to see Pharaoh and give him an apple or a carrot. As he saw me coming, he would whicker with welcome and trot stiffly over to greet me. As he munched his treat, he lowered his massive head to allow me to scratch his forelock.

One Saturday morning that spring, I arrived at the paddock to find Handley with tears in his eyes.

'M'dear, I'm afraid something awful has happened,' he told me, putting his arm around my shoulders. 'Pharaoh was taken ill last night – I found him lying in his stable. The vet came out and said it was his heart. It was the kindest thing to put him to sleep. He didn't suffer at all.'

We went into the stable. Pharaoh's massive grey body covered the entire floor. His eyes, with their long grey lashes, stared blankly into space. Struggling unsuccessfully to hold back tears, I knelt beside him and kissed his mealy nose.

'I've arranged for the local hunt kennels to pick him up,' Handley told me. 'They'll feed him to the hounds.'

Seeing my stricken face, he explained gently, 'He's awfully big to bury and it's much better that he's used now he's gone. It's the way it should be.'

Possibly because of my experience with the hawks, I could understand this. Hawks needed meat to live and so did hounds. I couldn't face staying to see Pharaoh taken away though, so I hugged Handley and left. For both of us, it was the end of an era.

Not long after this, I was offered the chance to exercise a pony. It belonged to the Aston family, who had a farm about a mile from Chilham. Lucy Aston was a friend of mine from school. The three elder Aston children had all learned to ride on the family pony when they were teenagers, but now they had grown up and moved away. Lucy showed no interest in riding, so the elderly pony had been left to live out his days in peace.

The farm was set in a shallow valley, off the main road which ran past Chilham to Challock. The farmhouse, Dane Court, was a large and attractive white house, covered in purple wisteria, with green shutters and a Kent peg tiled roof. To one side of the house lay a swimming pool and tennis courts. The farm buildings were at the rear, with a large Dutch barn, assorted sheds and a single wooden stable. I had spent many happy hours with Lucy swimming in the pool and playing on the farm. Then one afternoon I had spotted the pony in a distant field. I couldn't believe how lucky she was to have a pool, tennis courts *and* a pony, but whilst she enjoyed the first two, she told me she had no interest in horses whatsoever. A few days later, when I was invited to tea after school, I plucked up my courage and hesitantly asked Lucy's parents if I could ride the pony occasionally.

'We'd be delighted if you'd ride him.' Mr Aston's eyes twinkled behind his horn-rimmed glasses. He was a kindly, forbearing man, who rarely seemed to refuse any request. 'He's about fourteen and a half hands, so he should be a good size for you,' he added. 'He hasn't been ridden for some years, but we've still got his tack around somewhere, although it will need a good clean. I kept him shod in case Lucy should change her mind about riding him. It'll do the old chap good to have a bit of exercise – I should think he'll love it.'

The following Saturday, my mother dropped me off early at the Aston's, saying that she'd collect me at lunch time. It was a dismal morning, grey, with a steady drizzle. Mr Aston met me at the back of the house and showed me the stable with an assortment of tack, some of it tied together with string. He found an old headcollar, with a lead rope attached, and led me out to a large, wet field, where he pointed past a couple of dozen cows to a dark-brown pony grazing in the far corner.

'Take a pocketful of nuts – I'm sure he'll be pleased to see you.' He passed me a large fistful of cattle nuts out of the pocket of his jacket and left me to introduce myself.

'By the way, his name's Rocket,' he called over his shoulder.

I was on my own. Feeling very professional in a faded hard hat, a tweed hacking jacket which my mother had recently bought for sixpence at a jumble sale, and a brand-new pair of jodhpur boots, I grasped the headcollar in one hand, thrust the nuts into a pocket and climbed over the gate. As I approached Rocket, I could see that the years of idleness had taken their toll: he was exceedingly plump and his coat was matted with mud. I clearly had a big grooming job ahead of me.

When I was about ten feet from him, Rocket, who had been grazing solidly, lifted his head. I reached into my pocket and held out a handful of nuts encouragingly.

'Hello, Rocket, look what I've brought for you.'

He took a pace towards me and hooked his top lip over his teeth, stretching out his neck towards the nuts. As he took the first mouthful, I lifted up the headcollar. Jerking his head upwards in alarm, he wheeled on his back legs and shot off across the field with a surprising burst of speed.

Disheartened, I trudged in his wake. I was used to arriving for my rides to find Pharaoh already tacked up and gleaming. Although Handley had shown me how to tack up and how to groom, Pharaoh's silky coat had always been immaculate and anyway, I couldn't reach most of him. This morning I had imagined going for a long, leisurely ride to get to know my new mount. This was not a promising start.

Rocket had resumed his grazing in the opposite corner of the field. He continued to eat as I approached, rolling his eyes balefully in my direction. I hid the headcollar behind my back and produced another handful of nuts.

'Rocket, Rocket,' I wheedled. 'Look what I've brought you.'

Planting his feet squarely in the muddy grass, Rocket stretched out his neck and nuzzled up the nuts in a single mouthful. Cautiously, I edged the headcollar from behind my back and took the rope between my hands. As Rocket craned towards me, wrinkling his nose and sniffing for more nuts, I lunged towards his neck with the rope.

He danced backwards and I fell flat on my face. Cursing, I climbed to my feet and ruefully surveyed my new jacket. It was plastered in mud. Evidently, Rocket was not as thrilled at the prospect of exercise as Mr Aston had believed he would be. I had the sinking feeling that I was in for a long morning.

Now that the cattle nuts were finished, I wasn't in with a chance. I pursued Rocket for the next half hour, before giving up and heading back to the farmyard, tired and depressed. As I leant on the stable door, Mr Aston appeared.

'No luck?' he enquired, with an expression of concern.

'He grabbed the nuts and shot off,' I admitted. 'I've been trying to catch him ever since, but I can't get anywhere near him.' Covered in mud and flushed with the unwelcome exercise, I no longer felt at all professional.

'Come with me,' Mr Aston said kindly. 'I think I know what to do.'

He set off at a brisk pace towards one of the storage sheds, disappeared inside and re-emerged with a bucketful of nuts.

'This should do the trick,' he told me. He strode off towards the field, with me jogging behind to keep up. Reaching the gate he shook the bucket vigorously. Every head in the field turned.

'Yoi, yoi, yoi!' he shouted. The cattle began to make their way towards him, but they were overtaken at the trot by Rocket.

I watched in disbelief as Rocket buried his head in the bucket and Mr Aston, taking the headcollar from me, slipped it over Rocket's nose.

'He always was a bit of an old devil to catch,' he told me. 'I should have given you the bucket in the first place. Use it next time, but don't let him eat too much, he's terribly greedy.'

I took Rocket's lead rope from Mr Aston and, thanking him profusely, led the pony towards the stable. At least now we could make a start.

Inside the stable, which was strewn with muck left by the previous incumbents – cattle from the look of it – I tied Rocket's rope to a metal ring in the wall and stood back to survey my new charge. He was matted in mud and wet-through from the drizzle. I picked up a stiff body brush, which was missing most of its bristles, and set to. Rocket fidgeted and stomped while I brushed and brushed. I didn't seem to make much of an impression: the mud was too wet.

Lying in the corner of the stable, I spotted a couple of old hessian grain sacks. I picked them up and gave them a shake, coughing in the dust and chaff which spilled out of them. Armed with these, I started to rub Rocket down, pausing only to fetch him an armful of hay from the barn, in an attempt to get him to stand still. As soon as I dropped the hay into the manger, Rocket stopped fidgeting and started to munch. In the ensuing peace, I was able to make a tolerable job of drying him off, after which I resumed my labours with the body brush. Finishing him off with a soft brush about an hour later, I decided he looked quite smart. Despite the fact that his long winter coat was starting to come through, I had even managed to get a bit of a gleam to him. I then combed his mane and tail, which took another half hour as they were thick with knots.

The only item of horsey equipment which I owned at the time was a collapsible hoof pick, of which I was immensely proud. Handley had shown me how to pick out Pharaoh's hooves. He tapped a fetlock and Pharaoh lifted the corresponding hoof smartly, presenting it to Handley who held it steady while I picked it out. He showed me how to work delicately round the frog – the sensitive V-shape in the centre of the hoof – gently gouging out the cleft to remove any stones or pebbles. There had never been much to clean in Pharaoh's hooves, despite their size, as Handley attended to them every day.

Now it was time to test my new acquisition on Rocket. I stood with my back to his head, as Handley had showed me, and tapped his nearside front fetlock. Rocket paid not the slightest attention. I tapped it again, harder this time. He paused momentarily from his eating and looked over his shoulder with a pained expression. I decided that he hadn't got the message. Maybe I should tap harder still. I shut the hoof pick and rapped the fetlock smartly with it. Rocket whipped round and bit me hard in the

37

buttocks, ripping a chunk out of my jacket. He glared at me for a couple of seconds, as I massaged my wounded rear, then swallowed the scrap of tweed he was holding in his teeth.

Smarting with pain and indignation I stood back and considered my options. If Rocket and I were ever to make progress, I was going to have to get the upper hand somehow. He had, quite literally, run rings round me all morning. It wasn't good enough. Grabbing hold of the lead rope, I untied it and yanked Rocket closer to the metal tethering ring. I then retied it so short that he had only six inches to play with.

Satisfied that he couldn't bite me again, I turned my back and tugged at the fetlock, shoving Rocket with my shoulder at the same time to get him to shift his weight. To my surprise, it worked and I was grudgingly presented with a heavy hoof, caked flat to the level of the shoe with mud.

Picking delicately at the hoof as I had been taught had not the slightest effect, so I hacked away at the hard-packed mud until eventually I cleared down to the frog. As I picked round the frog, the stench of elderly manure was overpowering. I struggled on, the hoof seeming to get heavier and heavier. Rocket shifted his weight back on to his nearside, propping his bulk comfortably against my left shoulder.

Flagging with exhaustion, I was mightily relieved to reach the last hoof at the front, on the opposite side. Just as I was finishing it off, Rocket shifted his weight again, knocking the hoof pick flying across the stable. As I let go of his hoof to retrieve the pick, he plonked his foot heavily on to mine and, with a sigh of satisfaction, sunk his full weight on to it.

I was pinned to the spot. Shoving Rocket with both hands, I tried to get him to move his foot. It did no good whatsoever. I yelled and beat his shoulder with my fists. The only effect was to make him twist his hoof down harder. A bolt of searing agony shot through my foot. As tears welled in my eyes, I scanned the stable helplessly for some means of shifting him. I spotted my hoof pick, lying on the floor about five feet away.

38

Easing myself awkwardly into a sitting position, I lay on my side in the muck and edged my upper body across the floor. With my foot still trapped, it wasn't easy, but at full stretch I just managed to reach the hoof pick with my finger tips. Still sitting on my bottom, I grasped the handle firmly in my right hand, leaned back for extra momentum and, with all the force I could muster, stuck the sharp end of the hoof pick into Rocket's flank.

For an awful moment, I thought he wasn't going to move. He was so fat, I think he hardly felt it, but when the blow registered he shuffled sideways in surprise and continued to snatch peevishly at his hay. With my foot throbbing and liquid manure soaking through my trousers, I heard a car pull up outside.

'Hello darling,' my mother called over the half door. 'Did you have a good ride? What on *earth* have you been doing?' she asked, aghast, as I hobbled into the light.

Snivelling, I spluttered out my tale of woe. My mother listened sympathetically, eyeing my filthy, torn jacket and the toe of my new boots, which had been scuffed down to white leather.

'You'd better put him back in the field so we can go home and take a look at your foot,' she advised.

I untied Rocket and limped out into the yard, past the Dutch barn to the field. The sun had come out and the cows' backs were steaming as I took off Rocket's headcollar and released him. He trotted away from me without a backward glance, heading purposefully for a boggy depression in the middle of the field. Sinking to his knees, he rolled and rolled, rubbing himself blissfully into the mire until he stood up, caked from head to tail.

At home, a lot of skin from my toes came off with the damaged boot. My foot was bloody and bruised but, to my surprise, nothing was broken. Lowering myself painfully into a steaming bath and propping my bandaged toes on the rim, I vowed things would be very different next week. Come hell or high water, next Saturday we were going for a ride.

5

THE FOLLOWING SATURDAY dawned bright and sunny. I was relieved when the bucket of nuts brought Rocket trotting up eagerly and, as it was dry, his mud pack had hardened and was much easier to brush off. After about an hour, I had finished grooming him and was ready to tack him up. He clenched his teeth when I tried to put the bit into his mouth and blew out his belly when I tried to tighten his girth, but eventually we were ready for our first outing.

As I led him out into the yard, I wasn't quite certain what to expect. Would he be 'hot' to ride? To date, he had certainly shown plenty of spirit. I decided against mounting in the yard, in case he bucked me off, so I led him to an empty field beyond the grain storage sheds. Here the ground was softer and any further embarrassment Rocket might cause me would be less likely to be witnessed by the farm hands.

Rocket stood stock still while I mounted. As soon as I was astride, I gripped my knees into the saddle and waited for a response. Nothing happened. Tentatively, I nudged Rocket with my heels. Still nothing. Handley had taught me never to kick and indeed, in Pharaoh's case, it had never been necessary, a gentle squeeze with my heels had been sufficient to increase his pace. Clearly, a gentle squeeze was lost on Rocket so, throwing caution to the wind, I kicked him sharply in his ample girth.

Rocket ambled into a slow walk. After a few paces, I pulled him up to tighten his girth. He turned his head and tried to nip me in the ankle. I kicked him again and we set off round the field at an extremely sedate pace.

I was disappointed. I had no desire to be bucked off, but I had hoped that Rocket would show some of the liveliness he displayed when so energetically evading capture. On the contrary, he appeared to be a plodder. I rode him out of the field and headed for a farm track which led up through the woods, climbing to some apple orchards at the top of the valley.

As we progressed, it became patently clear that Rocket was only prepared to move at two paces: dead slow and stop. Deaf to all my commands, he only broke into a trot briefly, to help himself climb a steep section of track. I had been hoping, once we reached the orchards, to canter down the grassy rides, but Rocket would have none of it. While I egged him on, clucking, kicking and cajoling, he totally ignored me and mooched along, moodily snatching at apples.

I had just despaired of ever getting him to move any faster, when I heard a buzzing noise approaching over my shoulder. Glancing behind me in the direction the noise was coming from, I spotted three beehives. Craning my neck even further, I located the source of the noise. An angry swarm of bees was heading straight at us. Frantically, I kicked Rocket as hard as I could.

'Come *on!*' I yelled. To no avail.

Suddenly, just as the bees were bearing down on us, Rocket came to life. Stopping short, he lifted his head and pricked his ears. Bunching himself on his hocks, he leapt forward and shot off at a gallop. I was very nearly unseated, but managed to recover my balance and hung on for dear life. I had no desire to pull Rocket up until we had put considerable distance between ourselves and the swarm. We raced towards the end of the orchard, round a corner and tore down the ride towards the hill.

42

Surely the bees couldn't still be with us? Fearing we would both break our necks if Rocket didn't slow down before reaching the stony track, I yanked the reins and eventually managed to pull him to a slithering halt. Fearfully I looked back. No sign of the bees. His sides heaving, Rocket too glanced behind, then dropped his neck, clearly exhausted by our dash to safety.

Trembling, I slid off his back and stroked his damp neck. He nudged me with his nose and I fed him a polo mint. It was the first moment of truce between us. Taking heart, I got the feeling it wouldn't be the last. As the warm summer sun shone down on us, I slackened his girth and led him down the track towards home.

On occasion, I was able to ride further afield. My Aunt Margaret lived with my grandmother in a large house called Bucklebury, in Surrey. Over Christmas and at odd intervals throughout the year, my mother, Charlie and I would go to stay with them. Moggy, as my aunt was known to the family, hadn't ridden since she was a child, but when I started to learn, my enthusiasm prompted her to take it up again. After six months of lessons she bought a horse of her own, called William.

William lived in fine style in an expensive livery stables on the edge of Epsom Downs. During my visits to Bucklebury, Moggy and I would ride together most days, hacking out across the downs. Moggy rode William and I rode another horse from the stables. It was a magical area for riding. As we rode up on to the downs and turned along the edge of the famous racecourse, great swathes of turf lay ahead of us. The horses would start to hot up, until we gave them their heads. We could gallop for miles, in places just outside the rails of the course itself. As we passed Tattenham Corner, with the wind in my face and the only noise the pounding of hooves, I used to imagine myself riding a Derby winner, ahead of the field and heading for the winning post.

William was a dark bay of about fifteen and a half hands, well schooled and, for the most part, well mannered. However, he had one vice. In the stable, he was a biter. If Moggy had not caused this unfortunate trait, she had certainly aggravated it. Every time she visited William, she took him a bagful of treats. Slices of apple and pieces of carrot, lovingly prepared in a brown paper bag, were mixed in with extra strong mints, which he adored. William could spot the familiar bag as soon as we walked into the yard. He got used to being fed generously over the door when Moggy greeted him, in the stable while he was being groomed and even while he was being tacked up. As a consequence, he had developed the habit of snapping. Everyone had warned Moggy to stop feeding him snacks, but she doted on William and paid no heed.

During one wet weekend at home, the telephone rang. My mother answered it. As the conversation got underway, she began to sound very concerned.

'He did *what*?' she asked, in aghast tones. 'What did you do? Did it work? Is she alright?'

She listened for a few minutes more, then replaced the receiver, looking quite shocked. I waited with wide eyes; clearly something awful had happened.

'Moggy has had an accident,' she told me. 'Earlier today, she took your grandmother and one of the choir boys from church to see William at the stables. As they reached the stable door, William leaned over and snapped at her chest.' Shuddering visibly, she continued. 'He bit right through her clothing and tore off her nipple!'

My jaw dropped open and I winced. Poor, poor Moggy.

'Fortunately, William spat the nipple out.'

The unsavoury thought flashed through my mind that if it had been Rocket, he would have eaten it for sure.

'Your grandmother — showing great presence of mind — scooped the nipple up off the floor and drove Mogs to hospital, where they were able to stitch it back on.' My mother sank into a chair, looking quite pale. 'She's alright now, but that savage animal ought to be shot.'

Leaping to William's defence, I visualized the familiar brown paper bag, stuffed full of treats. 'It's Moggy's fault – everybody's told her. She gives him too many tit-bits.'

My unintentional pun went down in family history. After the wound had healed, even Moggy could see the funny side. William paid the price for his misdemeanour when brown paper bags became a thing of the past.

The next animal drama in our lives was caused by Wallis. Unlike Lucy, Wallis was not shy in his associations with the stray cats in the sawmills. He had many friends, whom he visited daily, but over a period of weeks I could see that he had formed a particular attachment with a little black stray, who looked up at him with adoring eyes.

When he was still a kitten, my mother had taken Wallis to the vet to get him neutered, but the vet had advised against operating at that stage.

'Leave him for another couple of weeks – it'll make him a nicer cat. No, no, there's no risk of fatherhood yet,' he answered my mother's question. 'He's far too young.'

Some weeks later, I spotted a tiny kitten, mewing plaintively by the end of a large pile of timber in part of the sawmills at the end of the garden. The kitten was tabby and white, a minuscule image of Wallis.

I sat quietly in the building and was soon rewarded by the sight of two more kittens, one black, like its mother, and one tabby. They were very small; I guessed they could only be a matter of a couple of weeks old. Investigating further, I discovered that the mother had made a nest in the pile of timber and that Wallis was a regular visitor.

My mother was unimpressed by the news. She took Wallis to be neutered straight away, but it was a case of shutting the stable door after the horse had bolted. The post-operative Wallis promptly lost all interest in his new family.

45

I became worried about the kittens. Without Wallis helping out, I wasn't at all sure that the little black stray could cope.

'They'll be alright,' my mother assured me. 'The mother will manage fine – I can't imagine Wallis was much help to her anyway. If you're really worried you can put a saucer of milk down in the building each evening, to make sure she gets enough goodness into her.'

From the outside of the building, I peered through the old diamond leaded light windows, observing the little black cat as she slunk in and out of the wood pile. She seemed to take good care of the kittens, but the strain of looking after her family was beginning to show: she looked painfully thin. Then one evening a week later, as I arrived home from school, my mother told me that she had found her run over on the main road.

This was a disaster. Without their mother, the kittens would starve. We went down to the sawmills but there was no sign of them.

'Can we move the wood to find them?' I asked anxiously.

'It's extremely heavy and if the pile slips, we might squash them. We can leave them some food, but I don't see what else we can do.' My mother was as concerned as I was.

All that night I tossed and turned, tortured by images of the kittens, cold, hungry and abandoned. By morning, I had come up with a plan.

'What we need is a tea chest and a sheet,' I told my mother. 'By tonight, the kittens will be starving hungry. If we can put some food in the tea chest and tempt the kittens inside, I can trap them.'

It wasn't much of a plan, but it was the best we could come up with. At dusk, my mother and I carried a tea chest down to the sawmills and positioned it at the edge of the log pile. We laid the chest on its side and, with the sheet tacked to the top edge, set a trail of tiny pieces of cooked chicken on the floor, leading to a saucer of chicken and milk at the back of the box. My mother, armed with a torch, went into the room next door, while I took up position on a stool at the side of the box, clasping the rolled sheet in both hands.

As darkness fell, it grew chilly. I sat as still as I could, shivering with cold and trying to stop my teeth from chattering. The light dropped rapidly, until I could scarcely make out my surroundings any longer. A broken window squeaked on a rusty hinge and tiles clattered on the roof as a gust of wind swept through the building. There was no noise from the pile of timbers.

About an hour later, just as I was wondering if I dared to stretch out my cramped legs, I saw a tiny dim shape move on the edge of the wood pile. Straining my eyes, I saw the shape begin to edge closer to the tea chest. It was one of the kittens. I couldn't make out what it was doing, but then I heard faint chewing noises. It must have picked up a piece of chicken.

I waited patiently, but it didn't come any closer. It was only a foot away from the mouth of the box. I willed it to go inside. Then, suddenly, there were two shapes. They moved closer to the box and a patch of moonlight fell on them. The black kitten and the tabby were following the trail of chicken. I scarcely dared to breathe. The tabby kitten seemed the bolder of the two. It moved to the lip of the tea chest. My heart was pounding so loudly, I thought it would scare them away, but then the tabby kitten disappeared into the box. Seconds later, I heard it lapping from the saucer.

Attracted by the noise, the black kitten moved cautiously to the entrance. It hovered there for a few seconds, then slipped inside too.

Suddenly, I was in a quandary. If I dropped the sheet now, I'd catch two, but what about the third kitten, the one which looked like Wallis? I would almost certainly ruin my chances of trapping that one too. Its siblings were going to finish the food and milk soon, then they would escape and I would have achieved nothing. I simply hadn't thought this far ahead. I was going to have to make a decision – and quickly.

At that moment I saw a third shape emerge from the wood pile and approach the box. I was going to have to wait now, but it was a gamble. Kitten number three found a piece of chicken left behind by the others. I could hear it eating, then, to my astonishment, it broke into a loud purr. My heart throbbed with pity. Poor little thing – it was so happy to find something to eat. It approached the box. All sounds of lapping from the interior stopped abruptly. Were they coming out? Then, with my heart in my mouth, I saw the third kitten disappear inside. I dropped the sheet over the front of the box.

The noise of my stool crashing on its side brought my mother running from next door. I was sprawled against the box, trying to hold the sheet tight to the sides.

'I've got them! All of them!' I yelled. 'But they're trying to get out and I can't hold them.'

The beam from my mother's torch caught one of the kittens pushing its head round the edge of the sheet. She dived forward and grabbed it round the neck. It spat and wriggled in her hand.

'Turn the box on its end. Quickly, or you'll lose the others.'

I tipped up the box and the saucer crashed to the base. There was a slithering noise and two little thuds as the kittens too hit the bottom. I pulled the sheet as tight as I could over the top of the box and between us, my mother and I managed awkwardly to carry the box and one struggling kitten back to the house.

In the warmth of the kitchen, I pulled back a corner of the sheet. The two kittens – splashed with milk and mewing – were huddled in a corner of the box. My mother dropped the kitten she was holding in with its companions and ran her lacerated hand under the tap.

'You've got some taming job ahead of you,' she said, ruefully rubbing antiseptic cream into a dozen tiny scratches. 'What on earth are we going to do with them tonight? We can't have them loose in the kitchen – they're completely wild.'

An inspired thought struck me.

'Bella loves kittens. Why can't she look after them?' I asked. 'We could put them into the potting shed with her. It's quite warm and they can't come to any harm in there.'

'I doubt Bella will wear it, but we can give it a try.'

In the potting shed, we used gloves to lift the kittens out of the tea chest, told Bella to lie in her basket and put the kittens in with her. The kittens shot straight out of the basket under some seed boxes. There was nothing further we could do. Putting down two more saucers of chicken and milk, we left them to it. Quite worn out by all the excitement, I slept soundly that night, happy in the knowledge that the kittens were safe.

Early the next morning, I looked through the potting shed window. A wonderful sight met my eyes. Bella was sound asleep curled up in her basket with all three kittens cuddled up against her. Carefully, I opened the door a crack and slipped inside.

Over the weeks which followed, Bella made all the difference to the kittens. Without her, I doubt if I would ever have been able to win their confidence. In the early days, they were like little spitfires, but through their acceptance of Bella as a surro-

gate mother, they came to accept people. Wallis shirked all responsibility, watching with disdain from a distance as Bella mothered the kittens. She of course was thrilled to have a brood all to herself at last and when they were tame enough to explore the garden, would lead them around with the three of them trotting obediently behind her.

By the time we found homes for them, the kittens were no different in behaviour to Lucy's litter. I desperately wanted to keep the tom, which was the image of its father, but my mother was unbending in her refusal. The original, she said, had caused quite enough trouble and the last thing she wanted was history repeating itself.

6

I WAS NINE WHEN I was invited to my first evening party. Parties up until that time had been daytime affairs, with afternoon tea. This invitation however, was to a party which started at 7 p.m., given jointly by the children of the Salmon family, who lived at the other end of the village.

Pippa, the youngest of the family, was a friend in my year at school. She had an older sister, Caroline, who was sixteen and very pretty, with long blonde hair. I didn't know Caroline well, but had seen her frequently as she was a sixth former at Ashford. The two girls had an older brother, Chris, who was nineteen and whom I had only seen from a distance. Chris was quite short for his age and wiry, with tightly curled reddish-brown hair. Their father was the local doctor and the family lived in a modern, detached house next door to the surgery.

The invitation promised a buffet with games and music. I looked forward to the evening keenly and when it finally arrived, I dressed with care in a black velvet 'midi' skirt and a burgundy crushed velvet top. I put carmen rollers in my hair and, after shaking out the curls, stood back to survey the results in the mirror.

Recently, I had shot up in height. At five feet seven inches, I was now only two inches shorter than my mother and I had the startings of a well-developed figure. During the summer, another school friend and I had enjoyed the distinction of being the only girls in our form who, because we were 'tall for our age', had been allowed to change for swimming in one of the rickety changing sheds beside the school pool, rather than on the lawn with the rest of the class. Staring at my reflection in the mirror, I could see the changes which had taken place imperceptibly in the last year. I looked quite grown up.

My mother drove me across the village square and down the hill towards the Salmons' house.

'I'll pick you up at ten thirty,' she told me. 'I'll wait in the car outside, you come and find me,' she added, sensitive to the fact that I would want to appear independent.

When I arrived – fifteen minutes late as my mother had advised – the party was already in full swing. There was no sign of Dr and Mrs Salmon.

Pippa explained. 'We got rid of mum and dad for the evening. They've left food. They won't be back before midnight,' she added.

Pippa had platinum blonde hair, cropped like a boy, and was wearing jeans and T-shirt. A bit of a tomboy, she was always in trouble at school. I envied her rebelliousness and tried to copy her whenever I could, but she was always the one with the bright ideas and a ready answer for her critics. In view of Pippa's character, I was expecting her to be the life and soul of the party, surrounded by an admiring crowd of other friends from school. I was very surprised, therefore, to discover that I was the only friend of her age there. All the other guests were friends of Caroline and Chris. Suitably flattered, I accepted a glass of Coke and enthusiastically joined in the party games, which were just getting underway.

Over the next hour or so, I couldn't help noticing that Chris Salmon was giving me some strange looks from across the room. I felt uncomfortable. Did he think I shouldn't be there? Had I got a smudge on my face? I went to the bathroom to check in the mirror.

When I rejoined the group, everyone seemed in high spirits. There was much joking and teasing; it was a totally different atmosphere to the kind of children's parties I was used to. They were preparing to play a game which required partners. To my utter astonishment, when it was Chris's turn to choose a partner, he chose me. How kind he was, I decided. He had seen that I didn't know anyone other than Pippa and was trying to make me feel welcome.

Pippa didn't appear best pleased. She looked even more put out when an hour or so later, Chris whispered to me to follow him outside. He led me round to the back of the surgery. It was very dark and I stumbled along behind him, thinking that maybe he had some surprise he wanted to spring on the others and needed some help with it.

In the darkness, Chris stopped abruptly in front of me and I cannoned into the back of him.

'What are we going to do?' I asked. 'Why are we here?'

'I just wanted to spend some time alone with you,' Chris said quietly. He took my hand in his and moved close to me. He smelled of soap.

I was completely taken aback. This was totally unexpected and I didn't know how to respond.

'Can I kiss you?' he asked, moving his body against me.

'Yes,' I breathed, half shocked, half flattered.

Chris took me in his arms and kissed me, tentatively at first and then deeper. He was about my height, which I found strangely off-putting. The smell of soap was overpowering. I couldn't really believe this was happening to me. I had never thought about boys before and Chris seemed so grown up.

'You're very pretty,' Chris told me, stepping back and holding my shoulders. I didn't know what to say, but Chris didn't seem to want a reply.

'We'd better get back,' he said, taking my hand once more and leading me along the back of the surgery. Before we went round the corner towards the house, he stopped and kissed me on the lips briefly once more, then dropped my hand and hurried into the house.

'Where have you been?' Pippa asked, as I slid into the dining-room. She was staring at my cheeks which had flushed pink with the warmth of the house.

'Outside,' I murmured vaguely, feeling a strange mixture of guilt and exhilaration.

Pippa didn't press it. We helped ourselves to some food and Chris disappeared into a noisy throng of friends. He didn't glance in my direction for the rest of the evening. Later, just as I was putting on my coat to leave, he appeared at my side.

'Are you off?' he enquired. 'Thanks for coming. Is your mother picking you up?' His eyes met mine. The message was clear. What had happened was to be our secret.

'Yes, she should be outside. Don't worry,' I added, to reassure him.

Outside, my mother was waiting in the surgery car park.

'Was it good?' she asked, as I climbed into the car.

'Wonderful,' I enthused. 'I was the only friend of Pippa's there.'

Instinctively I felt that I shouldn't tell my mother about Chris. I felt as though I had done something wrong. Later, in bed, I hugged my secret to myself, going over and over the incident in my mind. It had been some evening and I didn't know quite what to make of it. One thing felt certain, a new chapter had opened in my life.

7

WALLY WAS NOW a fully fledged member of the display team at the castle. Unfortunately, this meant that I didn't get to fly him often. At weekends I would put him on display and, later in the afternoon, I'd carry him up the big spiral staircase in the Norman keep and out on to the flat roof. The view from the top was worth the long climb. The roofs of the castle lay to my left. Below, the top lawn gave way to terraces, edged with red brick walls and connected by broad and crumbling brick steps. From above, the topiaries which punctuated the terraces looked like chess pieces, lined up in readiness for a game. Below the bottom lawn lay three small paddocks and one large one, extending to a wall at the estate's south-eastern boundary. Beyond the roofs, it was just possible to make out the lake, partially screened by its ruff of rhododendrons. To the right, the park field was dotted with colourful rows of visitors' cars. Beyond this, the estate stretched into the distance, separated from the top lawn by the ha-ha, which snaked towards the back drive. Leaning over the wall which ran round the top edge of the keep, I'd wait for Allan's signal down on the terraced lawns below. When Allan blew his whistle, I'd release Wally from the top of the keep and he would glide majestically down, over the upturned heads of the crowd, to Allan's outstretched glove. This was Wally's party piece and the visitors were entranced by the spectacle of him soaring high above them.

Allan's brief at the castle had grown. Lord Massereene had made him estate manager. In this new role, Allan started to develop other areas of the castle grounds, creating aviaries and enclosures for a whole range of exotic animals and birds. The three paddocks now held black-and-white Jacob sheep, soay sheep – dark brown all over and quite small – and diminutive Chinese water deer, which were a bit of a dead loss from the visitors' point of view as they spent most of their time hiding under bramble bushes. The large field beyond was fenced with stout netting to a height of ten feet. In here Allan put a herd of wapiti deer.

The wapiti stag was an enormous creature, weighing over a thousand pounds and crowned with an impressive set of antlers. Despite his size, he was a gentle creature at all times except during the rutting season. This Allan learned to his cost when, one fine spring day, he drove his car into the wapiti paddock to check the water supply. Resenting the uninvited presence of an intruder amongst his women folk, the stag charged the car. Head down, he punched a neat round hole straight through the passenger door. Allan, who had been in the process of climbing out of the car on the opposite side, leapt back in and, ramming his foot on the accelerator, raced out of the paddock at speed, pursued by the stag.

Around the lake, I helped Allan construct pens for a wonderful assortment of birds and beasts. Wallabies, flamingoes and demoiselle cranes were soon installed, next door to cattle egrets and several species of ornamental pheasant: Lady Amhurst, golden and silver pheasant – I quickly learned to recognize the different species, each with their distinctive plumage. The gaudy colours of the cocks were in sharp contrast to the dull mousiness of the hens.

The waterfowl, too, showed the same sexual dimorphism. My

favourites were the mandarin drakes, with their brilliant orange crests, and the Carolinas, whose heads were crowned with metallic green feathers. In my eyes, the least attractive of the waterfowl were the muscovy ducks. Considerably larger than the other species, with piebald plumage and comical red faces, they were rowdy in their behaviour, always the first to rush for food, pushing aside the smaller exotic ducks, which were left floundering in their wake.

When Charlie was home from school, he fished on the lake for carp. His early attempts were largely unsuccessful. Then one day we discovered, quite by accident, that the carp in the lake had a passion for cheese-and-onion crisps. I had been sitting beside Charlie while he fished, eating a bag of crisps, and had shaken the last few into the water for the ducks. Seconds later, the surface of the water boiled with fish and the crisp fragments disappeared, even before the greedy muscovies could get a look in. Intrigued by this, I went up to the castle gift shop and bought another packet. Together, Charlie and I mashed them into pellets with a little water and pushed a pellet on to Charlie's hook. Success was almost instantaneous. We never understood why the carp went for the crisps, but we kept the formula a secret while local fishermen marvelled at Charlie's success rate.

Allan taught me how to feed all the livestock in the pens and enclosures around the lake and when he was away lecturing on birds of prey to schools – sometimes for weeks at a stretch – I would help Ann by undertaking the feeding-round before school. It was pretty straightforward: all the feeding materials were stored in a small shed set back in the trees by the lake and all I had to do was carry buckets of water and scoops of various grains and pellets to the correct recipients. I enjoyed doing these rounds: the animals and birds got to know me and some of them became quite tame.

Last on my round was a pair of wild boar. They occupied a large, secure enclosure just behind the boathouse. Allan had explained that wild boar were very destructive. Like all species

57

of pig, they liked to root around for acorns and plant bulbs, unearthing vegetation in the process. In contrast to the rest of the pens, which were very neat and tidy, the wild boar enclosure – a thicket when it was first constructed – within a few weeks had been transformed by its occupants into a barren, muddy wasteland. Only the most substantial of the trees and rhododendrons had survived.

I liked the boar. They were completely different to domestic pigs, with muscular, brown, hairy bodies and short but slender legs, which carried them around the pen at a brisk trot. They kept themselves to themselves, the sow overshadowed by the boar, who bristled with self-importance. He had a fearsome set of tusks curling upwards from his lower jaw, but although he would trot over when I entered the pen to fill their food and water troughs, he never came closer than about thirty feet or showed any aggression towards me.

One morning, there was no sign of the sow. One of my duties at the lake was a head count of the occupants of the pens. Not wanting to upset the boar, I worked my way slowly around the outside perimeter of the pen, craning my neck to see if I could spot the sow under the rhododendrons. One area of undergrowth had been left largely intact by the boar. It was about six feet square, and too thick to see into, but as I passed it at the back of the pens, I could hear little squeaking noises coming from the middle of it. Peering into the thicket, I could just make out the outline of the sow. She appeared to be lying down. The squeaking noises continued. Full of excitement, I reported back to Ann.

'She's had a litter from the sound of it,' Ann told me. 'I'll check on her later. If I'm right, we must rope off the enclosure so the public can't get too close and bother her.'

That evening, Ann confirmed that the boar were indeed proud parents.

'I didn't go too close – the boar was quite protective – but I caught a glimpse of piglets suckling.'

58

The next morning I hurried through my round, eager to get a glimpse of the new arrivals. The boar appeared as usual when I entered the pen, but there was no sign of the sow or her litter. In fact, it was some days before I saw my first wild-boar piglet. I was pouring water into the trough when one appeared behind its father, ginger-brown, tiny and stripy – like a large chipmunk – with dark, beady eyes.

The following morning, I couldn't see any members of the family. Disappointed, I emptied their food into the trough noisily to see if any of them would appear. It was a warm start to the day and the early morning sun was streaming through the trees. In a pool of light, a little way away, the family were lying down, stretched out flat on their sides. They were so well camouflaged that I didn't even see them until the boar stood up.

Enchanted by the sight of the family sunning themselves, I went back to the metal five-bar gate which formed the entrance to the pen, to fetch a bucket of water, shutting the gate carefully

behind me once more. Returning to the drinking trough, I noticed the boar had moved closer. As I watched him, he started to paw the ground. He had mean little eyes, I thought, as I finished tipping the water into the trough.

The boar lowered his head, lifted it, then lowered it again. Suddenly, he charged. For a split second I was rooted to the spot, then fear gave me wings and I dropped the bucket and raced for the gate. I could hear him close behind me, but I didn't dare look back. Reaching the gate, I threw myself over it, tearing my trousers, my leg and my hands on the strand of barbed wire which ran along the top. The boar hit the gate behind me with his full force as I dropped to the ground on the far side. I lay in a heap shaking as he trotted victoriously back to his family.

After this incident, I never went into the pen again. New food and water troughs were lowered into the enclosure just inside the wire and to fill them I needed only to pour from the safety of the outside. Despite this, the boar still frightened me, making mock charges towards the fence, eyes blazing with fury at the intrusion into his family life. Often I thought he was going to burst straight through the fence but, inches from the wire, he'd screech to a halt and glare at me, before backing off for another go. The piglets grew rapidly, racing round the pen on sturdy little legs, squeaking in excitement, their noses covered in mud as they followed their parents, rooting and digging. I loved to watch them, but only from a discreet distance; I had learned my lesson.

One winter morning shortly after this, my mother, Ann and I set off on an unusual errand. We were to pick up a pair of goats from a nursing home some twenty miles away and bring them back to live at Chilham.

The goats had been my idea. I had an elderly aunt on my father's side who was staying in the nursing home at the time. Whilst my mother visited Auntie Carrie, I used to visit the animals which were kept in a field to one side of the house.

There was a donkey, some sheep, a couple of goats and their kids.

The owner of the home joined me one day as I scratched the back of the donkey, who was leaning blissfully against the fence while I worked my way along its back.

'The animals belong to us,' she said, 'but sadly the field doesn't, and we're about to lose our grazing from the farm next door. We are going to have to find homes for all the animals quickly. We only have a week.' She looked really anxious.

On the way home I pleaded with my mother to allow me to have the donkey, but to no avail.

'You've taken on more than enough animals to look after. Absolutely not,' she told me firmly.

I had grown fond of the animals during my visits to the nursing home. The sheep had all been sock lambs and were very friendly. Even the goats came over for a polo mint. I was worried about the animals' future and towards the end of the week I persuaded my mother to let me telephone the owner of the home, Mrs Walker.

'How nice of you to call. I've found homes for everything but the two adult goats. Nobody seems to want them,' she told me. 'If I can't find homes for them before Sunday, they'll have to be put down.'

Horrified, I went next door and told Ann the whole story.

'We could keep them in the paddock,' Ann suggested. 'If they have just had kids, they'll be giving plenty of milk – and goats' milk is delicious,' she added.

My mother was dubious.

'There's a lot of work involved in milking by hand,' she told me. 'You'd be expected to help out and you really don't have the time, but I suppose if Ann wants them . . . ', her voice trailed off.

Thrilled at the prospect of saving the goats, I telephoned Mrs Walker to tell her the good news. We arranged to pick up the goats the following day.

There was only one problem. We didn't have anything to collect them in. Allan had a large estate car, but he was away lecturing. Our old Morris Minor had got very sick and finally died. My mother had replaced it with a Morris Traveller Estate, purchased for the princely sum of thirty pounds. One of its more unusual features was the fine and varied crop of miniature mushrooms which it sprouted from the ledges where the rear windows slid back and forth. We decided that we had no option but to transport the goats in the Traveller. We flattened the rear seats and heaped the back with straw. With Ann and my mother in the front seats, there wasn't room for me, but I insisted on going too, declaring I was happy to share the back with the goats on the way home.

When we arrived at the nursing home, Mrs Walker was ready to help us. The field was empty apart from the goats: Lil, a pale biscuit colour, with white underbelly and blaze, and Cobweb who was grey, shorter in the leg than Lil, and plump. Both wore leather collars.

Loading two fully grown goats into the back of the car proved not to be an easy operation. Of the two, Lil seemed to be the more amiable, so we started with her. My mother backed the Morris just through the gate and Mrs Walker led Lil over to the car. Ann held Lil's hind-quarters still, while Mrs Walker and my mother took a front leg each and lifted them up on to the back edge of the Morris. I crouched in the straw, holding Lil's collar, ready to pull her forward.

'One, two, three, heave!' Ann lifted Lil's hind-quarters with a mighty effort and between us, we shunted and pulled Lil into the back of the car. She plonked down in the straw, with her legs curled under her, looking faintly surprised.

Now we had a problem. We couldn't put Cobweb in through the back doors of the Morris too, because Lil was blocking the way. We didn't want to risk Lil jumping out again, so the only option was to try to put Cobweb in through a side door.

Rudely uprooted from her grazing and towed by her collar to the car, Cobweb was not in a co-operative mood. We tried the same tactics. Ann, who was no lightweight, grabbed Cobweb round her plump belly and pushed her up to the side door. With the smaller opening, it wasn't nearly as easy to get her front legs up on to the floor of the Morris. Once achieved, she straightened them like rigid props. As my mother and Mrs Walker attempted to reposition her front legs, Cobweb wriggled and lashed out with a rear hoof, catching Ann a glancing blow on the shin. On the inside, I was vainly struggling to catch hold of Cobweb's collar as she tossed her head and weaved it threateningly from side to side.

'Don't let her go. We may not catch her again,' puffed Mrs Walker.

'Ouch! You devil!' Ann yelped as the angry goat kicked her again.

'We should have put Cobweb in first,' my mother gasped.

Despite the fact that the field lay beside a quiet country lane, we had begun to accumulate an audience. Two old men, a woman with a pram and a small dog had stopped to watch. It must have been a ludicrous spectacle: three women, pink in the face with exertion, struggling with a goat braced against the side of a Morris Traveller.

'Oi don't think she likes caars,' one of the old men offered, clearly enjoying the scene.

'Maybe she gets car sick' the other one suggested.

'What you need is one of 'em sheep trailers,' man number one pointed out. 'Then you could walk 'er straight in.'

The men propped themselves against the fence. Evidently they found the spectacle most entertaining. Even the dog seemed riveted. As they obviously had no intention of helping, we ignored them and resumed our efforts with Cobweb.

'Emma, see if you can move her front legs,' Ann commanded. 'Good girl. OK. Everyone *push!*'

With her back legs lifted off the ground and Ann's weight behind her, Cobweb finally shot into the car, landing on top of me in the process. We thanked Mrs Walker, who looked mightily relieved, and set off on the journey home.

I disentangled myself from Cobweb, but she refused to lie down next to her companion. Fixing me with that blank stare peculiar to goats, she lifted her tail and deposited a sizeable pile of black olives, then, spreading her back legs, peed copiously into the straw. She still wouldn't sit down, but ranged around unsteadily in the confined space, stumbling periodically against Lil and me. I began to regret my insistence on coming on this mission. Between the steaming breath of the two goats, the stinking results of Cobweb's apparent incontinence and the liberal quantities of goat snot deposited on the windows, we were beginning to get quite a fug up in the back.

We got some strange looks from other motorists, but eventually we made it safely back to Chilham. I had never been so relieved to climb out of a car. Lil and Cobweb were released into the paddock behind Carpenters and my mother and I took the Morris home to clean it up.

The following morning it was my task to milk the goats. Despite the problems of the previous day, I was rather looking forward to it. I had seen cows being milked by hand before. It looked easy enough: all you needed was a sparkling steel bucket, a three-legged stool and a cosy stall. I found a cleanish black bucket, a low four-legged stool and headed optimistically for the castle stable yard.

The stables at Chilham had been built in the days when horses lived in style. The yard itself was brick floored, enclosed on one side by an ornate wall and on the other three sides by buildings which made up the original working complex. The stables contained a range of herring-bone tiled loose boxes, now empty, with brass fittings and oak partitions topped with black railings. The boxes were flanked by feed storage rooms, a tack room, and housing for carriages. Above these were quarters for a stable hand and the head groom. Next to the stables there were more carriage rooms with a pigeon loft above. First I led Lil into one of the loose boxes and tied her lead rope to a ring, wondering if this was the first time a goat had ever graced such grand surroundings.

Settling beside Lil on my stool, I warmed my hands by rubbing them briskly together, positioned the bucket underneath her and reached for her teats. The angle was wrong, so I dispensed with the stool and knelt in the straw. I tugged firmly on one of the teats. Nothing happened.

This was very frustrating. I tried again. Still nothing. Lil turned her head and gave me a disdainful look. Tugging on each teat in turn, not a single drop emerged. In dismay, I went in search of Ann. I had had visions of presenting her with a warm bucketful of frothy milk, thereby demonstrating my proficiency in animal husbandry. This was not going at all to plan.

'There's something wrong with Lil's udder,' I told her. 'She doesn't have any milk.'

'She was bursting when I saw her earlier this morning.' Ann was puzzled. We went back into the stall.

'Show me what you were doing.'

I showed her and she laughed.

'You can't just tug like that. Here, let me show you. Start with the top finger and thumb and squeeze gently, then close your other fingers one after the other to stroke the milk down.'

Ann made it look easy. I tried and managed to produce a pitiful, disjointed stream which hissed weakly into the bucket.

'You'll soon get the hang of it,' Ann assured me. 'Bring me the milk when you've finished; I'm going to turn it into cheese.'

After she had left, I resumed my labours with determination. It took ages, but Lil was very patient and about half an hour later I had accumulated about an inch of milk in the bottom of the bucket. I had emptied as much as I could from Lil's two teats and the fingers of my right hand ached. I led Lil out into the paddock and caught Cobweb with the aid of a polo mint.

Tying Cobweb up in the stall, I had the nasty feeling that she was not going to be as patient as Lil. I sat down beside her, pushed the bucket under her udder and took a deep breath. It had to be done.

In one lightening-quick, fluid movement, Cobweb lashed

forward with a back hoof, kicked me in the knee cap and sat down on the bucket. I had expected some problems with her, but sitting down was not something I had anticipated. I extracted the bucket out from under the recalcitrant animal and considered what to do next.

Clearly, I couldn't milk Cobweb lying down, so I untied her, pulled her up and retied her. The second I reached for her udder, she dropped like a stone again and eyed me balefully. I rescued the bucket and weighed up my options. My eye lighted on the redundant milking stool. If I could jam that underneath her before she sat down, I might be able to get on with the job in hand. Although it had been too high to sit on while milking, the stool was about the right height to fit snugly underneath Cobweb.

I got Cobweb to her feet again and after several attempts managed to manoeuvre her against the side of the stall. Instead of lining up the bucket, I shoved the stool under her belly. Surprised, she collapsed on to it and there remained suspended, leaving her udder nicely exposed.

Victorious, but still wary of receiving another kick, I arranged myself and the bucket in position and gingerly started to milk her. At first she fidgeted but, draped over the stool, she couldn't pull away. After a few minutes, she gave up struggling and slumped in a resigned fashion, like a sack of potatoes. My milking technique still left a lot to be desired and it was a slow process, but after half an hour's hard work I finished milking her and looked with pride at the warm, scented milk in the bucket. Ann would be pleased.

As I clambered to my feet, Cobweb awoke from her reverie and kicked over the bucket. I threw myself forward to rescue it, but most of the precious milk was lost. The dribble left in the bucket had straw and other less savoury bits floating in it and looked most unappetizing. I pulled the stool out from under the goat and glared at her. She glared back. Clearly I had a lot to learn about goat husbandry. This was not a promising start.

8

WHEN I WAS nine years old, Ann offered me my first paid job. She had taken over the running of the tea-rooms at the castle and, during my long summer holidays, she offered me fifty pence a week to help out.

The main part of the castle, where Lord and Lady Massereene lived, was permanently closed to visitors. The house was Jacobean. Lady Massereene's daughter had once shown me a few rooms in the private section. The main entrance hall was large and very attractive, with a black-and-white tiled floor, oak panelling and a big fireplace. Off this a door opened into Lord Massereene's study, which smelt cosily of labrador and was comfortably furnished with an old leather sofa, decorated with sporting prints and stacked floor to ceiling with books. Behind the main hall lay a series of large reception rooms, with panoramic views across the terraces, over the paddocks beyond and out towards Mountain Street. A corridor to the rear led past the game larder to the rambling kitchen.

Upstairs, the castle was not in such good order. The years had taken their toll on the red bedroom, the green bedroom and the blue bedroom – originally named in accordance with their velvet curtains and soft furnishings – and now the fabrics in all the rooms were green with age. In the old nursery, I had been amazed to see ivy growing up the inside of the walls. Some of the rooms – including the huge ballroom over the main entrance hall – had fallen into disrepair and were never used.

Outside, an avenue of beech trees ran from the front of the castle to the main gates, which opened on to the village square. The terraced gardens lay to one side of the castle and at the rear, a large lawn was separated from the park field by the ha-ha. Along the edge of the park field lay another avenue of trees extending out into the estate beyond. Far out on the estate – too far for visitors to find it – there was a famous heronry where Henry VIII used to fly his falcons. The heronry was still occupied. Most of the herons migrated for the winter, leaving behind a few 'keepers' to mind it while they were away. They returned every year in February. Legend had it that if they had not returned by Valentine's Day, great misfortune would befall the owners of the castle.

The grounds of the house were open to the public five days a week, from Easter until the end of October. The entrance fee entitled visitors to unrestricted access to the gardens and grounds and included the falconry displays as an added attraction. The tea-rooms were housed in one wing of the castle, which also contained upstairs the original staff flats, now occupied by Jan, who helped Allan with the birds, and Bridget, who worked for Ann full time in the tea-rooms. Downstairs next to the tea-room was the old-fashioned castle kitchen with massive stone sinks and a gift shop, with a separate entrance from the outside for visitors. I worked hard in the tea-rooms, laying and clearing tables, taking orders and making endless sandwiches and pots of tea. The washing up took for ever: the old kitchen sinks were so deep that I had to stand on a chair to use them. I worked from two until six every day except Monday and Friday, when the grounds were shut. I worked out that my rate of pay was two and half pence an hour. This seemed like a good deal to me. I enjoyed working with Ann who, when we were quiet, regaled me with colourful stories about her life and the animals and birds she and Allan had kept during their years together. If we weren't too busy, I nipped out to help Allan with the falconry display at three o'clock.

The eagles Wally and Bugsy took pride of place in the displays. Allan would also fly two kestrels to the lure and a variety of other species. Sometimes he would fly a young hawk which was still on the training line or creance. This, he said, enabled the audience to appreciate a little of the patience which went into the training of a hawk. When I was able to help, I would fetch the next hawk which was to be flown from the display area where the hawks were tethered to Allan on the main castle lawn where the displays took place. I was handling all the hawks now except for Bugsy, the huge Imperial Eagle, who was too large for me to carry.

One hot afternoon, I dashed out of the tea-rooms rather late for the display. Before it started, I was supposed to have unwound the creance on the top lawn in readiness for the hawk in training. I was dismayed to find that the display had already started and Allan was in full swing flying Bugsy on the lower lawn. I grabbed the creance and started to run it out as quickly as I could. Intent on what I was doing, I did not see Bugsy heading towards me. Hearing Allan's warning shout, I looked up just as the huge eagle flew over the top of me. I felt a searing pain in my forehead and dropped to the ground with my head in my hands.

Allan called Bugsy back to him and, a minute later, he was at my side.

'Take your hands away and let's have a look,' he said gently.

Dazed, I sat up. My hands were covered in blood.

'He's raked you with a talon. He must have thought you were holding food instead of the creance. We'd better find your mother, it looks as if it might need a stitch.'

Three stitches later, I had a war wound to be proud of. I now understood why some visitors regarded me as brave to handle Wally and the other hawks. I had never been nervous of any of the birds and I was shocked that Bugsy could do this to me. Allan explained that Bugsy had not been deliberately malicious and I understood this. I was not going to let this incident put me off handling the hawks, in fact I felt I had a better understanding of their nature now – an aspect of it I had never paused to think about before.

The cut was quite deep and dead centre of my forehead. To give my mother her due, she did not make a fuss, or tell me the birds were dangerous, nor did she lay down conditions about my handling them in the future, but the scar was destined to be a permanent fixture.

At harvest time I went with Allan and his two boys Simon and Michael to the small paddock which lay beyond the avenue of horse chestnuts. Although rich in clover, the field was too small and awkward in shape for the estate's heavy machinery to harvest, so Allan laid claim to the crop to feed the goats and the Jacob sheep through the winter. Most of the hay had already been cut with a small tractor and cutter. It lay in crooked lines, like the crests of waves, stretching from one side of the field to the other.

Armed with a rake, I learned how to turn the sweet-scented grass over to dry. It was hard work. The sun beat down and the pollen made my eyes water and my nose prickle. As I worked my way down a row, turning it green side up to the sun, my initial progress was slow, but once I mastered the technique of wielding the rake, I got quicker. Field mice scuttled out of the grass ahead of me. One end of the field, which ran to a narrow point, had not been cut by the tractor, so Allan mowed this by hand with a long-handled scythe. Michael followed behind him, scraping the hay into a pile to dry.

By lunchtime, we were ready for a break. Our arms and shoulders ached and our mouths were parched. We sat under the cool of the trees and slaked our thirst with warm orange squash, tainted by Tupperware drinkers. A slab of home-made chicken pie with a thick golden crust, and a crisp Cox's apple restored our energy. Sitting with our backs to a tree trunk, I shut my eyes and cooled my forehead with the apple. Hay-making had sounded like fun, but it was much harder work than I had expected.

Over the weekend the hay was baled by old Jim Weller, the farm-hand. I was frightened of Weller. He was a terse character, without a good word for anyone. Short and grizzled, he stalked the farm buildings like a malevolent grey wolf, sneaking up on the boys and me as we played outside the granary, driving us away with a few bitter words. When the moon was full, it was rumoured that Weller would emerge from South Lodge to howl mournfully in the silver darkness. These reports allegedly came from eye witnesses. I was convinced Weller was a werewolf.

On Monday morning, Weller was just finishing off the baling as we arrived. Allan reversed a tractor and trailer between the trees.

'Thanks, Jim,' Allan called to him.

'Keep them damn kids away from them bales,' he growled. 'If they split them, I'm not coming back to tidy up. I shouldn't be doing this field in the first place – I've got enough to do.' Hunched over the wheel of his tractor, he chugged back across the park field.

I tried to pick up a bale. It was heavy, the twine bit into my hands. I staggered with it towards the trailer and tried my best to pass it up to Allan. The flat bed of the trailer was level with my shoulders. Allan laughed.

'They're too heavy for you, love,' he said. 'If you and Simon can help to move bales across the field, Michael can pass them up to me for stacking.'

Simon and I tried carrying a bale between us. Gripping the two strings, one in each hand, we walked crab-like at opposite ends. This was too slow, so we took one string apiece and found that we could walk normally. I slipped a hankie under the string

71

to protect my hand. Allan and Michael cleared the distant bales and we took short rests every twenty minutes or so, flopping exhausted against the growing heap which lay alongside the trailer.

Simon was several inches shorter than me. This made the bales awkward to carry and a few split, making me fear Weller's wrath. We swapped ends for each new bale, to even out the load on our shoulders. It was searingly hot. Thistles, baled with the hay, pricked the backs of our hands, leaving a red rash. We toiled on, escaping the midday heat for lunch under the trees again and a brief doze. Late in the afternoon, Simon and I at last reached the final bale, which lay by the hedgerow. As we lifted it, I heard a hissing noise. Coiled in the sun there was an adder, not two feet from my shoe. Its grey-brown back was bisected by a zig-zag of black. I watched, momentarily mesmerized, as it uncoiled, the characteristic V-shape on its head glinting in the sunlight. Then Simon saw it too. All tiredness forgotten, he dropped his end of the bale and ran yelling across the field. The spell broken, I followed in his wake.

'What's up?' Allan asked, as we arrived breathless at the side of the trailer.

'There's a snake – it hissed at us.'

'There's an adder over there!' Simon and I burst out at once.

'Provided you leave it alone, an adder won't hurt you,' Allan said. 'Another time, just back off quietly. It won't come after you.'

Allan had already taken three loads to the Dutch barn. As a reward for our labours, he gave Simon and me a leg up on to the last stack of hay for the ride back to the barn. I stretched out on the warm bales, plucking itchy blades of grass from my shirt and socks. Our clothes were dusty and sticky with perspiration and our shoulders felt as if they had been wrenched from their sockets. Simon's face was filthy and I knew mine must be too, but I was too tired to care. As the trailer rumbled across the park field, I sat up to catch the breeze in my face.

At home my mother, looking cool and fresh in a flowered

cotton dress, was digging the garden. She laughed as I walked across the lawn.

'You'd better go in and strip off in the kitchen,' she said. 'I'll run you a bath. Don't carry seeds all through the house,' she warned, as I peeled off my grimy clothes and dropped them on the kitchen floor.

My head ached from too much sun, and the bath felt like pure bliss. As I lay in the cool water, which was speckled with seeds and grass, my mother brought me an ice-cold lemon barley water. She sat on the stool beside the bath.

'You've really caught the sun,' and said. 'You'll be sore tomorrow.'

Lounging back in the bath I was reviving quickly, the exertion and prickly heat of earlier ebbing away in the soothing water. It had been a wonderful day.

After a few weeks working in the tea-rooms, I was transferred to the gift shop to sell trinkets, sweets, postcards, cans of cold drink and ice creams. It did wonders for my mental arithmetic, as I served crowds of impatient visitors. It was here too that I learned the difference between the British and the French attitude to queuing. My worst nightmares were the coaches of French school parties on sightseeing jaunts across the Channel. Many of the gift shops in Canterbury banned them, as they would lose far more to shoplifting than they would gain in sales.

At the castle, the French children would enter the shop *en masse*. The first thing they would do was to buy a few souvenir carrier bags. Then, while one of them engaged me in conversation in broken English, others would form a ring, blocking my view of the rest of the shop. Those who had purchased the carrier bags would then proceed to fill them up from the shelves and scoot off without paying, while the one talking to me would finally decide to purchase a postcard or an ice-lolly.

The gift shop was not the only place where the French

teenagers caused problems. They chucked the rustic benches around the lake into the water, broke panes in the greenhouses and swarmed through the fruit gardens like locusts. After one of their raids in the gift shop, I locked the door behind them in desperation and went in search of Allan. They had stolen so much that many of the shelves were almost bare. I had been powerless to stop them.

When I arrived at the display ground there was no sign of Allan. Pausing, I was incensed to see an angelic-looking French girl, who couldn't have been much older than me, pick up a stone off the path and hurl it at a tethered Little Owl. Little Owls are the smallest of our native owls, standing only about four inches tall. They are the sweetest looking creatures and I couldn't believe anyone could be so cruel as to try to hurt one. The stone bounced off the owl's chest and the girl bent over to pick up another. I sprang at her and grabbed her by the shoulders.

'How *could* you!' I yelled at her. 'You *horrible* person. Look at him! He's only tiny! You could *kill* him!'

Tears of anger and disbelief welled up in my eyes. That a girl my own age could behave like that was beyond me.

''E was sitting so steel,' she told me, clearly shocked at my reaction. 'I wanted to see 'im move.' She turned on her heel and flounced off in the direction of the coach.

At that moment, Allan appeared. Hearing my story, he flushed scarlet to the roots of his hair.

'Those bloody kids! I'll sort them out this time. I've had enough. You leave them to me,' he told me. I had never heard him swear before.

He called the police, who waited until all the teenagers were back on their coach preparing to leave and then boarded the bus and removed every article that they couldn't produce receipts for. Bags and bags of goods came back to the gift shop. I wanted the police to lock them up, but had to be content with the sight of their downcast faces as the coach left the car park. The girl who had thrown the stone had received a stern telling off from one of her embarrassed teachers and was in tears. It was some consolation.

Another hazard inherent in working in the gift shop was Oriel Massereene's dog, Alma. Oriel was Lord and Lady Massereene's daughter. Most afternoons she left Alma behind the counter in the gift shop, so that she didn't run loose with the tourists. Alma herself wasn't a problem. She was a sweet-natured Alsatian who seemed content to potter about behind the counter. The problem lay in her digestive tract: she had severe flatulence trouble. She broke wind constantly and the smell was excruciating.

This was bad enough, but what really bothered me was that, as she couldn't be seen behind the counter, I was painfully aware that every time it happened, the visitors thought it was me. The fact that I flushed pink each time another waft hit me probably didn't help.

A group of boys came into the shop one hot afternoon to buy cans of drink. They were about seventeen years old and one of them in particular was rather good-looking. I recognized him as the elder brother of a school friend. He had seen me helping with the falconry display earlier that day and started to chat to me about the birds. I was flattered by his attention and talked enthusiastically about the hawks. As the others drifted off, he winked at them and said he'd catch them up. It was quiet in the shop, so we continued to talk.

He was just asking me if I lived locally, when behind me Alma let rip with a particularly foul riposte. The conversation stopped short; I felt my cheeks colouring. Before I could attempt to explain, my companion wrinkled his nose and backed away.

'Must go,' he told me, exiting hastily.

Outside, I could hear him laughing with his friends.

'She *farted*!' His voice drifted in through the open door. 'It smelt *awful*! She's quite pretty, but I couldn't be doing with that!'

The boys were still laughing as they disappeared into the distance.

9

THE BIRDS OF prey at the castle attracted many volunteers who wanted to learn about falconry and generally help out. Of these, no one was keener than Eddie Hare.

Eddie came from Bunker's Hill, a rough area of nearby Dover. He joked that he had his own eagle: a colourful tattoo on his upper left arm. He was a karate enthusiast and kept his wiry frame in good shape with regular workouts. Most weekends he came to the castle to learn about falconry from Allan and help out with the hawks. Sixteen years old, good natured and with a keen sense of humour, Eddie longed to move out of Dover into the country, where he could keep his own bird.

The opportunity came his way to do this when he asked Lord Massereene for a job. He was offered the position of under-gardener at the castle, working under the expert eye of old Ballard. The only problem was that all the cottages on the estate were occupied, so Eddie was told that if he wanted a residential position, he would have to live in one of the old brick potting sheds next to the greenhouses, which lay to the left of the main drive.

I liked Eddie, he was always good fun to be around and he got on well with everyone on the estate. I helped him clear out and paint the potting shed, which was about eight feet wide by twelve feet deep, after which he moved in with half a dozen carrier bags containing all his worldly goods. It was rather dark in the shed – the windows were small and just below ceiling level – but there was electricity running to a couple of sockets and a single light bulb suspended from the ceiling. Eddie's most prized possessions were a stereo system – on which he played rock records at an alarming volume – and a lethal-looking marshal arts weapon consisting of two wooden rods joined together by a length of chain.

The most serious drawback of Eddie's potting shed was its lack of mod. cons. It had no bath or shower and no loo, only a tiny wash basin. The nearest proper facilities were up at the tea-rooms. This was not the sort of detail to which Lord Massereene would have paid attention when he offered Eddie a home there. He was so vague, it had probably never crossed his mind. It was brought home to him one evening when, wandering into the old castle kitchen, he came across Eddie, stark naked, running water into one of the sinks.

'Edward! What *are* you doing?' he enquired, flushing faintly with embarrassment.

'Taking a bath, m'lord,' Eddie informed him, not at all embar-rassed. Squeezing liberal quantities of washing-up liquid into the steaming water in the sink, he hopped in.

'Oh.' Lord Massereene seemed at a loss for words. 'Carry on,' he said finally and left.

A few days later, Lord Massereene was even more startled to see Eddie, dressed in a loin cloth, swing past his window on a rope. Hurrying outside, he looked up to see Eddie suspended from the roof. To amuse Jan and Bridget in the staff flats, Eddie had decided to dress as Tarzan, climb on to the roof, tie a rope round a chimney stack and swing past the girls' window making Tarzan noises. Unfortunately, he had made a miscalculation and, swinging past too many windows, he had now lost all momen-tum and was hanging stranded, beating on the window to be let in. As a startled Lord Massereene watched, the window opened and Eddie disappeared inside.

Considering the number of pranks that he pulled, it was surprising that Eddie lasted at the castle, but he worked hard in the gardens, which were perpetually understaffed. Complaints about the gardens from visitors – many of whom had not taken in the fact that the castle itself was not open when they paid their entrance fees – were not uncommon. One visitor was heard to remark unkindly that all the borders were herbaceous and most of those were stinging nettles. Ballard was a professional gardener, but one of advancing years, and rather slow and doddery. Stephen and Jimbo made up the rest of the gardening task force. These two were known as 'the Smurfs', due to their small stature and the fact that, regardless of the weather, they wore pointed woolly bobble hats. I used to wonder if their heads were pointed underneath, but I never got to find out.

Lord Massereene was not over generous with the wages he paid. The junior gardeners were paid just below the taxable threshold. Stephen, having worked for the same salary for a couple of years, finally plucked up the courage to go up to the big house to ask Lord Massereene for a pay rise. Ushered into his employer's study, he stuttered out a request for an extra pound a week. Rather to Stephen's surprise, Lord Massereene – who only ever seemed really on the ball when discussing money – agreed that this rise would indeed be possible. He went on to point out that if he paid the extra pound, this would put Stephen into the lowest tax bracket and the government would take two pounds away from him. He therefore offered Stephen the choice: take the salary increase and lose two pounds, or stay as he was. After considering these options for a day, Stephen told Lord Massereene that he thought he'd stay as he was.

Around this time, Lady Massereene acquired two new dogs. Taa and Arton were pharaoh hounds, a species none of us had ever seen before. With skinny bodies, pointed ears, sharply pointed pink noses and long, thin legs, the two of them resembled ginger rats on stilts. Each afternoon, Lady Massereene would tie a head scarf over her deerstalker hat, don a camelhair cape and head out into the grounds with a cigarette hanging out of the corner of her mouth and the two dogs on leads. Large, blonde and statuesque, she moved through the gardens like a galleon in full sail. Anyone who showed an interest in her new charges was treated to a knowledgeable dissertation on the lineage of the pharaoh hound. Apparently they went back to the days of Ancient Egypt, whence they derived their name as guardians of the entrance to the tombs. As a species, they were extremely rare in Britain at the time and Lady Massereene had purchased them for breeding. Unfortunately, however, their pedigrees – which arrived after the dogs themselves – revealed that they were brother and sister.

Taa and Arton had singularly unpleasant dispositions and when they were let out to roam the grounds at will, they would bite anyone they encountered. They terrorized the Smurfs who, once they had been bitten a few times, were understandably petrified of them. Digging the long borders along the terraces, Stephen and Jimbo would work back to back, glancing up constantly in case they were ambushed. If a pharaoh hound was spotted on the horizon, the Smurfs would dash for the iron gate leading into the quiet garden, where they would be safe. Taa and Arton were not stupid. Seeing the Smurfs run, they wouldn't head straight for them, but instead would streak along the top lawn and down the steps at the far end to cut off their escape route. It was a race, sometimes the Smurfs won, sometimes they didn't.

The dogs soon developed a fearsome reputation. Complaints were legion – even old Ballard was bitten by them – but Lady Massereene refused to hear a word against them. To make matters worse, they never put a foot wrong when under her gaze, staring at people beadily when they were on the lead, but never attempting to bite. Even Lord Massereene hated them. Finally, Lady Massereene was persuaded to fit Taa and Arton with muzzles.

All the staff were vastly relieved, nobody more so than the Smurfs, when the dogs' reign of terror came to an end. Sadly, however, relief was to be shortlived. Taa and Arton learned how to remove their muzzles with their paws and could once again be seen stalking hapless victims, their muzzles hanging uselessly round their necks.

About ten miles from Chilham, there was a zoo park, housing a large collection of wild animals in spacious, well-laid-out enclosures. I visited the park one summer's day with a school friend on a birthday treat. Having spent some hours in the park, seeing everything there was to see, we stretched out on the grass in front of the café, whilst my friend's mother unpacked a picnic. Lying on my stomach in the grass, looking idly at my surroundings, I noticed a cage I hadn't spotted earlier, almost hidden in the trees beyond the café. Not wanting to miss anything, I climbed to my feet and went over to investigate. To my astonishment, inside a chicken-wire aviary no bigger than six feet square, there was an eagle. It was repeatedly flying off a thin wooden perch, hitting the wire and dropping to the ground. Its feathers were in awful condition.

I was horrified. Everything was wrong with the cage: it was too small, the perches were unsuitable and there was no solid back or sides to the enclosure to make the eagle feel secure. The bird was clearly distressed and, being completely wild, had obviously been deliberately tucked away out of sight of the public. It was golden brown all over and looked a lot like Wally.

Upset, I returned to the rest of my party and explained what I had seen.

'I have to do something,' I told the mother urgently. 'The poor bird's in a terrible state.'

The others came over to see for themselves and after some discussion, I went into the café to enquire about the eagle.

'It's wrong to keep it like that,' I told the girl in the café.' It's going to injure itself if someone doesn't get it out of there.'

The park manager was called.

'It's not been here long,' he told me. 'It's very wild still.'

'Would you sell it?' I asked him.

'I don't know. Look, here's my number, give me a ring later,' the manager said. 'I'll talk to the owner.'

All the way home I fantasized about buying the eagle. I had a few pounds saved from my pocket money and my job in the gift shop. I prayed it would be enough.

When I got back, I told my mother the story and she let me telephone straight away. The manager answered. Breathlessly, I asked him if they'd reached a decision about selling the eagle.

'I spoke to the owner and he said he knows there's a problem with the bird, therefore he's prepared to sell it for thirty-five pounds.'

My heart sank. This was a massive amount of money, far more than my savings and, I knew, more than mum could afford to give me.

'Can I call you back?' I asked, 'I'll let you know later.'

My hope was that Allan would want the eagle, but much to my surprise, he didn't.

'I've got enough hawks at present and no room in the mews for another eagle,' he explained.

'But somebody has to buy it.' I was really worried. The vision of the eagle repeatedly throwing itself against the wire kept running through my mind.

I went for a walk up to the castle, mulling on the problem, and bumped in to Eddie with Jan and Bridget. I knew Eddie dreamed of owning an eagle, but I also knew he couldn't afford thirty-five pounds; he never had any money. Nevertheless, I told them the story in case they could come up with anything helpful.

'I could buy him,' Bridget announced. 'I'll borrow the money from my father.'

She was as good as her word and, two days later, one dishevelled eagle arrived at the castle. Allan identified it as a female African Tawny Eagle and Bridget named her Sheba. I was sad that I hadn't been able to buy Sheba myself, but the important thing was that she was out of that cage.

Bridget didn't stay at the castle for long, but during the time before she left, Eddie managed to save up enough money to buy Sheba in instalments. There wasn't much room in the potting shed with the two of them in there, but Eddie no longer needed to joke about owning an eagle.

10

THERE WAS A nasty commotion in the garden. A deep bark – too deep for Bella – was followed by some loud yowling and hissing. I overtook my mother on the way out to find Wallis on the wall between the front gardens of Carpenters and Deepwell House, next door. Wallis looked like a bottle brush. Swollen to twice his normal size, he was leaning off the wall into next door's garden, batting a portly Dalmatian with a paw. As we arrived on the scene, Wallis delivered a particularly vicious blow with claws outstretched and cut the Dalmatian on the end of its nose. The dog turned tail and ran off howling. Seconds later, a window opened to reveal a grey-haired man with glasses and a bristly, nicotine-stained moustache.

'Is Jay causing problems?' he barked at us. 'I must introduce myself. I'm Alex, Alex Jardine. My wife and I have just purchased Deepwell and we are in the process of moving in. Why don't you come round and have a drink?' he added affably.

We acquiesced and made our way next door, where Alex greeted us enthusiastically, kissing our hands with great aplomb. He was smugly plump – rather like Jay – yet animated. His eyes shone with sincerity behind his glasses and he moved with the slightly ponderous air of one on important business. He ushered us towards a faded velvet-covered sofa, surrounded by boxes and packing cases, in a large and dusty drawing-room.

'Yvonne! Yvonne! Where has she got to? Ah! Yvonne, come and meet . . . I'm sorry I've forgotten your names – Mary and Emma. They live next door.'

A harassed-looking blonde woman in her fifties appeared briefly and disappeared again at Alex's behest to find a bottle of sherry. In contrast to Alex – who radiated health and vitality – Yvonne wore the resigned look of one who is in the middle of mayhem and knows for certain that there is to be no reprieve. Jay appeared with the cut on his nose still oozing blood and I apologized and mopped it with my hankie. Alex didn't appear to notice. He put me in mind of Captain Mainwaring out of *Dad's Army*.

'What do you do?' my mother enquired politely.

'How nice of you to ask,' Alex said charmingly. 'I paint actually – fish mainly. I've got one somewhere round here I can show you . . . Yvonne! Yvonne! Where's that large oil I've just finished of the trout?'

Yvonne reappeared bearing a tray with four engraved glasses and a dusty bottle of sherry.

'I couldn't find a decanter,' she apologized. 'Everything's here somewhere, but there are so many boxes to unpack . . . ' Her voice trailed off and wearily she waved a hand at the serried ranks of packing cases.

'Splendid, splendid. Come and join us for a drink, old girl. By the way, have you seen Charles?' Alex settled himself comfortably in a large armchair and accepted a glass of sherry from his wife.

'Not recently, I'll see if I can find him. I think he's fly-casting in the field.' Yvonne put down her own glass and headed dutifully towards the door.

'Leave him, he needs the practice,' Alex commanded. 'If you can find my rod, I'll give him a lesson myself this afternoon.'

Far from looking dismayed that her husband intended to leave her to continue the unpacking on her own, Yvonne looked faintly relieved.

Charles, their son, was an only child in his late teens. Artistic, like his father, he had a rather startling blond Afro hairdo. He had left school to go straight into art college, but hadn't liked it and left at the end of his first week. He now divided his time between fishing on the nearby Stour, practising his casting in the garden and painting. He was also a member of a local pop group. To Lord Massereene's fury, the group used to rehearse in the old sawmills at weekends. The volume was so loud that the whole area would pulsate with noise until the tiles were virtually shaken from the roof. As the crow flies, the castle was probably half a mile from the sawmills, but the raucous strains of Charles and his head-banging cronies could be clearly heard even at this distance.

The Jardine family was completed by 'Gran', Alex's mother. Frail and wizened with age, Gran repeated herself constantly and would mutter to herself under her breath. She liked porridge for breakfast and the stove in Deepwell nearly always had a saucepan of porridge perched on it, either in its cold and solid state or hot and steaming, with the occasional bubble erupting like Vesuvius. Alex on the other hand liked kippers and each morning an overpowering smell of fish would pervade the air outside our back door.

The Jardines had moved to Chilham to run medieval banquets in the Norman keep at the castle. While guests at the banquets dined on venison and syllabub, they were entertained by minstrels, a fire eater and falconry. To my delight, Ann, who also became involved, asked me to assist her.

'Alex is insisting that everyone must dress up in medieval costume,' she told me. 'Allan's not all that keen to dress up in tights, so I wonder if you would like to help out? I can run you up a costume on my sewing machine.'

The banquets were scheduled to take place on Friday and Saturday evenings. The following Friday, dressed in what can best be described as a polyester caftan, I carried Wally up the back drive behind the substantial figure of Ann, who, swathed in a larger version of my outfit, carried Bugsy. As we climbed the steps to the keep, Alex, who had ignored his own instructions and was in a dinner jacket and a frilly dress shirt, greeted us at the door.

'Splendid, splendid,' he said, beaming at us from behind his bushy, short-clipped moustache like a benign musk-rat. 'We're not quite ready for you yet, so come and have a drink while you're waiting.'

He led us down the spiral staircase into the dungeon. I followed with a degree of trepidation. Out of curiosity one day the previous summer, I had been down into the dungeon after releasing Wally from the top of the keep during a demonstration. It was not an experience I had any desire to repeat. The cold, musty darkness down there had a decidedly sinister feel and I had been anxious to escape back into the daylight. It was easy to believe the tales of the white lady who haunted the dungeon. It was said that she had been bricked up in the walls during Norman times for being an 'unfaithful mistress'.

As I followed the reassuring bulk of Ann through the heavy wooden door into the dungeon, I was amazed at the transformation which had taken place. The rough flint walls were decorated with tapestries, suits of chain mail and a selection of medieval weaponry, including a lethal-looking flail formed from a spiked ball attached to a length of chain. A slate-topped bar, festooned with hops, had been constructed on the far side of the small room, backed by gleaming rows of optics. Sophisticated discotheque equipment, including coloured strobe lights and a revolving mirrored ball, added to the bizarre scene. I wondered what the white lady would make of this brash intrusion into her sanctum.

After a quick drink at the bar, Alex sprayed his mouth liberally with breath freshener to disguise the whisky and we followed him up the steps to the first floor, where the main banqueting hall was packed with a noisy throng of revellers. Alex cleared his throat loudly several times on the threshold to gain their attention, then finally resorted to clapping his hands.

'My lords, ladies and gentlemen,' he announced grandly. 'May I present our falconers.'

It was an introduction with which I became very familiar in the months which followed. The banquets became extremely popular with groups who came to celebrate office parties, birthdays, wedding anniversaries and a host of other special events. After Ann had given a brief talk on falconry in medieval times, it was my task to reverse Wally on to the gauntleted arm of guests so that they could have their photographs taken. After several hours of having their goblets plied liberally with ale and mead by skimpily clad serving wenches, some of the guests were sadly the worse for wear and it was a tribute to Wally's equable temperament that he put up with being manhandled from one person to another.

Back on the home front, the Jardines extended Deepwell by taking in part of the sawmills. They added a huge snooker room, another sizeable drawing-room, several more bedrooms and an additional bathroom. Yvonne told us that she was grateful for the extra bathroom. Charles and Alex, she explained, would return from fishing expeditions with their catches still alive. These they released into the bath, where they would remain for several days while being painted. As a fish artist, Alex was exceptional and about a year after his arrival at Chilham, he was asked to produce a set of stamps for the Post Office.

In their garage, which lay at the far end of Deepwell's long drive, Charles and Alex hung carcasses of venison for the banquets. Charles taught me how to gut and dress a deer, which was far bigger than anything I had tackled before when cleaning meat for the hawks. Deer pelts, in various smelly stages of drying out, were pinned round the walls of the garage, liberally covered in a noisome mixture of saltpetre and bluebottles. Charles even attempted to teach me how to fly-cast on the lawn, but I spent

most of the time hooking the walnut trees in the front garden. Alex purchased a strip of the paddock in front of Carpenters from Lord Massereene and started a vegetable garden, which he tended himself that first summer, wearing an extraordinary straw sun hat tied under his chin with blue ribbon.

The banquets were soon so successful that a new manager, Mike, was employed to help. For a short time Mike lodged with us in Carpenters and it was through him and a strange quirk of fate that I landed a small speaking part in a feature film.

I was spending the night with a school friend when the telephone rang at about seven o'clock in the evening. It was my mother. She told me that Mike had a friend who was the casting director on a film called *O Lucky Man*. The casting director had contacted him on the off-chance that he might know of a young girl she could cast in the role of the vicar's daughter. The film was being shot in the nearby village of Challock. Apparently a girl had come down from stage school in London to do the part, but the director, Lindsay Anderson, was not happy with her. Mike mentioned me as a possible stand-in.

The pressure was on to find a replacement and the casting director wanted to come and see me that very evening. Directions were duly given to her over the telephone. My mother warned me that the casting director would also consider my friend Kyla as an alternative choice. In a state of high excitement, Kyla and I were allowed to stay up until she arrived. I was anxious lest she choose Kyla instead of me. I wished fervently that I had been at home so that she would not see Kyla, who was tall for her age and very pretty, with dark, wavy hair. It was a wet and stormy night and our visitor finally arrived at ten-thirty, having got lost looking for the remote house. She appeared at the door like a drowned rat, spoke briefly to the two of us, said I would be ideal and disappeared again. I was thrilled to have been chosen and tried hard not to gloat. Poor Kyla was visibly crushed.

The next day I was taken out of school to meet Lindsay Anderson. Allan's son Simon came along too and was cast in the role of my younger brother. The star of the film was Malcolm McDowell. My mother told me that he had been in a cult film called *If*. I had never heard of Malcolm McDowell and I did not know what a cult film was, but when we arrived on location at Challock parish church, I had no trouble identifying the star. He was wearing a gold lamé suit. Together with the director, he spent some time chatting to Simon and me, explaining our roles and introducing us to the rest of the cast. We were booked for three days and my mother was booked as our chaperone. We were allotted a location caravan to ourselves, which was parked alongside the catering marquee. Our day started with breakfast.

'Would you like everything in your roll, ducks?' the woman behind the trestle-table asked me.

'Yes please,' I said. I had no idea what 'everything' amounted to, but I was eager to find out.

'Everything' turned out to be a full English breakfast inside a huge bun – fried egg, sausage, bacon and mushrooms. It was delicious. Men with walkie-talkies and expensive-looking anoraks rushed in and out, grabbing a couple of rolls apiece in paper napkins and disappearing again. My mother, Simon and I sat at one of several long tables, observing the flurries of activity with interest.

A woman came into the marquee, accompanied by a girl whom I judged to be about ten – the same age as me. The two of them seemed to be arguing. As they passed our table, the girl – who had long dark hair and a sulky expression – lapsed into silence and looked daggers at me. I was at a loss to understand what I had done to merit such a villainous glare.

The casting director then appeared and joined us at our table.

'That's the girl from stage school whose part you are playing,' she whispered. 'She's going back to London this afternoon. Mr Anderson thought she was too precocious.'

Seeing us glance sympathetically across at her, the girl flounced petulantly out of the marquee, pursued by her chaperone, her breakfast untouched.

'It'll matter awfully to her,' my mother said quietly to me. 'Film schools are very competitive. It will be humiliating for her to go back to London after she thought she'd got the part. To work with a director as famous as Lindsay Anderson would have been a big break for her.'

I felt genuinely sorry for the girl.

Our scenes were to be shot in the rolling downland surrounding Challock church. Although it was spring, the church had been decorated as if for Harvest Festival. I quickly came to realize that nothing in the film world was quite as it seemed. In the cemetery, moss-covered gravestones which appeared to have been there for centuries were suddenly plucked from their resting places by props men and repositioned in a way that expertly disguised the fact that they were made from polystyrene.

With the camera running, Simon and I played tag in the graveyard. I felt completely unselfconscious. The camera was set up at quite a distance and I was never certain when it was running and when it was not, so it felt no different to playing with Simon at home. Lindsay Anderson seemed happy with the sequences and praised us enthusiastically when we had finished for the day.

On the second day we did very little work and divided our time between sitting in the caravan, waiting to be called, and eating ravenously in the marquee. My mother and I were enjoying the film catering; we were on a tight budget at home and it was wonderful to have three huge meals a day. By the afternoon, though, I began to grow bored.

'Can't we go and watch them filming?' I asked my mother.

'No, not at the moment,' she told me firmly.

'Why?'

'They're filming some scenes in the church which would be unsuitable for you and Simon to watch,' she explained tentatively.

'What sort of scenes?'

'X-rated scenes,' my mother said abruptly.

I was none the wiser, but later in the afternoon things were enlivened when we were called to do a sequence which involved a hay ride in a cart. It was just like haymaking on the estate with Allan and the boys.

On the last day of filming, we were driven up to the top of the downs in a Land Rover. With the camera running, we were asked to run with Malcolm McDowell down into the valley. I liked Malcolm, he was sweet to Simon and me and kept toffees for us in the pockets of his gold lamé jacket. I was sorry when the last day drew to a close. At the end of shooting, we were paid ninety pounds each by the casting director.

'Would you consider letting Emma go to Africa to work in a film?' she asked my mother. 'I'm casting another production and looking for a young girl to play opposite the boy who starred as Billy Casper in *Kes*. The film is about eagles.'

I caught my breath. What an opportunity! And to work with Dai Bradley who had been my idol ever since I had seen him flying his kestrel in *Kes*.

'How long would it take?' my mother asked.

'Oh, about three months.'

'I don't think I could take Emma out of school for that long,' my mother said, in a tone which brooked no argument.

I was devastated. How could she turn down such an offer on my behalf? I had loved my first taste of filming. As far as I was concerned, my mother was denying me the chance of stardom. As soon as we dropped off Simon next door, I asked her why.

'You remember the little girl who came down from film school for your part?' she said. 'You remember how unhappy she was? How much it clearly mattered to her?'

'Yes,' I said. 'But I don't understand what she's got to do with me.'

'I don't want you ending up like her,' my mother said bluntly. 'She'd grown up too quickly.'

I did not think much of this explanation and it was months before I really forgave my mother. Meanwhile, the Board of Film Censors awarded *O Lucky Man* an 18 certificate. I was not to see the film myself until several years later.

11

I HAD HEARD ABOUT another falconry establishment with the reputation of being the biggest and best in the country. It was run by Phillip Glasier, who used to be professional falconer to the actor, James Robertson Justice. The Falconry Centre, which was based in Gloucestershire, boasted an unrivalled collection of eagles, hawks, falcons and owls and also ran falconry courses for the public. I badgered my mother to let me go on a course and finally, one summer when I was thirteen, she relented and allowed me to telephone and enquire.

I was surprised and extremely disappointed to learn that the courses were only run in the winter. Speaking to Phillip himself, I poured out the story of how I had come to learn about hawks, explaining that I had been flying them for five years and desperately wanted to learn as much as possible. My enthusiasm must have struck a chord with Phillip.

'If you really want to come down, you can help out for two weeks,' he said. 'You'll have to work hard, you won't get to fly a hawk and I won't pay you anything,' he added gruffly.

It was all arranged. My long-suffering mother booked us both into a bed and breakfast in Newent – the closest town to the

Falconry Centre – and we headed west for the holiday of my dreams.

My mother dropped me off outside the centre very early on my first morning. Phillip came to the door to let me into the museum-cum-reception area. He had a goatee beard, silver-grey hair and a forthright manner. Walking into the museum was, for me, like walking into paradise. Falconry equipment, old photographs, hawk eggs and countless other items of paraphernalia relating to hawks were housed in glass cabinets or displayed on the walls. Outside, row upon row of tethered hawks of all shapes and sizes stretched into the distance.

The hawks were kept on a proper 'weathering ground', in three-sided, roofed shelters made from tightly packed Norfolk reed. Most of the birds lived outside year round in these shelters, which were called 'weatherings'. The perches were sunk into a base of neatly raked sand and, on fine days, the hawks were put out on to the lawn in front of the weatherings and offered a bath in a wide, shallow dish of water. Tidy, clipped yew hedges separated the lawns from the paths where visitors walked. The paths followed a U shape, with another large lawn in the centre, where the biggest birds were tethered. Beyond the 'hawk walk' lay breeding aviaries and a field to one side where the flying demonstrations took place.

Some of the species at the centre I had only seen in books and there were others which I did not recognize at all. To me, the most impressive sight was the row of large falcons. Phillip told me he used them during the displays, when he flew them to the lure. I had only seen Allan fly the smaller kestrels to the lure before, so I was extremely keen to see one of the bigger falcons in action.

Back in the museum, Phillip gave me my first job. I was to clean the museum from top to bottom, sweeping the floor and dusting all the glass cabinets. When I had finished this – which took most of the morning – I was allowed to help with the task of filling up the hawk baths. The highlight of the day came when

I watched one of the displays and marvelled at the breathtaking speed of a lanner falcon stooping to the lure.

I learned a lot during the two weeks. Phillip had a sharp tongue, but he was extremely kind to me. My experience in the gift shop at Chilham came in useful when I was stationed at the reception desk to collect entrance fees, but my favourite times were when I was allowed to handle the hawks. I greased endless jesses, fetched, carried, cleaned and generally made myself as useful as possible. To my delight, Phillip relented about me flying hawks while I was there and each afternoon he included me in the training of one of the lanner falcons. I sat in the sweet meadow grass of the flying ground and watched him put the young bird through its paces. When he reckoned I had watched enough, Phillip taught me how to call the falcon and how to approach it on the lure, being sensitive to its every movement. I became totally absorbed, drinking everything in like the elixir of life. It was the best two weeks I had ever had and, at the end of it, Phillip paid me two pounds.

I returned home to Kent positively glowing with the experience, only to discover that I had left behind my precious leather falconry glove, which my mother had paintstakingly cut out and stitched for me. She had made it a couple of years previously on the eve of my first television appearance with the hawks. The BBC had come to the castle to make a short film on falconry. During a recce the day before filming, the producer had asked if Simon and I could be interviewed. Up until that time I had been managing with an adult's falconry glove, several sizes too large for me, so my mother asked Ann for a glove pattern, scaled it down, bought some leather from Canterbury that afternoon and made a glove to fit me overnight, in order for me to have it for filming the next day. I telephoned Phillip and asked if he could find it and send it on to me.

'We've got loads of gloves here – how will I recognize it?' he asked me.

'Well . . .' I was embarrassed. 'When my mother was making

it she accidentally cut out the thumb hole on the wrong side, so she embroidered an eagle on a leather patch and stitched it over the gap.'

'Sounds perfectly revolting,' he snapped at me. 'I'll see if I can find it. By the way, do you want a kestrel?'

Pogle the kestrel arrived by train in a Red Star parcel. I opened the box carefully in the kitchen at Carpenters and a pair of beady, bright eyes greeted me. Catching her in the box wasn't easy. She sunk her needle-sharp talons into my hand several times as I reached in, trying to corner her. Finally, I dropped a tea towel over her and lifted her out while she made clear her annoyance with a high-pitched scream.

I had prepared leather jesses for her and while my mother held her – struggling and protesting – I fitted these around her legs as I had been taught. As soon as she was equipped, I attempted to get Pogle to sit on my glove. Every time I positioned her, she flopped off and hung by her ankles. Wally had done the same thing initially, but it had been easy enough to put my right hand on his chest and lift him on to the glove again. Each time I tried this with Pogle, she either bit me or managed to grab me with her talons. My right hand was quickly covered with numerous cuts and small but painful puncture wounds.

Eventually, Pogle stood on the glove, but if I moved a muscle, she bated again. Despite the fact that she was tiny compared to Wally and, indeed, to most of the other hawks next door, she was full of spunk and fire. She stood only six inches off the glove. Her chest was a biscuit colour, streaked with darker brown, and her back was a glossy mantle of chestnut feathers speckled with black spots. She sat stiffly on my fist, with her feathers pulled tight against her body, ready to react instantly to the slightest provocation. Looking into her blazing eyes, I got the impression that she was going to prove a strong character.

After a couple of hours both of us were tired, so I tied her to a perch which I had prepared for her in a shed at the bottom of the garden. I was proud of my 'mews' for Pogle. I had moved a load of firewood out of the shed, swept, cleaned and polythened the floor and covered this with a layer of newspaper. On a shelf below the windows sat a small pair of balance scales and weights which I had purchased from a kitchen shop. Beside this lay my precious copy of *Falconry for You*. To one side of the door, I had amateurishly hammered in a row of nails on which to hang my glove, a dreadful attempt at a hood which I had made, a spare pair of jesses and a clean leash. I thought it all looked very professional.

Over the days which followed, Pogle made slow progress. She fed from my glove after a couple of days but, to my frustration, she flatly refused to jump for food. If I moved my glove too close, she would snatch the food from her perch. If I kept my fist out of her reach, she leant forward precariously, but remained stubbornly on her perch. After a couple of fruitless days tempting, wheedling and cajoling – during which she hardly ate a thing – I went next door and borrowed a kestrel called Humphrey, who was already trained. Putting Humphrey on another perch next door to Pogle, I jumped him for food while Pogle looked on. The example worked. Returning to Pogle, I stretched out my hand and she jumped immediately. After that we were under way.

Seven days later, Pogle was doing five stoops to the lure. I flew her to beef, but she also needed whole food to give her roughage, so I trapped sparrows for her in a sparrow trap supplied by Allan. On wet days, I flew her indoors. This was not a practice described in *Falconry for You*, but it was a way of keeping her exercised in bad weather. I started off by calling her across the kitchen to my glove. She seemed totally unaffected by being indoors and came first whistle. I opened the door to the dining room and called her the full length of the kitchen and through the open door. After a few days' practice, I could put her in the kitchen, leave all the doors open through the house and head for the drawing room. She was very responsive to my whistle and as soon as I called her, she took off and came to find me, flying round three corners in the process. Soon, I could get her to find me upstairs. I spent hours each evening with her on my glove as I watched television and she grew very tame, preening and standing on one leg, with the other foot tucked up into her feathers, a sign of contentment and well-being in a hawk. I felt that the bond between us was strong.

Each day I rushed home from school to fly her, longing for the moment when I could release her to take to the wing. The blazing anger which lit her eyes when she arrived had been replaced by trust, yet Pogle would never be completely domesticated. I had learned that it was not in the nature of a hawk ever to be subservient to a human being. Unlike dogs, birds of prey have no desire to please man. Trained hawks offer a falconer no tangible affection or loyalty, but instead something much more: the chance to work in partnership with a free spirit. To hold Pogle on my glove, release her to the heavens, then recall her from aloft, seemed to me like a recurring miracle.

One windy Saturday in November, six weeks after her arrival, I flew Pogle in the garden. She was fat that day – looking back on it, I realized she was too fat – and during her second flight to the lure she climbed steeply as a gust caught her. She glanced down at me briefly before turning and flying away. I ran after her, but she kept going and going, like a puff of thistledown blowing on the wind. I lost sight of her after a couple of fields, as she headed deep into the estate.

Over the next twenty-four hours I searched and searched for Pogle. By Sunday night I was in despair. I had flown her, as usual, with her jesses on and I knew that these could snag and trap her. I cried myself to sleep that night and dreamt tortured dreams of Pogle hanging upside down from the branch of a tree, flapping weakly until her strength failed her. I woke pale and exhausted and, to my utter dismay, my mother insisted that I went to school. It was one of the longest days at school that I can remember. I couldn't concentrate on anything at all and got into trouble for staring out of the window. When I finally walked into the kitchen late that afternoon, my heart was heavy. I had no hope whatsoever of hearing good news. My mother turned to greet me.

'She's back! Some scrap-metal merchants went to a dump on the estate and found her there, trapped by her jesses on a bramble. They took her to Allan, who brought her to me.' Her face darkened. 'She's hurt though, you'd better have a look at her. I've put her in the downstairs loo.'

I rushed into the loo and found Pogle propped on soft towels draped over the toilet seat. Both her legs were badly bruised and her ankles were terribly swollen. She could not stand, but sat on her haunches instead, with her lower legs stretched out in front of her. Her eyes were dull and she seemed to have lost all her fight.

I prepared a dish of warm water and antiseptic and gently bathed her legs, which were clearly painful. To my relief, she could still open and clench her toes, so I knew her ankles weren't broken. After I had finished bathing her legs, I offered her some beef, cut small, with a pair of tweezers. She accepted a few pieces hungrily. This was a good sign and the food seemed to pep her up a bit. She looked more alert and started to make herself comfortable, settling down on her chest like a broody hen. Lying there, she looked so sweet and confiding. I turned the light off and left her to sleep, relieved beyond measure that she was back, praying that her ankles would mend.

The next morning before school, I gave Pogle a dead mouse. She could not hold it in her feet to eat, but before I could retrieve it, she tucked it underneath her and lay down on it. I tweezer-fed her beef again, but she seemed to want to keep the mouse as security. She looked a little brighter and seemed to be taking in her surroundings, bobbing her head as she looked around.

When I returned from school that afternoon, my mother reported that the invalid had sat up on her haunches for part of the day, accepted a little more beef and had had a doze in the

101

afternoon. My mother had grown fond of Pogle too during the couple of months that I had had her. This was just as well, as with me away at school each day, she had been landed with the task of playing nursemaid to a convalescent kestrel.

As Pogle grew stronger, her spirit returned and she became wilful and disruptive. Because of her sore ankles, she couldn't be tethered. As the swelling subsided, she started to use her feet a little. Soon she could hop off the loo on to the floor. After that, the door to the loo could not be shut as it opened inwards on the small space and Pogle used to sit on the floor behind it. This effectively gave her the run of the kitchen and, as soon as she felt up to it, she started to explore.

Although she still spent much of her time lying down, her legs could soon support the weight of her landing, so she started to use her wings once more. After a few short practice runs, she flew up to the highest shelf in the kitchen and settled there in her broody hen position, wedged between a couple of ornate antique mugs. I think it was only then that my mother began to realize the full destructive potential of having a kestrel loose in her kitchen. Until now, cleaning up after Pogle had been a matter of washing the towels she sat on and changing the news-paper in her new sleeping quarters. Now she was mobile it was a different matter altogether.

She developed a favourite roosting spot on the kitchen window-sill behind the sink. From this vantage point, she could watch sparrows on the terrace outside and keep a wary eye on Bella, who had her basket under the sideboard opposite. After a few days, Pogle felt the urge to get to a higher perch, whilst maintaining her position at the window, so she started to roost on the extractor fan. There was only just enough room for her to fit on her stomach between the fan and the lintel over the top of the window, but she would squeeze herself into the four-inch gap and leer down at us while we did the washing-up.

In between extended bouts of resting, Pogle made a terrible mess. She flew round the kitchen, passing droppings liberally.

102

She could even put out both of the pilot lights on the gas cooker by muting on them as she flew over, leaving the kitchen reeking of gas. She perched on items of crockery and breakages became frequent. If newspaper was left beneath her roosting point to make it easier to clean up after her, she shredded it into confetti, distributing thousands of tiny pieces all over the kitchen as she flapped her wings. She paddled on the draining board and picked up a pair of my mother's tights and flew round the kitchen with them. Food which she did not want to eat straight away, she surreptitiously stashed in a small gap between the boiler and the wall, until I found it much later by tracking down the smell of festering meat.

Sometimes she went down to floor level and sidled up to Bella, until she was eyeball to eyeball with her. If neither of us was there to stop her, she intimidated poor Bella to the point of stealing meat from her bowl. An entry in my mother's diary on Christmas Eve, six weeks after Pogle had been found injured, reads, 'While we were out, she broke the only good cup that I had not put away in a safe place. She had paddled in the sugar bowl again and mixed it with the salt. The kitchen smelt like the lower end of Calcutta – wish I was blessed with the temperament of Mother Theresa. I am not!!'

After six months she was finally fit enough to be jessed once more. It was time for Pogle to make a fresh start. I retrained her and got her properly fit; then, that spring, we put her into an aviary with one of Allan's male kestrels, Ivor, who had a broken wing. We hoped that the pair might breed but, although they got on well together, roosting side by side and even exploring the nest box, they took it no further. After a couple of months, Pogle became restless, staring upwards with her eyes fixed on the sky. I was acutely conscious that her future was in my hands.

After a great deal of soul searching, I decided to release Pogle. Ivor was too crippled to be released, but Pogle was in perfect health and there was no reason why she should not raise her own family in the wild. I knew she could catch mice and I thought her chances of survival were good. After all the time she had spent with us and all we had been through together, I could not justify confining her for the rest of her days. One fine July morning, my mother and I walked across the paddock behind the house to Pogle's aviary. With a lump in my throat and my eyes smarting with tears, I opened the aviary door. Without hesitation, she darted out. We watched as she flew like an arrow into one of the big walnut trees behind the house. She sat there for a while, then took off. I shielded my eyes and watched her until she was lost in the early morning sun.

12

EVEN WITH BINOCULARS, I couldn't see much under the black stetson. I watched intently as the young man wheeled his mount round on its hocks and shot off at a gallop across the paddock. He could certainly handle a horse.

The village was agog. Lord Massereene had invited Max Diamond's Jousting Association of Great Britain to move its headquarters to the castle. Jousting displays were now going to be a central attraction at Chilham during the spring and summer months. Recently, the stable block had become a hive of activity. Shiny chrome wheelbarrows were propped up by the muck heap. Shovels and pitchforks leant against the back wall of the stables, and several chickens, some farmyard ducks and two geese appeared in a small wire run below the rear stable steps.

Between the stable block and the back drive of the castle lay the farmyard, strewn with an ancient and malodorous layer of manure mixed with straw. A covered walkway ran round the inside of the yard and off this opened the doors to food storage rooms, an old milking parlour, several stalls and, in the corner nearest the back of the stables, a bullpen leading off a large loose box, which had been unoccupied for many years. The buildings were of mellow red brick with leaded light windows, and roofed with old Kent peg tiles in muted shades of pink and ochre. To me it looked exactly as a traditional farmyard should look.

The yard was presided over by Dougie, the shepherd. In his twenties, Dougie was about six feet two, with a long, lugubrious face and dank, dark, shoulder-length hair. His Kent dialect was enriched with adjectives which helped him to describe, in no uncertain terms, the joys of working with sheep on an estate where it looked as if money was tight, facilities limited and essential materials non-existent. Mollie, Dougie's wife, darted through our lives like a little bird. For a shepherd's wife, she wore the most unsuitable clothing. Pegging the family's washing up outside their small cottage at the edge of the stable yard, Mollie generally wore pastel crimplene skirts, frilly blouses and gingery stockings with open-toed strappy sandals. She was quite a bit older than Dougie, but they had a lot in common, including their vivid and highly descriptive vocabulary.

On a cold morning in December, soon after the new activity had started up around the stables, I went in search of Dougie with the excuse that I needed some baler twine, but really to gain a closer look at what was going on. There was no sign of Dougie in the farmyard, but just as I was turning to leave, a noise alerted me to the bullpen on the far side of the yard. As I watched, a magnificent dark bay stallion emerged through the open doors of the loose box. Snorting and arching his neck, the stallion paced around the confined pen, nostrils flaring. He was not particularly tall – not much more than fifteen hands high – but he had stunning conformation, with a thick neck, muscular quarters and a long, wavy mane and a forelock which reached the tip of his nose.

I edged closer to watch the stallion, mentally scanning the pages of one of my horse books to see if I could work out what breed he was. What struck me most was the curious way he moved: high stepping with hooves flicking out to the sides as he trotted round the pen. As I approached him, he turned fiery dark eyes on to me, then, to my disappointment, he disappeared back inside his box.

Later that afternoon, four riders appeared in the paddock behind Carpenters, careering around on glossy, fine-boned horses. Watching from my bedroom window, I noted jealously that the stallion I had seen earlier was being expertly ridden by a young woman. The other three horses were ridden by youths. My eye was constantly drawn by the rider in the black stetson. I wished he would take the hat off so I could see him properly.

That evening, quite unexpectedly, I was introduced to the mystery rider. I was in the Dungeon Bar waiting for Ann and me to be called for our turn in the main hall, when a young man appeared at my elbow. Even without the cowboy hat, I recognized him. He introduced himself as Steve Ford.

'I saw you riding in the paddock earlier today,' I said shyly. He was well-built but not tall – about my height – with blond hair which fell to his shoulders and a tanned face. His blue eyes were drawn to Wally.

'We were just giving the horses some exercise. They're mainly Spanish Andalusians. They hadn't been out since Max brought them down here and they needed to let off steam,' he explained.

'Who was the girl on the stallion?' I enquired.

'That was Sue on Cordobes. She rides him in the tournaments. It's a good gimmick to have a female knight, the crowd love it. The other two were Gareth, my best friend, and Mel, Sue's boyfriend. Is this your eagle – can I hold him?'

Surprised, I handed over the spare glove and Steve lifted Wally off my fist. I was even more surprised to see that he seemed to know what he was doing.

'Have you handled hawks before?' I enquired, curious.

'I used to work at the Hawking Centre in Crediton,' he told me. 'I took the job of head falconer there when I left school. I've only got a kestrel at the moment. For the last couple of years I've been doing semi-professional stuntwork, including jousting.'

I was staggered. He was handsome, he rode horses *and* he was a falconer.

'I'm staying with Max for the weekend to visit the set-up, then I'm moving here next month to train the horses and the squad of guys who ride them.' His eyes settled on mine. 'I'll be living in the groom's flat in the stable yard. If you're any good with horses, I'd appreciate a hand exercising them.'

Tossing and turning in bed that night, I thought about the way things were changing in my life. Many of the people I had known since we came to live on the castle estate had moved on or were on the point of leaving. Eddie had left several years ago, taking Sheba with him. In the last month, I had been shocked to learn that the Oswalds were leaving too, with all the hawks, including my beloved Wally. Even old Ballard was close to retiring. Apart from the Jardines, I thought I was destined to be left Dougie, Mollie and the Smurfs for company. Now a new door was opening. Steve was moving on to the estate, bringing with him an exciting and romantic world of horses and jousting. I fell asleep that night to dream of knights in armour, flashing swords and noble steeds.

Steve arrived on the estate in late January. He blotted his copy book early on by announcing that he had found a ginger dog with long legs hanging by its muzzle from a barbed-wire fence at the far end of the horses' paddock. He had released it, he told Dougie.

'Should have left the bugger hanging there.' Dougie was deeply put out, as indeed were Stephen and Jimbo when they heard how Steve had rescued one of the pharaoh hounds. The Smurfs went into a decline until they heard a few days later that Taa – the more aggressive of the two – had been found run over on the main road. Lady Massereene requested that they bury the dog in the rose garden. Some hours later, two figures in bobble hats could be seen dancing joyfully on a pile of freshly dug earth.

Steve's new quarters were far from lavish. The main room was large, but very dark and dingy, with peeling paint and a concrete floor. Light was provided by a single, dim bulb and a small window which opened on to the stable yard. The room contained a large stone sink in the corner, an ancient Belling stove and an airing cupboard which housed the hot-water tank. Max supplied a few items of furniture: a bed, a ripped black vinyl sofa with orange cushions, a small table with two chairs, and a sideboard. Off the main room, there were two tiny cubicles containing a concrete-floored shower and a loo.

Steve spread a black plastic hayrick sheet on the floor, fixed a curtain across one corner, behind which he hung his clothes, and moved in with Corky the kestrel – who slept on the end of his bed – and a record player. Shortly after his arrival, I was thrilled to receive an invitation to lunch.

We dined on steak and kidney pie with rice and baked beans, to the strains of Rick Wakeman's album *Myths and Legends – King Arthur and the Knights of the Round Table*. Over lunch we talked enthusiastically and easily about hawks, horses and Steve's past.

'How old were you when you first started flying hawks?' he asked me.

'Eight,' I said. 'How old were you?'

'I was twelve when I first flew one, but I was eight when I first became interested. It was the year Goldie the Eagle escaped from London Zoo.'

He passed me a faded yellow scrapbook. It contained a dozen press clippings featuring the Goldie story. It struck me that the scrapbook was similar in many ways to one which I had compiled when Ann and Allan had first moved to Chilham, which documented with photographs my training of Wally.

By the end of lunch, I had begun to build up a picture of Steve. I couldn't get over the coincidence of meeting someone in whom a passion for hawks and falconry burned as brightly as it did in me. In 1977 it was a rare sport, only practised by a handful of people across the country. In the afternoon I ran back to Carpenters across the paddock from the stable yard and found my mother in the kitchen.

'Steve used to be a professional falconer at the Hawking Centre in Devon,' I told her breathlessly. 'But then he left to start jousting as Knight of the Eagles with Max Diamond.'

'That's nice,' my mother said vaguely, intent on a steaming pan of garden gooseberries, which she was turning into chutney.

'He's hoping to get the job as falconer here at the castle when the Oswalds leave.'

The vinegar in the chutney stung my eyes and the pungent aroma was so overpowering it made my nose run. Even Bella's nose wrinkled, but before the two of us escaped into the garden, I got my mother's sanction to ask Steve to supper the following night.

The next day my nose was still running, but not from the chutney. Overnight, I had gone down with a heavy cold. Early that evening, while my mother laid up supper on the small round table in the drawing-room, I went upstairs to get ready. I put on my best jeans and my favourite red and black striped rugby shirt, then stood in front of the mirror on the door of my wardrobe to study my appearance. I had shot up in height recently. At five feet eight and three quarters, I was only a quarter of an inch shorter then my mother. My dark hair now curled half-way down my back and I had a slim, well-developed figure. All I could see looking in the mirror that evening, though, was my red, running nose. I applied a little make-up to try to disguise it. I was really fed up. Why did I have to look so awful when I so much wanted to look my best? Life was grossly unfair.

Steve arrived at the kitchen door punctually at six-thirty, dressed in clean jeans, a collarless shirt and tall Spanish riding boots. As usual, he wore his black cowboy hat pulled well down over his forehead. I let him in, trying not to sound too thick-headed, and Bella gave him a warm welcome while he hung his hat on the peg inside the door. In the drawing-room, I shyly introduced him to my mother.

To my relief, they appeared to warm to each other from the

outset and the evening progressed well. Steve was lively company and he entertained us with colourful tales of his exploits with the jousting troupe.

'My father's a senior probation officer,' he explained. 'He wanted me to work with people because he didn't think I could make a career out of hawks and jousting. In fact both my parents disapproved, but that didn't stop me. The same day I left school in Exmouth, I left home and walked straight into a job with hawks.'

I hoped this was not striking any ominous chords with my mother. I had two career options in front of me, etched in stone at the time of my birth by an omnipotent parental hand. One was to read medicine; the other was to follow in my father's footsteps and read law. Currently I was leaning towards law, as I had recently discovered that I could take my articles while actually working in a law firm, thereby earning my keep and avoiding going away to university, which had never held any attraction for me. Despite my dutiful resolve to follow a 'proper' career, I envied Steve his freedom. It seemed to me that I was destined to progress from slaving over books in school to slaving over books in a law firm, with no light at the end of the tunnel.

My mother went up to bed at ten o'clock. My cold had taken a turn for the worse and, forced to abandon all attempts to disguise my snivelling, I was now streaming into a succession of paper hankies. I didn't know whether it was the cold or the company, but I was beginning to feel a little light-headed. I so much wanted to make a good impression on Steve, who looked to me like a blond hero out of a magazine.

About an hour later he left, thanking me for a wonderful evening. I climbed the stairs and knelt on the window seat on the landing, watching the light from his torch as he crossed the paddock. When the light was lost from view, I went into my mother's room and sat on the edge of her bed. She put her book down and looked at me.

'Well?' she enquired.

'I think he's wonderful,' I enthused. 'But he kept a polite distance.'

'I'm not surprised with your cold – what did you expect?'

'Can I invite him again?' I asked anxiously.

'Ask him whenever you want to,' my mother said, smiling. 'I like him, he seems very straightforward and it's a real coincidence that you have falconry in common. The odds against that must be incredibly slim.'

Steve came to supper each evening for the next two days. On the third evening, my cold had developed into flu and I looked hellish. My mother went to bed early again, tactfully explaining that she had an excellent book to finish. Steve and I sat in the flickering firelight, marvelling at the uncanny similarity between Alex Jardine and Arthur Lowe, whom we were watching on television. In the dim glow, our eyes met and we stopped laughing. Leaning forward, he kissed me gently on the lips. It was a few days before my fifteenth birthday, yet I felt again the burning certainty which I had felt about my future with hawks: like a bolt from the blue I knew that I wanted to spend the rest of my life with Steve.

13

POTENTIALLY IT WAS bad news. Eddie returned to the castle the day after the Oswalds had departed, with Sheba and a young wife called Jan in tow. I saw them going up the back drive heading for a meeting with Lord Massereene. A few hours later I heard that Eddie had been given the job of falconer at the castle.

Lord Massereene had promised Steve the job, but I knew his reason for changing his mind. Eddie had Sheba and Steve only had Corky. A kestrel did not have the allure of an eagle when it came to displays and publicity. Having lost touch with Eddie, I felt bitterly resentful that he should waltz back on to the estate and steal the job from under Steve's nose. The question which it inevitably posed was, would Steve stay at Chilham?

I had fallen in love with Steve. With it came feelings I had never experienced before. The minute I heard the news I was tortured by thoughts of his leaving; he had often told me that he had only accepted the job with Max because of the promise of the job as falconer. Would he stay for the jousting alone? Would he stay because of me? I didn't know; all I knew was that his answer mattered to me more than anything had ever mattered to me before. In fear and trepidation, I went to find him in the stables. He was grooming Cordobes when I found him.

'I've heard,' he said, without looking up from the horse's gleaming flank.

I did not have the courage to ask Steve the question which was burning inside me, but watching him energetically wielding the body brush, I felt tears pricking in my eyes. A shaft of sunlight streamed through the door of the box and lit his blond head as he concentrated on his work. If he left, my heart would break for sure.

He stepped back and inspected his handiwork. Catching a glimpse of my face, he registered surprise. He came over to where I was standing and took my shoulders in his hands.

'I won't leave, if that's what you're thinking,' he told me. 'I love you; I'm not going anywhere.'

Sobbing with relief, I buried my face in his chest, hugging him tightly.

'I love you too,' I said. 'I thought you would go.'

'I couldn't, not now, so wipe your eyes and cheer up,' he said, kissing me on the forehead. 'We'll get more hawks of our own anyway and work something out. Alex has promised me that we can continue to do the falconry at the banquets, if we can get another hawk.'

In his new role, Eddie revamped the static display ground. Thoughtfully but inaccurately he translated the signs which read DO NOT FEED THE BIRDS into French as NE MANGE PAS LES OISEAUX. Meanwhile, Steve attempted to buy a couple of new hawks. Good hawks were not easy to come by, so I telephoned Phillip Glasier to see if he might be able to help. He told me that he had a Long-legged Buzzard 'sitting on a perch twiddling her toes' and that if I wanted her I could have her for fifty pounds. Steve's wage was only twenty pounds a week, but he had some money saved from doing staged saddle falls during jousting tournaments – for which he got ten pounds a time extra – and so he purchased Ebony, who was soon flying free and hunting rabbits on the estate.

With Corky and Ebony, we were set to do the banquets. Our

meagre earnings from the banquets paid for the hawks' meat and the Sunday joint, which became Steve's contribution to the housekeeping at Carpenters. He ate with my mother and me two or three evenings a week and frequently he cooked too, revealing a culinary talent which had been belied by our first lunch.

It was a beautiful spring that year. I gradually became involved in every aspect of Steve's work as he looked after the horses and prepared for the summer jousting tournaments. When the work was done, we would saddle up Cordobes and Steve's jousting horse, Fabiola, and ride out into the cool woods across the estate.

On Saturday mornings, I did Steve's washing-up in the large stone sink in the corner of his flat. This was a real labour of love, as he never washed up a thing through the week, stacking plates, cups and mugs one on top of another, until the sink was filled with a precarious stack of crockery, which got smellier as I dug deeper. He had no fridge, so food, which was kept in the sideboard, went off very quickly. Each week he would start a 'stewpot' with chopped lamb and several handfuls of pearl barley. He added to this surprisingly tasty concoction through the week, reheating it each evening with the addition of a chopped carrot or a handful of sliced potatoes when it began to thin out. Towards the end of the week it had turned into a soup and, by the weekend, the pan with traces of furry remnants burnt on to its base was balanced on the top of the pile in the sink. There was no draining board, so I had to stack everything on the floor in order to fill the sink with steaming water to make a start. At the bottom of the pile I invariably came across two bottles with an inch or two of green milk in the bottom.

Max Diamond was a human dynamo. In his early fifties, he was strongly built, with a forceful manner and powerful presence. His hair and bushy moustache, which curled up at the corners, were pure white. Rheumy blue eyes, shot with fine red veins, reflected his love of beer. He had a keen sense of humour, but his quick temper was legendary and his language was the most colourful I had ever heard. Whilst Alex's favourite word was 'splendid', Max's was 'poxy' and the stable yard constantly reverberated to his dulcet East-End tones. He lived and breathed jousting, and rode in the tournaments as the Black Gauntlet, insisting on winning every event. When I played darts in the pub with Max and Steve and other members of the troupe, teams were divided into 'The Red House' and 'The Blue House', just as they were during tournaments.

Apart from the jousting, Max's principal claims to fame were as a songwriter and author. He wrote the hit sixties song sung by Charlie Drake, 'My Boomerang Won't Come Back', which sold nearly a million copies, and a humorous book entitled *Joust a Minute*, written in the same colourful language in which he spoke. Even Max was surprised by the number of expletives which survived into print, especially as the publicity material rashly described it as 'a book for the whole family.'

'They left in all the effs!' Max said. 'I told 'em to take them out – 'cept the one about the Sicilian landing, that was an important one. Still,' he added cheerfully, 'many people've complimented me on the book. They say reading it's just like hearing me speak.'

Faced with this larger-than-life character, it came as something of a surprise to meet Joan, Max's wife. Quiet, educated and possessed of a delicate beauty, Joan had an air of serenity and a polite and cultured manner which was totally at odds with Max's rancorous tirades. Considerably younger than Max, she presided at the jousting tournaments as Queen of Light and Beauty. Max and 'Joaney', as he called her, had a three-year-old son, Peter. Much to his annoyance, Max was constantly mistaken for Peter's grandfather.

Despite his shortcomings, Max was good-hearted and allowed me to enter his intoxicating world of horses, costumes and tournaments with kindness and generosity. I was drawn into a medieval existence, accompanied by my very own knight in shining armour.

Steve borrowed my mother's car to pick me up from the station after school each afternoon, and soon he was spending every evening with us. He would sometimes cook supper and help me with any homework which required a drawing. He was delighted when his biology diagrams scored higher marks than they had ever earned him at school. In many respects, he was like a cross between a boyfriend and the big brother I so sorely missed. I hated it when he went back to his miserable flat at the end of each evening. In the mornings, as I dressed for school, watching him across the paddock feeding the chickens and mucking out Cordobes, I would long for the moment when he met me off the train at the end of the day. While other girls in my class were talking about who they were going out with that weekend, which discotheques they were going to and what time their parents wanted them home, I would hug to myself the knowledge of my relationship with Steve.

That spring, my mother and I went on holiday for two weeks to Minorca. I missed Steve badly and was thereby rendered totally immune to the pesterings of Spanish waiters who wanted to take me out in a pedalo or to a discotheque. The two weeks passed slowly and when my mother and I were finally on our way home from the airport, I at last brought up the subject I had been mentally rehearsing for the entire holiday.

'Steve spends every evening with us now,' I started off.

'I'd noticed,' my mother said dryly.

'I hate it when he goes back to his flat each evening,' I said anxiously, testing the water.

'He'll freeze there next winter,' my mother said. She had seen Steve's room and had been not at all impressed.

This was as good encouragement as any, so I took the plunge.

'I just know I'll always be with Steve,' I said, tripping over my words in my anxiety to get them out. 'You'll always know where I am and who I'm with. You'll be spared the worry of me going

117

out on dates . . .' I took a deep breath. 'Would you let Steve move into Carpenters?'

My mother flashed me a searching look. For a long moment, she did not answer.

'I think we could probably put up with him,' she said finally.

I was amazed. I had never seriously thought that she would agree and it was some years before I fully understood her reasoning. I had hardly seen my father since mum had divorced him, a state of affairs which she had in many respects encouraged. She had wanted to keep Charlie and me away from him, needing that reassurance. Out of loyalty and love for my mother, I too had painted a black picture of my father. Then, without warning, Charlie switched camps and went to live with my father. We had gone to pick him up from boarding school for the holidays one Christmas when I was eleven, and arrived at the school only to be told by Charlie's house-master that he had already left with my father. Uncomprehending, I had cried for days. I missed him terribly and it had been a savage blow for my mother.

The court welfare officer had warned my mother that the dramatic severance from both my father and my brother might cause me to resent men in future. My mother's family was dominated by women: my grandfather had died when I was very young, leaving behind my grandmother and three daughters. Since Charlie left, I had effectively been isolated from day-to-day domestic contact with men. Then, suddenly, Steve had come along. My mother was relieved beyond measure to see me form a strong relationship with him. In many respects, she too had benefited from having a man about the place. Steve fixed things, helped out and offered support in a range of ways. Inviting Steve to live at Carpenters seemed like a natural progression to both of us.

Steve could scarcely believe that I had asked my mother if he could move in. He was even more stunned to hear that she had said yes. He didn't hesitate to accept the invitation and moved his few bits and pieces into the spare room at Carpenters the same day. His presence there made me feel secure.

It meant quite an adjustment to have a man around the house again. The door to the only bathroom in the house had no lock, so Steve had to sing while he was in the bath. My mother did not like him smoking in the house, so he had either to go outside or surreptitiously blow smoke up the chimney. If my mother had any unfavourable comments about Steve, she directed them at me.

'It's not *Steve's* laundry which bothers me,' she grumbled a couple of weeks after he had moved in, 'it's his horse's. I can scarcely get it in the machine and it smells awful.'

During the jousting tournaments, the horses wore flowing robes called caparisons. Fabiola's voluminous caparison – stinking of sweat and laced with hairs – had to be bundled each week into the ancient washing machine. Recently it had started to make some curious grinding noises.

Although I loved having Steve living with us, I had not bargained for the subtle change in the status quo which it evoked on the domestic front. Steve sided with my mother in all matters concerning me; the two of them would check up on my homework, deprive me of favourite activities if I had school work to do or appeared overtired, and jointly register their disapproval of the way I wore my hair or the clothes I chose. To my fury, I came home from school one day to discover that they had colluded in throwing away my favourite dressing gown. When I sulked they laughed at me.

At times it felt as if they were really ganging up against me, yet if either of them had a complaint about the other, I was expected to sort it out. With his five-year advantage and the support of my mother, Steve gradually came to exert a degree of control over me considerably greater than in a normal boyfriend-girlfriend relationship. It was a small price to pay for the realization of my desire to share my life with Steve, but at times I felt rebellious.

119

I had no room to manoeuvre at home, but I vented my frustration at school. Whilst working just hard enough to keep my reports and exam results good, I skived off classes every afternoon, sneaking into town with a friend to wander round the shops or go to the park. We never got caught and I took particular pleasure in this small act of defiance, which would have enraged both my mother and Steve had they known.

During the jousting tournaments, each knight had his own squire, basically an assistant on foot. Dressed in tights and an undistinguished brown tunic, I acted as Steve's squire. I passed him his sword or his lance, ran after and caught Fabiola after Steve had performed one of his falls, and set out various props in the arena. I quickly became competent in this menial role and my moment of glory came when the *Blue Peter* film crew came to Chilham to film a tournament and I was chosen as squire to Peter Purvis.

As a *Blue Peter* presenter, Peter was required to master a wide variety of unusual skills for the benefit of the programme. Jousting he wisely viewed with a degree of trepidation. I sympathized: even for someone who was an accomplished rider, it was a considerable challenge to ride one-handed, carrying a heavy lance and fitted with a helmet through which vision was limited to a tiny slit.

'Does anyone ever get hurt?' he asked me, as I armed him for the practice run against Max.

'Steve had his ear removed by a lance during a tournament in the Cardiff Military Tattoo,' I told him. 'But that was ages ago, before I knew him. I haven't seen anyone get hurt since Max fractured a small bone in his wrist.'

'You're a big comfort,' Peter said, with feeling.

'I'm sure Max will take it carefully: he knows you're a beginner,' I said soothingly.

'I can see why knights traditionally fell in love with their squires,' he joked as I handed him up his helmet.

I flushed pink. At the end of the day, despite the fact that I had never collected milk bottle tops for starving children in Africa, nor come up with a prize-winning device made from old washing-up bottles and sticky-back plastic, I got my *Blue Peter* badge.

The highlight of the 1977 jousting calendar was the Queen's Silver Jubilee Tournament. Huge crowds were expected. Max was contacted by an American film company to ask if they could film the event for their television sports channel. The crew duly arrived a couple of days before the main event and set about capturing some of the 'colour and pageantry' of the preparation for a tournament. After filming the troupe preparing the horses, armour and costumes in the stable yard, under Max's volatile, sergeant-major-style commands, the director began to think up other sequences to film before the tournament began. To my surprise and delight, he asked if some of these sequences could involve me.

One of the suggestions was simple enough: I was asked to put on the dress I wore for the banquets and wander around with a hawk on my wrist in the picturesque surroundings of the lake. The other suggestion was more exciting: they asked me to ride 'two up' behind Steve. The sequence – which would show a knight and his lady riding off into the sunset – was to be used as the close to the film.

I had seen sequences like this in films: the heroine clasping her arms around her hero's waist, as they galloped into the sunset. I was sure I was up to the task. One of the heavier horses, Duke, was led out to the park field and Steve, in full armour, climbed aboard. His was the easy part, in my opinion. I was then helped on to Duke's well-padded rump and sat astride. Fortunately my dress had a very full skirt and train. This was arranged over Duke's rear quarters so that my dignity was preserved. However, once Duke started to move, I began to feel extremely unsafe. I started to understand why the film actresses clasped their heroes so tightly.

'We're not going to have to go any faster than this, are we?' I asked Steve nervously, as Duke shuffled into a walk.

'We're going to gallop!' he said. 'The cameras aren't even rolling yet. Hang on tight.'

Before I could protest, Steve kicked Duke sharply in the ribs and the horse lurched forward. I nearly lost my balance but, hang on to Steve as if my life depended on it, I somehow managed to regain my precarious seat. As we accelerated from a canter into a full gallop, the speed and the excitement began to take effect and I began to enjoy myself.

Quite how I managed to stay on, I will never know, but we completed our run across the park and, as Steve pulled Duke to a standstill, I slid off, legs shaking. The inside of my thighs were chafed and red, but when a video of the completed film arrived several months later, I had to admit that it had been worth it.

14

I WALKED NERVOUSLY INTO the banqueting hall, to be greeted by
a chorus of wolf whistles and cat calls. As I turned to face my
audience, a bread roll whizzed past my ear. Inwardly I cursed
Steve and my mother for landing me in this position. Nobody
had warned me that the group would be a stag party. I could see
Alex hovering in the doorway.

'They're a bit lively tonight,' he had told me before I went in.
'But don't worry old girl, I'll get hold of their attention for you.'

His worry was somewhat misplaced. I now appeared to have
their attention and I wasn't at all sure that I wanted it. Why oh
why had I ever agreed to do a banquet on my own? I had never
spoken in public before – and what a group to cut my teeth
on.

Steve and my mother had gone to the south coast with Ebony,
to film a commercial for Chrysler cars. My mother had been dis-
concerted to receive a school report which showed my atten-
dance record for the summer term as less than fifty per cent. She
and Steve, in agreement as usual, had been adamant that I could
not take another three days out of school to help Steve with the
shoot, so my mother had gone instead. Smarting with the pain
of not being able to accompany Steve on our first proper film

job with the hawks, I had been left to hold the fort, including doing the Friday banquet.

Despite my lack of confidence, I could scarcely refuse to do the banquet. The last few months had been a time of flux. Steve had taken me to visit his parents in Devon the previous Christmas and, unwittingly, he had returned a day later than Max had been expecting him. As he walked into the stable yard, Max lost his temper and fired Steve. Alex came to the rescue.

'Look here, old chap,' he told Steve. 'Why don't you work for me? You can be my driver.'

Alex did not have a driving licence and Charles had only a provisional one, so the long-suffering Yvonne had to drive the two of them everywhere they went. On top of their social engagements, fishing trips and visits to numerous pubs, she also had to do all the purchasing for the banquets, ranging from weekly trips to the cash-and-carry to journeys to distant deer farms to collect carcasses of venison. Hearing that Steve was unemployed, Alex had come up with a bright idea which would simultaneously rescue Steve from the dole queue, improve the quality of Yvonne's existence and ensure his own transportation to and from various fly-fishing venues, via the best hostelries *en route*.

The position came with fringe benefits. Alex had offered us the use of the unconverted section of the sawmills at the bottom of garden, in which to house our hawks. He allowed Steve to include shin of beef for the hawks in the banquet's regular order, repaying the company at cost. This represented a big saving on our bills. Despite this generosity from Alex, however, the driving was only on a part-time basis and it soon became clear that our hawks – ten of them in all by now – were going to have to earn their keep.

It was thus through the misfortune of Steve losing his job with Max that we came to open the Bird of Prey Centre. To boost Steve's chauffeuring earnings and our income from the banquets, the two of us decided to offer falconry courses, fully trained hawks for films and television, and bird of prey flying demonstrations for country fairs and shows. Using Carpenters' address and telephone number and inspired by a piece which had been printed in the *Kentish Express* a few months earlier headed 'Stephen is the killer birds' best friend', I had begun to seek press coverage for our new venture. My mother suggested advertising the falconry courses in the *Country Gentleman's Magazine* and before long I had booked our first residential students.

The job for Chrysler had in fact come from an article which was published about our new venture in the *Observer* colour supplement. The article was written by a photo journalist called Robert Hallman. I had met Robert the previous year, when he came to the castle to photograph the jousting. He had instantly been struck by the photogenic qualities of the hawks and had since made regular excursions from London to compile a portfolio of the hawks. Armed with a Hasselblad, he had taken some stunning pictures, which he had little difficulty selling to the *Observer*.

The sight of Alex hovering anxiously in the doorway of the banqueting hall that evening forced me to pull myself together. Steve and I were hugely indebted to him and I could not possibly let him down.

'Good evening,' I said, addressing my jeering audience as firmly as possible. 'This is Sam, an African Steppe Eagle. I've come here this evening to tell you a little about falconry in medieval times.'

I had heard Steve deliver this talk so many times that I knew it off by heart. I was thankful that Sam, a new acquisition, had a hood covering his eyes so he was unable to see my rowdy audience. He had only done two banquets before. He was still quite nervous of strangers and, after the talk, we had the dreaded photo session ahead of us. Sam had never been passed round for photographs before, as Ebony had always fulfilled this role. Leering, beery faces swam in front of my eyes. They were not going to make it easy for me.

'*The Book of St Albans*, written in the fourteenth century, outlined a code of conduct which restricted the keeping of certain species of birds of prey to various social ranks. For instance, only an emperor was allowed an eagle . . . '

'Get 'em off darlin'!' a plump man with a puce face called from the back of the hall.

'A king was allowed a gyrfalcon, a big white falcon from the Arctic regions,' I pressed on tremulously.

'I think it's cruel,' my heckler piped up again. 'Look at that poor bird, shackled to 'er arm. You should let it go!'

Forty sets of eyes fixed themselves on me threateningly.

'It's not cruel!' Indignation at the accusation got the better of my timidity. I had had enough. The last two days had been miserable: left behind with all the stock to look after, on top of going to school and endlessly rehearsing this rotten talk.

'Sam flies free every day of his life. If he wanted to fly away there'd be nothing to stop him,' I said, seizing the shocked pause which my outburst had provoked. 'To me that's a pretty good indication he's happy with his life even if you're not!'

'Good on yer darlin!'

'You tell 'im!'

'Why don't you shut up, Billy? Let the young lady talk.'

I appeared to have won the battle. With renewed confidence, I finished my spiel, asked them all to be quiet, removed Sam's hood and handed him over for photos to a couple of the guests who were still sober enough to stand steadily. Sam, bless him, behaved impeccably. I was just preparing to lift him off the arm of the final guest and make good my escape when Billy, my antagonist, appeared behind Sam. I was about to ask him to move away from behind Sam, when I saw the eagle start to lift his tail.

'Get out the way!' I warned. It was too late.

The man's jaw dropped open just as Sam fired out a huge dropping. It hit him square in the mouth. Rooted to the spot, I watched in riveted horror as he spat it out.

'Good shot, int 'e?' Billy said. To my vast relief he was too drunk to care.

I left the room to raucous laughter and a big round of applause.

'Well *done* old girl,' Alex said, taking my arm on the steps. 'Come and have a stiff drink, I expect you could do with one after that.'

In the dungeon, I accepted a gin and tonic. Hawks rarely drink anything at all but, to our surprise, Sam put his head down into my glass, threw out the slice of lemon, then took a sip of the gin and tonic. Lifting his head, he smacked his beak as the liquid ran down his throat. I did not stop him; I figured we had both earned it.

Since forming the Bird of Prey Centre, our collection of hawks had grown steadily. As it became known in the area, vets, RSPCA inspectors and members of the public handed in injured wild hawks for us to nurse back to health. It was helpful to receive these waifs and strays from a vet, who had usually carried out the veterinary work already, thereby saving our minimal resources. Vets were also more likely to have fed the bird on a suitable diet, although Steve did collect the odd individual from a hospital cage in which there was an open can of dog food in the corner. When we collected an injured hawk, we always checked what the bird had been eating – if indeed it had eaten at all since its injury – so that we could continue to feed it on whatever had been stimulating it to thrive during its first days in captivity. We were stumped, however, when Steve asked a vet in Gravesend what food he had used to tempt a Short-Eared Owl, which had suffered the trauma of having a wing amputated.

'Well, actually, she's been eating cats' testicles,' he told us, looking rather embarrassed. 'And for roughage, I've been feeding her budgies – blue ones mainly.'

Only those birds which made a complete recovery could be released, so Steve laid waste the garden at Carpenters to construct aviaries, where owls and kestrels which were permanently damaged could be paired up for breeding, after a period of convalescence. Much of the intensive nursing work was carried out by my mother, who kept her charges in a warm spot on a shelf above the boiler in the kitchen. To our delight, that spring we bred two kestrel chicks, Basil and Elliot, from Corky and a young injured female kestrel whom we called Digit.

On a working level, Steve and I were gradually identifying our individual strengths and weaknesses, enabling us to work effectively as a team. Steve excelled in front of an audience. Gifted with great confidence, he could entertain and captivate all age groups. Consequently he fronted all the demonstrations while I, who lacked his easy confidence with crowds of people, acted as his assistant. However, I quickly learned that Steve had neither the aptitude nor the inclination to handle the business side of the new venture. Reconciling the bank account, replying to correspondence, negotiating the purchase of new hawks and handling the logistics of bookings – these were tasks which fell to me. It was a trade-off which both of us appreciated, and which increased our reliance on each other.

On a personal level, too, our relationship was going from strength to strength. Although he was the natural leader, Steve made no bones about the fact that he adored me. He was concerned about and interested in anything which pertained to me, from the pressures of studying for my exams to the type of medication I took to counteract my streaming summer hayfever. I blossomed under his protective mantle and relished sharing my life so completely with him.

Between helping Steve with the Bird of Prey Centre and keeping up with school work, I was debating options for my future. My mother had made it clear to me that she did not mind how enthusiastically I devoted myself to Steve and the new business, provided that I worked for my 'A' levels and then followed a 'proper' career. I had finally determined to read law, avoiding university by taking my law exams while articled with a local firm. I needed of course to find a firm which would be willing to take me on. As I was mulling on this, Alex came to the rescue again and introduced me to his solicitors in Canterbury, an old established firm called Gardner and Croft.

'Old Tiggy Croft'll look after you,' he told me, his eyes twinkling behind his glasses. 'Why don't you go and spend a couple of days there to see if you like it? I'll make the arrangements.'

Thus it was that I presented myself in the tiny reception of Gardner and Croft, to spend a couple of days shadowing David Geene, one of the firm's senior partners.

I judged that David must be in his early forties. He had dark hair, greying at the temples, and kind eyes. He welcomed me into his spacious first-floor office, which had large windows facing out on to Castle Street. The room was lined from floor to ceiling with books, most of them leather bound in sombre colours. A marble fireplace and ornate plasterwork on the ceiling combined with a large leather-topped desk and some comfortable chairs to enhance the impression of gracious living. The graceful room reminded me of the times I had visited my father's office as a young child. His had been similarly well appointed, but devoid of life and fun, a place for hushed voices and serious conversation. David had the same weary grey tinge to his complexion that my father used to have after a long day at the office.

I sank into a deep leather button-backed chair in front of his desk, as David outlined my itinerary for the next two days.

'I have a few clients to see this morning and I thought you might like to sit in. You could take some notes – that would be helpful,' he said. 'Then, this afternoon, I've asked one of our young associates to take you to the local magistrates' court to hear a couple of minor allegations of theft and a speeding offence.

'Tomorrow, one of my female colleagues has her first session with a client filing for divorce,' he continued. 'You might like to sit in on that, and I've got a conveyance and a couple of wills to draft in the afternoon, so you can help me then. It's a good cross-section, typical of the type of work we do in this firm. It should provide you with the opportunity to decide whether you'd enjoy it here and also give us the chance to get to know you.'

Apart from the trip to court, it sounded pretty dull. I found it very difficult to get excited by the prospect of petty litigation.

The first client arrived and I moved to a chair near the window to take notes on a yellow legal pad. A young girl – perhaps two years older than me – with heavy black eye make-up and straggly blonde hair, had been accused of stealing cigarettes from the supermarket where she worked.

It was interesting hearing her version of events, but as I scribbled, my mind strayed to Steve and the hawks. It was a bright, sunny day and I had left him putting the birds out to weather on the lawn at Carpenters. That afternoon, he planned to work with a young buzzard we had recently acquired, manning it and trying to get it to feed on the fist.

The sun streamed through the open window. I struggled to pull my thoughts back to my work. It was hard to concentrate on such a beautiful day. In the distance, I could hear a blackbird calling. Its call was drowned by the angry honking of a car horn in the street below. Looking down, I saw people in business suits scurrying to and fro.

In the afternoon, I went in search of the young lawyer with whom I was scheduled to attend court. His office was three floors up. As I climbed the stairs, they got steeper and narrower and, when I finally reached the top, I was surprised by how small and dingy his office was in comparison to David's. His plain wood desk was scratched and stained with ink and the two chairs were of the grey, typist's variety, with adjustable backs. His reference books had overflowed the two small bookshelves and were stacked in untidy piles on the floor. I stepped over them to reach a chair.

'Fortunately, I don't have to see many clients up here,' he told me, reading my mind. 'You don't get a smart office here until you're a partner. Depending on your ability, and a little bit on the luck of the draw, it can take quite a few years after you qualify before you reach those dizzy heights.'

On the way to the courthouse, we chatted further about the legal profession.

'I'm hoping to be articled while I complete my law exams,' I told him.

'It's extremely hard work to qualify through a correspondence course while you're articled,' he said. 'You're expected to earn your keep in the firm at the same time and that puts you under a lot of pressure. You'll have to be quick too: in a year's time the Law Society is stopping correspondence courses for all but those with the highest grades at 'A' level.'

This was not good news. Preparing for my 'A' levels in sixth form at school would take a full two years, by which time I would be too late. I returned home that evening very despondent.

'There may be a quicker way to get your 'A' levels,' my mother mused, as we ate supper. 'I'll telephone Canterbury Technical College tomorrow and enquire.'

The following evening, my mother told me that on the strength of my eight 'O' level passes, I would be accepted on a one-year 'A' level course at the Technical College in Canterbury. Gardner and Croft were prepared to offer me a place as an articled clerk, provided that I passed my 'A' levels. Arrangements were made for me to leave Ashford School at the end of the summer term, to start the new course at college in the autumn. Although I was relieved that we had found a route to my career which I could follow without leaving Chilham, I was depressed by the finality of the arrangements. My future was signed and sealed, now I was obliged to deliver.

15

'DO YOU HAVE an eagle you could supply for a Dracula film?' I was getting used to unusual requests from the handful of agencies in England which specialized in supplying animals for films.

'We've got an African Steppe Eagle,' I said.

The questioner was more interested in the bird's habits than its species.

'Would it sit on a rock in a studio and eat a rabbit?'

'Yes, he could manage that,' I told her.

'Can you be at Shepperton studios Tuesday of next week at eight-thirty in the morning?'

'We'll be there,' I promised.

She gave me some brief details of the film. John Badham was directing Frank Langella in the lead role, with Laurence Olivier as Count Van Hessling.

'The film will be true to Bram Stoker's book,' she assured me. 'The director wants everything to be as authentic as possible.'

I travelled with Steve up to Shepperton on the appointed morning, holding Sam hooded on my fist. The first person we met on the sound stage was the continuity girl, who was complaining bitterly to a lighting technician.

133

'Nothing is bloody enough for Mr Badham,' she continued after we had introduced ourselves. 'He made his name with *Saturday Night Fever* and now he wants to prove that he can make a good horror movie. All he wants is blood and guts.'

Part of the sound stage at Shepperton had been skilfully converted into two floors of a Victorian lunatic asylum, complete with spiral staircase. As we waited to be called for Sam to do his bit, we watched some scenes being filmed. The extras dressed as mental patients were incredibly convincing. They remained in character even while in the canteen – a couple of them danced a little jig as they waited in the queue at lunchtime. I commented on this to the continuity girl, who joined us at our table.

'The reason they're so good is because they *are* loonies,' she told us. 'They were recruited from the local mental hospital. You see those people over there holding the strait-jackets? They're attendants from the hospital in case any of them get out of order.' I didn't know whether to believe her or not.

On our way back down to the sound stage after lunch, I bumped into Donald Pleasance, who also had a role in the film. He held the studio door open for me and I thanked him.

'You're most welcome,' he told me. 'Nobody ever holds doors open for me.'

We had been asked to provide our own dead rabbit. A props man asked to see it. He had explicit instructions from the boss.

'Can you gut the rabbit?' he asked Steve. 'Mr Badham wants to see the guts spewed out over the rock which we've built for the eagle to sit on. He doesn't think the real guts will show up enough on camera though, so I've been to the butchers and got a load of chicken giblets. I'll mix them with a bit of Kensington gore and that should do the trick.'

It appeared that the continuity girl was right.

The dead rabbit was nailed belly up on the fibreglass rock, with its head towards the camera. The props man donned a pair of rubber gloves and stuffed the gutted rabbit with messy fistfuls of scarlet-stained intestines until it bulged. Gore trickled down the rock.

'Ready for yer guv,' the props man spoke into his walkie-talkie.

The director appeared, with his entourage in tow. He inspected the props man's handiwork.

'Where's the eagle? Great, what a wingspan! He's magnificent. Put him on the rock will you, central if you can.'

Having had a hasty conference, Steve and I were worried about Sam ingesting Kensington gore, the red paint used to stain the guts. Steve tied a large chunk of beef to the rabbit's back, out of camera shot. This attracted Sam and he concentrated on tugging at it while the shot was filmed. John Badham seemed pleased with the sequence and pronounced the shot 'in the can'. A year later when the film reached British cinemas, I was disappointed to discover that the sequence had never been used.

Thanks to the animal agents, we enjoyed a steady trickle of film work. Soon our hawks featured in advertising campaigns for products and services ranging from nail varnish and racing bikes to British Airways. I learned more with each job that I did and my expertise in handling the hawks on set improved. One week, we received a call to go to Chesil Court Studios in London to do a stills shoot with a talented young photographer called Paul Bussell.

The shoot, I was told by the agency, was to advertise car tyres. The manufacturer was producing a series of advertisements for magazines, designed to depict the tyre's amazing grip.

They asked me to take our largest eagle to sit atop a car tyre, so that its feet could be photographed in close-up, gripping the surface of the tyre. We duly arrived at the studios at the appointed hour with Sam, our only eagle at the time.

I rang the bell and a girl's head appeared round the door.

'We've brought the eagle for the tyre shoot,' Steve told her.

'You are going to stay with it aren't you?' the girl enquired, eyeing Sam's crate anxiously.

'Yes, of course.'

The girl seemed relieved. Opening the door properly to let us in, she introduced herself, 'I'm Yolanda, Paul's assistant. Last week we had a pair of otters loose in the studio. The man who delivered them from the zoo left as soon as we had signed for the box. We had a big glass tank in the studio for them, containing gallons and gallons of water.

'It took us ages to set it up,' she continued. 'We'd dressed it with rocks and weed and spent hours lighting it. We'd been expecting handlers with these animals, but instead a note came with them saying that as they weren't trained, there was no point having a handler and we should just release them into the tank. Then it said, "Beware, they bite!"'

'We had awful difficulty getting the otters out of the crate and into the water,' she said, shaking her head ruefully as she recalled the scene. 'In the struggle, the tank was overturned and flooded the studio. Paul nearly had a seizure and the otters shot under a pile of backdrops, where thank God they stayed until we telephoned the zoo to come and pick them up.'

I was horrified that the poor creatures had been so terrified.

'We've also got to shoot limpets and tree frogs – you know, the little green ones with the orange suckers – for this series of tyre adverts,' Yolanda said over her shoulder. We followed behind, carrying Sam's crate between us.

In the dim light of the studio, we were introduced to Paul. He led us towards the set to show us where he wanted Sam to sit. The studio was not large and we had to be careful where we stepped, as the floor was strewn with cables which fired an impressive array of studio lights. In the centre of the room, half a car tyre had been mounted in front of a skyscape background. Lights with reflective silver canopies were positioned close to the tyre on both sides and a large camera was set up about three feet in front of the set. It was going to be very enclosed for Sam, perched on the tyre.

'Believe it or not, one of the most expensive parts of this

whole shoot is that transparency behind the tyre,' Paul said, indicating the skyscape.

The transparency was about three feet square, showing a cloud-studded sky at sunset. It was backlit to project light through the clouds, making it look very realistic.

'I took a whole range of sky photographs and submitted them to the client. That was one they chose, but the cost of blowing it up to that size was enormous. We've only got the one and we spent all day yesterday lighting it, so I'd be very grateful if you could try not to knock it when you put Sam on the tyre.'

Steve and I exchanged uneasy glances. This job had sounded easy, with no flying to do and only Sam's feet in the shot. There was no way we could have realized in advance how tight the set was. I began to pray that Sam would behave: he could not afford to open his wings even slightly or he would hit the lights; if he tried to fly off the tyre, he would hit the camera. I was comforted by Paul's attitude. He was energetic and friendly and seemed keen to include us in the finer points of the shoot.

'Why aren't you doing the shot outside, with a real sky?' I asked.

'Because I'd never get the lighting right outdoors. You have much more more control in a studio,' Paul explained. 'Have a look through the viewfinder on the camera. You see that grid? I need his feet to be precisely in the middle.'

We had a look through the viewfinder. The camera was the biggest I had ever seen. The aperture was about ten inches square, marked with a faint set of grid lines.

'It's a ten by eight Sinar plate camera, large format,' Paul said. 'Each frame costs a packet, but the quality's matchless.'

I took Sam out of his travelling crate for Paul to inspect him.

'I'll need those straps off his legs — that won't be a problem will it?'

'He's used to doing shots without them,' I reassured Paul, as Steve and I removed Sam's jesses and cut off his bells.

When everything was set, I edged my way between the

camera and a light and carefully placed Sam on top of the tyre, in such a way that he did not need to open his wings to balance himself.

'I'll take a few Polaroids first,' Paul said. 'Can you move him two inches to camera left?'

I nudged Sam, who obligingly shifted his weight and repositioned his feet over the chalk marks on the tyre. Paul squinted through the viewfinder, then stepped back and squeezed the trigger lead. With everything so precisely set up, he didn't even need to be looking through the camera when he fired off the shot.

Flash bulbs popped on all the lights. To my relief, Sam didn't budge. It was strange to me that hawks never appeared to mind flash, despite the fact that their eyesight is reputed to be eight times better than ours. They seemed to have the ability to adjust their pupils instantly to extreme fluctuations in the level of light, without wincing or blinking.

'Ignore the quality,' Paul told us, showing the first of the Polaroids to us. 'It's not a patch on the proper plates.'

Yolanda made a few small adjustments to the settings on one of the lights and Paul fired off two more Polaroids. When he was satisfied, he loaded the camera with the proper film.

'This is for real now.' He took another squint through the viewfinder.

To my horror, as he stood up, his finger poised on the trigger, I saw Sam's tail start to lift. Helplessly I watched as Paul fired the camera and simultaneously Sam fired a large liquid dropping. It splatted dead centre of the backdrop, a foul-scented, sticky brown mass that dribbled down the transparency on to the floor. There was a stunned silence.

Then, apologizing profusely, I retrieved Sam, and the others dismantled the set. The ruined transparency was carried into Paul's office and laid on his desk. We stood around anxiously while he studied it.

'I think I can turn it into a cloud!' he announced brightly. He turned to Yolanda. 'Fetch me a fine paintbrush and I'll have a go.'

Mopping off the surplus dropping with some tissue, Paul set to work with his brush. After fifteen minutes, he straightened up.

'There!' he said, beaming. 'You can hardly see it. It's lucky it was a sunset shot – at least the colours are similar – it just looks a little more stormy than it did.'

Relieved, we trooped back into the studio, where Paul and Yolanda set about the task of resurrecting the set. When they had finished, Yolanda went out to get some sandwiches for lunch and Paul went into the kitchen to make some coffee. As he re-emerged with a tray of steaming mugs, we heard a noise from the kitchen behind him.

'Wanker, wanker, wanker!'

Steve and I stared at each other in amazement.

'Wanker, wanker, wanker!' It was a loud, cheerful voice.

'I'm sorry about that,' Paul said. 'It's my parrot, do you want to come and meet him?'

Full of curiosity, we followed him into the kitchen. A Green Amazon parrot was climbing up the bars of his cage.

'He's called Panama. His language is a real embarrassment,' Paul said. 'I keep him out here so he doesn't upset my clients, but he hates me and every time I go into the kitchen I get a flood of abuse.'

Panama shinned down the bars of his cage, lay down on the floor and did a most un-birdlike sideways roll. Righting himself, he came over to the bars and presented the side of his head to me to be scratched. Bad language notwithstanding, he seemed to be the sweetest character.

'He likes women,' Paul told us. 'But not men for some reason. I got him from a pet shop where they used to keep him in the window. That's where he learned to swear I reckon. I tried repeatedly to buy him, but the manager of the store refused to part with him, he was such a big attraction. He kept trying to

139

palm me off with other parrots. Then one day as I was passing, I popped in again. 'You can take him right now, just give me the money,' the man said. I paid him on the spot, brought Panama home, let him out of his cage and he nearly bit my finger off. Something bad had happened to him in the shop I reckon. The manager admitted that's why he sold him to me, but I never found out exactly what had happened. Whatever it was, it was probably a man who did it to him and it's turned him a bit mad.

'He's got a very low boredom threshold,' Paul went on, as I scratched Panama's head through the bars. 'I try to keep him occupied, but it's difficult when I'm working. When he gets fed up, he starts screaming for attention and swearing. I give him toys, but he destroys most of them. He loves anything which makes a noise.'

Panama disappeared under a sheet of newspaper. Lurking under this paper tent, he peered beadily at us.

'Fuck off!' he commanded in imperious tones.

'I've got something he'll like,' Steve said, disappearing into the studio. He returned seconds later with one of Sam's brass hawk bells, on the bewit – the leather fixing strap – which we had cut off earlier.

He shook the bell by the cage, then handed it to Panama, who

accepted it politely. Rolling on to his back, he held the bewit in his beak and kicked the bell repeatedly with his feet.

'He likes that,' Paul said. 'That should keep him quiet for a few hours – I hope he doesn't break it.'

It should be OK,' Steve told him. 'It's tough enough to withstand Sam chewing at it.'

We left Panama with the bell and returned to the studio. Sam, having blotted more than his copybook that morning, behaved impeccably for the remainder of the afternoon and Paul got the shot he was looking for. Before we left, we went back to see Panama. He was still carrying Sam's bell in his beak.

'Oi, you!' he said, dropping the bell.

I went over to the cage.

'Wanker, wanker, wanker!' he screeched at me, with ear-splitting clarity.

A year later I was working with Pete Seaward, a photographer who knew Paul and Panama. Laughing, he updated me on the latest incident in the Panama saga.

'The people in the flats above the studio complained bitterly about Panama. He used to swear and screech at four o'clock in the morning. Finally, Paul was forced to give him away.

'He hadn't been at his new home very long before he escaped,' Pete continued. 'He flew off to the roof of a closed-order convent in Ladbroke Grove. He was up there all night swearing his head off. Eventually the new owners 'phoned Paul to see if he could catch Panama.

'The nuns brought this long ladder while all the time the parrot was screeching, "Oi! Fuck off! Fuck off! Ha, ha, ha. Wanker!" Paul couldn't reach him, but he took off again and flew into a tree in a children's playground. All the children came out to watch. Apparently Panama kept up an unceasing flow of foul invective until he finally managed to catch the blasted creature.'

It was a sobering thought that parrots can live to the age of sixty.

141

16

ONE EVENING IN September 1978, Steve came up behind me and put his arms round me. Turning to face him, I noticed that he had the look of someone with something important to say.

'I think we should get engaged,' he told me. It was more of a statement than a question.

'Are you going to ask me properly?' I asked him, my face betraying my answer before the question had been posed.

He dropped on to one knee.

'I love you, will you marry me?' he asked, his tone serious.

'Yes, you know I will,' I said, flushed with pleasure.

'We won't be able to afford to get married for quite a while and we certainly can't afford a house of our own at the moment, but we can have a long engagement,' he told me. Then he grinned. 'I'd better go and ask your mother.'

My mother gave her consent joyfully and the three of us went out to The Plough for supper to celebrate. I felt that my mother must have felt vindicated in her decision to allow Steve to move into Carpenters and to permit me to devote myself to him so completely at such a young age. Sitting in front of a roaring fire in the cosy atmosphere of the pub, we toasted our future. The next day, Steve borrowed some money from my mother and took me into Canterbury, where he bought me a ring in the shape of a flower, with a tiny aquamarine in the centre.

After the joy of leaving school and the freedom of the long summer holidays, my days were now back in a routine. As I travelled on the bus to college, one glorious golden morning in October, I was reading through some history notes which I was supposed to have learned for a test, when the bus pulled up at one of its regular stops on the outskirts of the village of Shalmsford Street. Glancing idly out of the window, trying to imprint Lord Palmerston's dates as Prime Minister on my memory, I was alarmed to see a woman waiting at the bus stop fall down in a dead faint. She crashed on to the pavement and lay unmoving.

Other passengers on the bus commented and looked out of the window, but to my amazement, nobody went to help the woman. She lay beside the bus in a heap as the other people waiting at the stop climbed aboard and the driver prepared to move on. Horrified at the people's callousness, I leapt up and, stuffing history notes into my briefcase, jumped off the bus.

As I reached the woman's side, she was coming round and trying to sit up. I propped her up as best I could and she recovered sufficiently to tell me that she lived in a nearby farm cottage. She leant heavily on my arm as we walked the short distance home. To my relief, her husband was there, so I was able to pass her over into his care. The bus had long gone, so I started to walk back towards Chilham, about five miles away.

The countryside was gilded with the colours of autumn. I whistled to myself, swinging my briefcase as I walked. This was infinitely preferable to sitting a history test; I was grateful to the poor woman for getting me out of classes for the day. Soon I left the hamlet behind me and followed the road past a couple of apple orchards and out into open country. The sun warmed the top of my head and I could hear a wood pigeon cooing in the hedgerow. Despite the beauty of the morning, however, I

144

couldn't quell a little voice which was persistently nagging in my head.

'You're engaged to be married,' the voice said. 'Your husband will spend his life in the country working with hawks, but what about *your* dream for the future? Will you spend your time looking for excuses like this to escape the drudgery of office work?'

In the long term, if the Bird of Prey Centre was successful, I could see my legal salary supporting an assistant for Steve, someone who would then be doing the job I would rather do myself. It was a depressing thought.

As I neared Chilham village, my thoughts were interrupted by a half-grown puppy. He looked like a collie cross, with a black head and back, a feathery white chest and long wispy black tail with a white tip. He had been trying to eat grit at the side of the main road, but when he saw me, he dropped on to his belly and started to crawl towards me, wagging his tail in an ingratiating manner. He was not wearing a collar and as he was clearly lost and dicing with death on the edge of the road, I looped my belt round his neck and took him home to Carpenters.

Steve and my mother were surprised to see me home so early and even more surprised to see my companion. The dog was starving hungry, so while they fed him, I telephoned the police to see what the procedure was with a stray dog. They told me no one had reported a missing dog, but over the weekend they had received reports of a car stopping on the main road, out of which had been thrown a black-and-white puppy and a black-and-white kitten. The kitten had already been picked up. The desk sergeant said that if I wanted to take the dog down to the station, it would be kept there for a week, then, if it was not claimed, it would be put down.

I looked at the puppy. Having wolfed his food, he was lying at my feet, looking up at me with his nose between his paws. He obviously had a sweet temperament and it was quite unthinkable to have him destroyed. Fuming about the sort of people who could so cruelly abandon a dog, I gave the desk sergeant Carpenters' telephone number and told him that unless the dog was claimed, I would keep him. I called him Havoc.

A month after Steve and I got engaged, the telephone rang.

'Eddie's had a car accident.'

It was Lord Massereene's secretary.

'One of his front tyres blew on the motorway and his car rolled down a bank. He's suffered some nasty injuries, including a broken heel, so he's going to be in hospital for quite some time. Lord Massereene was wondering if Steve might be willing to take over the demonstrations until he comes back? If indeed he comes back.'

'I'm sure Steve would be delighted to help,' I said, my mind racing.

'Lord Massereene would like to come and see Steve to discuss terms,' she said. 'He's tied up today, but I think he may pop down tomorrow.'

'We'll look out for him,' I assured her.

Eddie's parents called to ask if Steve could look after Eddie's hawks while he was in hospital. For reasons they didn't make clear, they too seemed doubtful that Eddie would return to the castle. Could this be Steve's chance to land the job of falconer?

The next day Lord Massereene appeared over the garden wall, with Barra the labrador at his heel and the usual smidgen of bloodstained loo paper on his chin. Steve and I were sitting on the patio wall playing ball with Havoc and watching the hawks which were preening on their perches on the lawn. Including the aviary stock, we now had twenty-five birds in total.

'Lots of birds,' Lord Massereene commented, leaning on the wall. 'Didn't realize you had so many. Understand you've agreed to take over from Edward for the time being – decent of you – need to talk to you at some stage about working long term.'

He appeared ready to wander off again, he really was impossibly vague. In my eagerness to pin him down, I invited him to

146

dinner the following evening. He seemed slightly taken aback but he accepted the invitation.

My mother was away, so the following day, while Steve tried to work out on the back of an envelope what he should charge for doing the displays, I nervously prepared to cook the best meal I could manage.

'Apparently chocolate mousse is his favourite pudding,' I said, breaking plain chocolate into a bowl. One of my aunts had been a professional chef for Cadbury's and had taught me how to make a delicious chocolate mousse.

'I've bought some of that tasty chicken liver paté from Browns in the village – we'll have it with crusty bread. Then we're having chicken casserole with rice.'

In the early evening, I got changed for dinner in a high state of nervous anxiety. I desperately hoped that my suspicions about Steve being offered the job were correct. I felt sorry for Eddie, but I had not forgotten how he had been given the job I hoped Steve would get.

Lord Massereene arrived late. After a drink before dinner, we sat down to eat at the circular rosewood table in the dining-room. To my frustration, although he tucked into the food with enthusiasm, Lord Massereene did not seem to want to talk about Eddie or the job. As I carried the chocolate mousse to the table, Steve took the initiative and broached the subject.

'You said you wanted to talk to us about the future?' he enquired, as Lord Massereene spooned up his first mouthful of mousse.

'Hum – very good mousse, very good,' Lord Massereene muttered.

There was a long pause.

'Hum – yes,' he continued thoughtfully. ' I don't think young Edward will be coming back – wondered if you wanted the job?'

'I would be interested,' Steve said quite nonchalantly. 'I assume the position would include North Lodge?'

This was the crucial question. North Lodge was Eddie's

147

house. It was one of the two castle gatehouses which flanked the main gates to the castle, overlooking the village square. If the position came with the house, we would have our own place to live.

'I, er, have other plans for North Lodge. Couldn't you continue to live here?' Lord Massereene said hopefully.

He was a wily old bird. If he could persuade Steve to take the job but continue to live at Carpenters, he could rent out North Lodge. Steve and I looked at each other. The chance of North Lodge was important to us, but it was a gamble to hold out for it. If I was honest with myself, I knew we needed the security of a regular salary regardless of whether we could get North Lodge or not. Recently, Charles Jardine had passed his driving test and the Bird of Prey Centre had been struggling as Steve's income from chauffeuring Alex had virtually dried up.

'I'd only be interested in the job if it included North Lodge,' Steve said firmly.

I was torn between admiration at his stand and nervousness that he would blow our chances.

'I'll have to think about it,' Lord Massereene said.

He left a short while afterwards, leaving us anxiously weighing up the odds. The next day the telephone rang. I answered it. It was Lord Massereene's secretary.

'Lord Massereene wondered if you might be willing to move into a flat in the castle?' she enquired.

This was progress of a kind, but it was not much of an option. I envisaged the flats over the tea-room and gift shop in the castle. The rooms were claustrophobic, dark and musty with small windows.

'I think we'd be too far away from anywhere we could house the hawks,' I said.

'I'll explain that to his lordship,' she said.

We had to wait another twenty-four hours before she came back to us again. Hearing her voice, Steve beckoned me over.

'Would two thousands pounds per annum and North Lodge

be acceptable?' she asked Steve. 'Eddie's collecting his things over Christmas, so you could move in over the New Year.'

We both had our ears to the receiver.

'I think that would be fine,' Steve said.

He replaced the receiver and hugged me joyfully. Sensing the atmosphere, Havoc bounded around us, wagging his tail. We had a home of our own.

17

'**M**Y BUDGERIGAR HAS died. I wonder if you would be kind enough to bury him for me?'

Puffing nervously on her cigarette, Lady Massereene extended a shaky hand in Steve's direction. In it was clasped the small body of a green and yellow budgie.

It was late November. Steve and I were sitting on the elderly leather sofa in Lord Massereene's office, trying to finalize details of the new breeding centre we wanted to build at the castle over the winter. If we were moving to North Lodge, we needed to move all our birds out from the garden at Carpenters.

Lady Massereene really did seem unhappy and I felt for her as Steve took the budgie.

'Of course I'll bury it,' he told her. 'I'm so sorry.'

I could see Steve didn't know where to put the little bundle of feathers. He moved it awkwardly from hand to hand, then finally put it in his coat pocket.

'One gets very attached to budgies,' Lady Massereene said sadly. 'They're such characters.'

Walking back to Carpenters after the meeting, we talked about Lady Massereene. Neither of us knew her well, but I understood her unhappiness, it was like losing one of the hawks. Then Steve had a bright idea.

'Why don't we buy her another one?' he suggested.

That afternoon, we drove into the pet shop in Canterbury and selected a green and yellow budgie as close in markings to the old one as we could find. Later, as we hammered on the heavy front door of the castle, we were not sure what her reaction would be. Lady Massereene opened the door herself. She looked faintly surprised to see us.

'We've bought you another budgie,' I explained.

'Oh, that is so *kind* of you.' She genuinely seemed quite overcome. 'I would never have bought another one for myself. Come in, won't you?'

We followed her through the private wing of the castle and into the kitchen, where a bird cage was hanging from a stand with its door swinging forlornly open. Steve fished the new budgie out of the small cardboard pet box and released it carefully into the cage. Lady Massereene looked quite pink with pleasure.

Later that day, we received a bottle of whisky, two beautiful glass tankards engraved with tawny owls, and a note of thanks. After that, whenever we saw Lady Massereene walking in the grounds, she would come over to talk to us, although we never came to trust Arton, her remaining pharaoh hound.

I was nearing the end of my first term at college when I received a telephone call one evening from Robert Hallman, the photographer whose pictures had earned us so much good publicity in the past.

'I had a meeting today with a literary agent,' he told me, sounding quite excited. 'I've been thinking for some time now about trying to get my photos of the hawks published in a book.'

I was intrigued.

'The agent thinks he can place a book on falconry with a publisher, but it needs someone to write it,' he continued. 'I suggested that you might be able to.'

There was a pregnant pause. I drew in my breath sharply.

'I'd love to have a go,' I admitted. For years I had nursed a secret desire to write a book. I had even started one once, on Whitney.

'The only snag is, the agent asked me how old you are,' Robert said. 'I had to tell him that you are only sixteen, so he's asked to see a sample of your writing. Do you think you can put something together this weekend?'

'I'll try – I'll start work straight away,' I told him, my heart pounding.

It seemed ironic that only the previous week, Steve and I had agreed that if we could only get a picture of one of us with a hawk published in a falconry book, it would help to make our name in the falconry world. I could hardly take in the fact that I was being given the opportunity to write an entire book on the sport I loved so much. Feverishly, I dug out the chapter I had written on Whitney; it was going to take some work to get it good enough to submit.

Steve and my mother were full of encouragement. Whether they seriously thought I had any chance of being accepted as author of this book, I did not know, but they read my piece and made suggestions. I worked solidly on the chapter over the weekend and my mother typed it on her old manual typewriter. On Monday morning on my way to college, I mailed it with my fingers firmly crossed.

In preparation for moving in to North Lodge, Steve and I needed to create housing for the hawks close to our new home. The garden at Carpenters had not been the same since Steve had taken a saw to my mother's lilac trees in order to make space for the row of wire aviaries, which now extended the full length of the lawn. Although my mother would miss the constant interest of watching the hawks, she was a keen gardener and I knew she would be pleased to get her garden back. Recently, Alex had started to talk about selling off the sawmills for development, so we needed to create mews space too.

Lord Massereene gave us permission to use the complex of sheds above the greenhouses, so we started by clearing Eddie's potting shed and the sunken building next door to it. We were in the middle of this task one Sunday afternoon, our clothes covered in dust and our faces streaked with dirt, when we heard a shout from outside.

'Allo! Mr Ford? This is Jimmy. Gareth sent me.' It was a broad Cockney voice.

Speaking to Steve on the telephone some weeks earlier, his friend Gareth — now a professional stuntman — mentioned that he had met a young lad who was very keen on falconry.

'He's as strong as an ox and he's got a heart of gold,' Gareth told Steve. 'If I send him down, will you teach him a bit? In return, he'll help you out. He lives in south London, but I think you'd find him a useful pair of hands at weekends — he's very willing.'

We were greeted by a young man of about eighteen, clearly dressed in his Sunday best. He was wearing drainpipe trousers, Doctor Martin boots and an immaculate navy Crombie overcoat with a red handkerchief tucked into the top pocket. He had an ingenuous, round face, with close-cropped Sid James hair, long sideburns and a gold stud in his left ear.

'How'd yer do? M'name's Jim — Jimmy Plainson.' He pumped our hands enthusiastically.

We quickly learned that Jim was enthusiastic about everything he did. Not even stopping to take off his coat, which was soon filthy, he waded in to help us straight away, and seemed more than happy to work furiously all day, provided that he could see the hawks at the end. As Gareth had promised, he was a gem.

'If you come down next weekend, I could teach you how to fly Ebony if you like,' Steve said, as we showed Jim the hawks later.

'I'll come down after work on Saturday,' Jim said, looking like

154

someone who had just been given the moon. 'I work in a butchers see, on Saturday mornings, so I'll fetch down a nice bit o'steak.'

Over successive weekends, Jim more or less became a permanent fixture. He was one of the kindest, most genuine people one could ever wish to meet and Steve and I became very fond of him. With his help, we transformed the potting shed and surrounding buildings into spacious mews for the hawks and started work on our aviary complex for the breeding stock.

Jim lived at home in Tooting with his parents. Like his father and his father before him, he was a dustman, in fact as far as we could gather, the Plainson family were the Tooting Refuse Mafia. The money Jim earned from the council seemed like a small fortune to us. He was always immaculately dressed and he never failed to impress us when, peeling off a filthy T-shirt at the end of a hard day's work, he would drop it into the bin and replace it with a brand new one from his bag, fresh out of its wrapper.

'Y'see, Em, Stevie, I don't like me mum to have to do too much washing, bless her,' he explained.

Jim was covered in tattoos and when he got to know us better he showed us his favourite. Taking off his shirt he revealed a goshawk in full flight, with wings outstretched, so large that it covered most of his back. The feet of the goshawk were extended in anticipation of catching a rabbit, which was scurrying across his kidneys. Although tattoos were not my thing, I had to admit that it was beautifully executed.

'There's more, but I can't show you, Em,' he said. 'I'll show Stevie though, if y'don't mind leaving us alone for a minute.'

I disappeared and when I returned five minutes later, Steve's face was a picture.

'There's another rabbit,' he explained to me. 'Lower down on Jim's back – much lower,' he emphasized. 'It's disappearing down a hole.'

'It was painful to have it done,' Jim elaborated, his artless face

155

beaming. 'But worth it – never fails to get a laugh down the pub.'

When he first started coming to see us, Jim used to travel from Tooting on the train, but about a month after we got to know him, he turned up in a canary yellow Ford Camaro. I had never seen one of those flashy American vehicles before and I was staggered to learn that it cost Jim a pound a day in insurance. I was still too young to be able to take my driving test, so when Steve was busy, Jim appointed himself my chauffeur, driving me to collect any injured hawks which people had picked up, normally road casualties or the victims of overhead wires.

From my point of view there were two drawbacks to the Camaro. Firstly, it was fitted with air horns which – to the obvious amazement of pedestrians and other motorists – played the first line of 'Dixieland'. Secondly, it had a built-in megaphone, like those fitted to cars used for electioneering. Into this contraption Jim would bellow 'All right darlin'?' at any astonished girl we happened to pass.

By late January, we were able to move in to North Lodge. It had taken considerable effort to get the house ready. The afternoon after new dark-green carpets had been laid – a present from my mother – the door opened and Lord Massereene walked in.

'Come to see what you're doing,' he said, marching straight into the drawing-room without stopping to take off his wellington boots, which were covered in mud.

'Hum, is that a one hundred watt light bulb?' he asked, pointing at the single bulb suspended from the ceiling.

Stunned by his sudden appearance nobody could speak for a moment, then Steve went to check the bulb.

'Yes, it is,' he told Lord Massereene, who was now pacing round the room like a caged lion, leaving a trail of caked footprints in his wake.

'Cost you a lot to run, you should change it for a forty watt,' he muttered in disapproving tones, and left.

I surveyed the quagmire covering our new carpet in disbelief.

156

'How *could* he?' I stormed. 'He just walked straight in; he didn't even knock. Look at the carpet, he's ruined it five minutes after it's been laid. He's even managed to splash mud up the wall!'

'He does own the place,' Steve pointed out.

'I don't care,' I said. 'He's got no manners at all. From now on we're locking the door, so he has to knock and then I'll insist that he takes his boots off before he comes in.'

I waited until the mud on the carpet had dried before attempting to clean it, but Chilham's clay soil left a faint ginger imprint which I was never able to eradicate completely.

Lord Massereene's behaviour was all the more annoying because he had not commented on the valiant work which Steve, my mother and I had done to render North Lodge habitable. My heart sank the first time I walked into the little house. Inside, it was filthy and ringing wet; the cold hit you like a damp blanket.

I was the lucky one. My college term had started, so while I caught the bus each morning, Steve and my mother – wrapped up like Eskimos in thick coats and armed with buckets, scrubbing brushes and scouring pads – set about the unpleasant task of getting the floors and walls of North Lodge clean enough to paint. I joined them each afternoon, greatly appreciating any progress that had been made in which I had not had to participate.

'I had to take up the stair carpet this morning with a shovel,' my mother reported to me with a shudder one lunchtime.

The lodge was built from red brick, with a Dutch gable beneath a Kent peg tile roof. Upstairs, it had two decent-sized bedrooms and a third which was not much more than a box room. Downstairs, it had a little hallway, a spacious drawing-room and a kitchen, with a tiny bathroom beyond. The back door opened on to a walled yard, backed by a brick shed. From the yard, a door opened on to a large and untidy sloping garden at the rear.

Beneath the filth, the lodge did have some attractive internal

157

features. The hallway and kitchen were floored with red quarry tiles. An original dresser was built in to one of the walls in the kitchen, with a carved cornice and open shelving above two large cupboards. All the windows were leaded lights and the ceiling in the drawing room was made entirely from solid oak beams, with ornate scroll work. The lodge looked out over the village square.

We bought furniture out of the local papers. One of the advertisements read, 'Double bed, good condition, £7.50'. It listed a Canterbury telephone number, so I 'phoned up.

'I've seen your ad in the paper for a double bed – do you still have it?'

'Yes, would you like to come and see it?'

'Yes please, my name is Emma Braham.'

'Emma! This is Mrs Wordsworth, your biology teacher. What *are* you doing buying a double bed?'

It took rather a long time to explain.

A year or so earlier, Dougie and Mollie had moved into South Lodge opposite. From Mollie, I discovered that locking the front door at all times was a wise precaution, and not just to prevent his lordship from tramping in unannounced.

'One day shortly after we moved in,' she told me. 'I came downstairs to find a family of tourists sitting in my front room, on my settee, watching my television! The bleedin' cheek. You want to watch them visitors. Never leave your door unlocked or next thing you'll find them in your kitchen making tea!'

The first night we moved into North Lodge, I felt quite strange. I was worried about my mother in case she was lonely; I felt guilty leaving her on her own. Despite the comforting presence of Steve, I felt a little frightened too: I had moved away from the protective umbrella of my childhood and now, with Steve's salary of forty pounds a week plus our earnings from the banquets, it was up to us to succeed. I was still only sixteen, yet I had entered a whole new world of responsibility: running a house, paying bills, cooking, cleaning, making ends meet. I felt painfully inadequate. Shivering under the duvet in the unfamiliar surroundings, I was transported back to my first days at Carpenters, when I had been plucked from the womb of Medlar House.

In the cold light of day my fears drained away, to be replaced by pent-up excitement. The world was my oyster and all I had to do was use my wits and apply my energy. My spirits were only slightly dampened when I went down to the bathroom and discovered that my face sponge, the toothpaste and the water in the loo were frozen solid.

18

WE HAD BEEN raided. I unlocked the sunken mews that morning and found one of the perches unoccupied. The leash was still tied through the tethering ring, but it had been cut through the middle with a sharp knife. There was no sign of the hawk.

It was little Gringo who was missing, I realized, as a lump came into my throat. Gringo was an American Broad-Winged Hawk with one eye. Small, brown and mottled, with a black-and-white barred tail and a sweet temperament, he had not been with us long. Because of his one eye, he had been very twitchy when he first arrived: he seemed permanently scared that there was something lurking behind him. He focused awkwardly with his good eye, craning his neck like Long John Silver. After a couple of weeks of handling him, I had just begun to win his confidence.

All the other hawks were still there. I checked them quickly: Ebony, Sam, Sutek, a lugger falcon, and a buzzard called Nomad. I shut the door and ran frantically round to North Lodge to find Steve. He was in the kitchen, preparing Havoc's breakfast.

'We've been broken into!' I yelled breathlessly as I burst through the door.

Dropping the can he was opening, Steve overtook me as we ran back towards the mews.

'It's the sunken mews,' I panted. 'I haven't checked the others yet.'

None of the other hawks in the potting shed mews were missing. The curious thing was that the padlock on the sunken mews was intact. There were no signs of a forced entry. The building had no windows but, looking up, Steve spotted the small skylight propped open. The drop to the floor of the mews was a good twelve feet.

The skylight was grimy and covered in verdigris. Shrouded by the tall yew trees which ran along the rear of the building, it allowed very little light to enter the mews, even propped open as it was now.

'Why would someone do this? Why Gringo?' I was at a loss to understand.

'We've had a lot of local publicity recently: maybe someone was trying to steal him,' Steve speculated. 'Or it could be a mis-guided do-gooder who wanted to set the hawks free. They prob-ably picked on Gringo because he was the smallest and easiest to handle.'

'He'll never make it if they've set him free,' I said, horrified at the thought. 'He can't hunt in the wild with one eye.'

'I'd better call the police,' Steve said.

Watching his retreating back, I slumped down on the steps down into the mews. Poor, poor Gringo, what had become of him? Would the thief return for more? What about Ebony, Sam and the rest of our precious collection?

My eye was drawn to Ebony. She had stopped preening and was looking up with her head cocked to one side, as if some-thing had caught her eye. Following her gaze, I peered upwards into the gloomy darkness. Faintly, I could just discern a small black shape on a beam. Climbing to my feet, I strained my eyes. The outline was hawk-shaped. My heart beat faster, it was Gringo!

Quickly, I slipped out of the mews and shut the door behind me. I bumped into Steve coming in the opposite direction as I ran round the corner, at the bottom of path leading to the breeding centre.

'I've found Gringo! He's in the mews up on a beam!'

'Get a ladder,' Steve said urgently. 'I'll climb up on to the roof and shut the skylight.'

Gringo was manned but not yet trained. If he got out of the skylight, we would almost certainly lose him.

Inside, with both the skylight and the door shut, I shone the torch while Steve climbed the ladder towards the beam where Gringo was perched. My job was to try and stop Gringo landing close to one of the other hawks, who might grab him. As Steve approached, Gringo spotted him with his good eye and took off in alarm, flying round the inside of the mews several times before landing on the floor in a corner. Edging my way quietly over to him, I reached carefully for the cut end of his leash. I had it. Safely back on my fist, Gringo seemed none the worse for his adventure.

'It's lucky he flew up to the beam and didn't go near Sam or Ebony. Either of them would have killed him,' Steve said.

Ten minutes later, the village bobby arrived. He reckoned that whoever had broken in had had a struggle to climb back out of the skylight.

'From the outside, they'd never 'ave realized that the floor was sunken and it was such a tall climb back out again,' he said. 'Last thing they'd 'ave wanted was to be found locked inside when you opened up this mornin',' he added, smirking at the thought.

'Reckon whoever did it was forced to let the 'awk go afore 'e could climb out,' he said, scratching his head as he looked up at the skylight. 'Must've been some local wag, after a bit of bragging and a few pints too many at the White 'orse', he continued. 'I 'ave my suspicions, but unless you catch 'im red 'anded, there's no way we can prove it.'

'Best thing you can do sir,' he said, turning to Steve, 'is to invest in the biggest guard dog you can find, as a deterrent like. Take 'im for a walk around the village. Let everyone know you've got 'im. Tends to put folks off do big dogs.'

I could see the wisdom of his advice, but we could not afford to buy a guard dog. Instead, I called the RSPCA to see if they knew of a suitable dog for re-homing.

'We've got a Doberman in Deal,' the girl told me, after I explained the situation and gave a description of the type of home we were offering. 'And an Alsatian in Chatham.'

'I'd prefer the Alsatian,' I said. I had no experience of Dobermans, but when I was very young, the family had had an Alsatian called Major, whom I remembered with affection.

'Why is the owner parting with the dog?'

'The family can't afford to keep him any longer,' she explained. She gave me the address and telephone number.

'There's just one last thing: he's white. Does that matter?'

'I don't see why that should make any difference,' I said, surprised. I had never seen a white Alsatian before.

Later that afternoon, we drove up the motorway to Chatham to have a look at the dog. Wending our way through a large, modern housing estate, we found the small house among hundreds of other identical properties. Back to back, in serried ranks, the houses had pocket handkerchief gardens at the rear.

'I can't believe they've kept an Alsatian in one of these,' Steve remarked as we pulled up under a street light.

'It's the right road and number,' I said doubtfully.

A thin young man with stubble on his chin answered the door.

'You've come to see Rebel, have you?' he enquired.

'That's right,' Steve said.

The man showed us into a tiny living room at the front of the house. Four small children were sprawled on the carpet in front of the television. On the worn furniture lay four cats, dozing peacefully in the warmth from the gas fire.

'He's in the kitchen,' the man told us. 'The kids love him and he's sweet as anything with them, but he's so big, there's no room for us all when he's in here too.'

He opened the door to the kitchen and Rebel bounded into the room. My first impression was of a woolly polar bear. The

164

dog was truly huge, creamy white all over, with a black nose and eyes. I had never seen such a massive Alsatian. His tail wagged furiously as he greeted me, licking my hand with a wet pink tongue. The children came over and gathered round the dog. He licked each of them on the nose in turn.

A woman carrying a baby in her arms followed Rebel into the living room. Behind her, through the kitchen door, I could see two blue budgies in a cage.

'So you've come to get our Rebel?' the woman said.

Steve and I looked at each other. On the journey over we had agreed that we were only going for a look. If the dog was not ideal, we could not afford to take him.

'Yes please,' I said. I was already in love with this gentle giant of a dog, he was like an animated teddy bear.

The kids did not complain, but one by one, they put their arms round Rebel's neck and hugged him. I felt awful to be taking him away from them.

'We love him,' the woman said. 'He's ever so good – even with the cats – but he's just grown too big and now Pete's lost his job. It was fine when he was a puppy . . . ' Her voice tailed off. The smallest girl was in tears; even the father's eyes were moist.

'Can we give you some money for him?' Steve asked.

'I couldn't take anything for him; all we want is for him to go to a good home,' the man said. 'The RSPCA told us about your set-up, it sounds like he's fallen on his feet.'

'You're welcome to come and see him any time,' I said.

'We may do that one day,' the man said, rummaging in a drawer.

'You be good,' he told Rebel, as he handed Steve a blue nylon lead.

Clipping it on to Rebel's collar, we thanked him and led our new acquisition out to our blue Mini Traveller. Willingly, he jumped into the back, where he filled the entire space. He seemed to be very well trained. As we drove away I glanced back at the family gathered in the doorway.

'I wonder if they'll come and visit Rebel,' I said.

165

Back at Chilham, we had our plan to put into operation. Taking heed of the policeman's words, we decided to take Rebel across to the White Horse that evening. If the perpetrator was indeed a regular in the pub, we hoped the sight of Rebel might put him off another break-in attempt.

'I'll take Rebel, you take Havoc,' Steve suggested.

The appearance of an enormous white Alsatian in the pub caused quite a stir. Shortly after we had sat down, to my alarm I heard growling under the table. Before I could stop him, Havoc suddenly leapt on Rebel and we had a full-scale dog fight on our hands.

Yelling at Havoc — who was definitely the aggressor — we managed to separate the dogs, pulling them apart by their leads. It was all over in less than a minute. Apologizing to Trevor, the landlord, we led the dogs back to North Lodge.

Whether it was the fight, or whether Rebel's appearance alone would have been sufficient, we never knew, but by the next morning, word had spread around the village that we had a huge, savage dog. Our deliveries suddenly stopped. Our milk was left outside the main gates and the post was pushed under the wooden door at the side. This was a more dramatic reaction than we had anticipated. We had no desire to be totally ostracized by the village, we merely wanted to dissuade further break-ins. However, although it was quite some time before we could sleep peacefully through the night, it appeared that the policeman's theory had been correct. We had no more trouble.

After their initial test of wills, Havoc and Rebel became the best of friends. They went everywhere together and were united in their hatred of Arton, the surviving pharaoh hound. They lay in wait for her in the undergrowth, bushwhacking her as she patrolled the main drive in search of Smurfs. Appearing from the shrubbery at speed, Rebel knocked her over like a steam-roller and lay on her, while Havoc danced around nipping any piece of ginger fur which protruded from beneath Rebel's bulk.

Rebel was superbly well trained. Ordered to sit and stay, he would sit rooted to the spot for an indefinite period, even if left on his own. He was excellent with the hawks too and before long he could be trusted to lie behind the barrier on the static display ground, when the hawks were on display to visitors. As the weeks passed, we discovered that there was only one problem with Rebel: he did not bark. Neither Steve nor I wanted him to be over-protective of us but, as a guard dog, it was unhelpful that he was totally silent. It was as if being part of a large family in such a small house had conditioned every streak of aggression out of him. Now – regardless of the provocation – he remained entirely mute.

We concealed this fact vigorously: it would certainly have spoilt Rebel's image as a guard dog. It was difficult, therefore, to know how to cope with a telephone call from Alex in the small hours of a Saturday morning.

We were asleep when the call came through. There had been a banquet earlier that evening at which the guests were Royal Marines stationed in Dover. The banquet was a farewell treat for the men, who were off on a tour of duty in Northern Ireland the following day. Having already consumed vast quantities of beer, they had been a rowdy audience. In view of their forth-coming posting, I could not blame them for letting off steam, but I had not been sorry to leave the keep that evening.

Alex's voice on the other end of the telephone sounded uncharacteristically ruffled.

'Sorry to call you at this hour, old girl,' he said, 'but we've had a spot of bother with the Marines.

'They started to use the optics behind the bar as a coconut shy, throwing full cans of beer at them; then they tried to hang one of the wenches from a hook in the ceiling,' he continued, sound-ing a little overwrought.

'Their commanding officer has got most of them back on the coach, but two are on the loose somewhere. I wonder if Steve could take that huge Alsatian of yours and go and see if he can round them up?'

167

In view of Rebel's nature, I was sceptical of his ability to strike fear into the hearts of two rampaging Marines, but I said we would try. Quite apart from anything else, we did not want them going anywhere near the hawks. Steve collected Rebel from his kennel in the breeding centre and I put Havoc on a lead too. As Steve walked Rebel up the front drive in the darkness, I shadowed them in the bushes with Havoc. We eventually caught up with the two soldiers, who were staggering drunkenly arm in arm, singing loudly and tunelessly. Havoc, concealed in the undergrowth, barked ferociously.

The sight of Rebel – looming pale in the moonlight and apparently barking fiercely – appeared rapidly to sober them up and they took a couple of steps backwards. From my hiding place in the shrubbery, I could see that Rebel was wagging his tail.

'Go back to your coach, lads, or I'll let him off the lead,' Steve told them firmly.

Rather to my surprise, they turned tail and staggered off. Five minutes later, the coach – containing a full complement of men – headed out through the main gates. As it drove past North Lodge, I was alarmed to see it sway, glancing against the wall. There was a crash and a large, ornate flower pot shattered on the ground. I caught sight of the commanding officer's grim face through a side window of the coach, before it disappeared across the square.

The next morning, the commanding officer was back with half a dozen of his men, who looked considerably the worse for wear. It was 5.30 a.m. They could hardly have slept: the coach had not left until one o'clock in the morning. He knocked on our door.

'I'd like to apologize for the behaviour of my lads last night,' he called up as Steve opened the bedroom window. 'We've come back to clear up the mess and pay for the damage.'

'I cleaned up the flower pot last night,' Steve told him. 'But you'll need to see Lord Massereene about paying for it; it's one of a pair with the other lodge.'

'I'm returning this too,' the commanding officer said, colouring slightly. In his hands, he was clasping a stone eagle which normally sat on the wall beside the plant pot. 'I found it on the bus on the way home.'

'We hadn't even noticed it was missing,' I said truthfully, joining Steve at the window.

Turning to go, the commanding officer suddenly looked back over his shoulder.

'By the way, is that dog of yours loose?' he said. 'I don't want to bump into him. He scared my lads witless last night. Said they'd never seen such a huge animal.'

'You're quite safe,' I reassured him, shooting an amused glance at Steve. 'He's in his kennel.'

A week later, while swotting for my 'A' levels, I received a telephone call.

'My name's Geoffrey Household,' he introduced himself. 'I own a literary agency called Limelight Limited. Robert Hallman sent me the chapter you wrote on the owl and I must say, I enjoyed it very much.'

I caught my breath, this was the call I had been waiting for.

'I'd like to meet you in London next week if you would. I've secured a good publisher for Robert's falconry book. They think you'd be fine to write it. How's Tuesday for you?'

'Tuesday's fine,' I breathed, hardly able to get the words out.

'Let's have lunch then. I'll book a table at L'Escargot in Greek Street. See you there around one o'clock?'

'I'll look forward to it,' I managed, my heart pounding.

Bursting with the news, I ran from the house and found Steve on the top lawn. I threw myself into his arms.

'We've got it!' I told him joyfully, still scarcely able to take it in. 'The book – I've just had a 'phone call from the agent. I've got to go up to London next week. Can you believe it?'

Steve was as excited as I was. The following Tuesday, I waited on the platform at Chilham station. The train was late, and I began to fear that I would miss my connection. I paced the platform in frustration. As stations went, Chilham did have its compensations though. Immediately beside the London-bound platform lay a flooded gravel pit, which was a haven for water-fowl. As I watched, a Greater Crested Grebe glided serenely past, with its long curved neck arching gracefully beneath fanned orange-brown head feathers. The untouched beauty of the lake, dotted with water irises and clumps of slender rushes, contrasted starkly with the graffiti-covered concrete bridge over the railway line and the bent railings which divided the platform from the nearside edge of the lake.

I checked my watch for the umpteenth time. I had missed my connection for sure now. Chilham station did not have a pay phone, so I had no way of contacting the restaurant and asking them to warn the agent – who was travelling up from Devon to meet me – that I had been delayed. My frustration mounted. When the train finally arrived, it was a full hour late.

As I settled in my seat, an announcement was made over the tannoy.

'British Rail would like to apologize for the late arrival of this service,' a nasal voice informed us. 'This is due to a fatality on the line at Chartham.'

Sadly, this was not unusual. Chartham was the stop between Canterbury and Chilham. In the countryside beyond Chartham, there was a psychiatric hospital called St Augustine's Hospital. Fatalities on the line at Chartham invariably meant that one of the patients had thrown themselves in front of a train. This was confirmed by a businessman in a smart suit sitting opposite me.

'This one jumped off a bridge,' he told me. 'Timed it beauti-fully apparently. The guard said it was an awful mess. Damned inconsiderate really – these people never think of the poor bas-tards who have to clear up after them.'

While I digested this unsavoury piece of information, I was still selfishly worried about my lunch appointment. Cursing the luck which was threatening one of the most important meet-

170

ings of my life, I prayed Geoffrey Household would wait for me.

I had no time to telephone when I arrived in Ashford, throwing myself on to the next train to London just as it was leaving. I finally reached the restaurant in Soho at ten minutes to two. To my relief, Geoffrey was still waiting for me. I apologized profusely, explaining the reason for the delay, painfully aware that it sounded like a bizarre excuse.

'Don't give it a second thought,' he told me, as we ordered *moules* and *coq au vin*. 'By the way, I hope this won't put you under too much pressure, but the publishers want you to write two books, not one.'

My astonishment must have shown in my face.

'You see,' he continued, 'they produce a series of small, heavily illustrated paperbacks and they like the idea of doing one on falconry. Robert's photographs will suit the format ideally. The only snag is, they get their annual output of paperbacks all printed at the same time in Hong Kong, it's cheaper that way. They've only just thought of adding this one on falconry and the others are already written. Do you think you can get it done by early next week? They only need ten thousand words, then you can have another six months for the hardback.'

'I can try,' I stammered. I had no idea what ten thousand words looked like.

The waiter delivered steaming bowls of mussels with crispy French bread.

'Don't let it spoil your lunch,' Geoffrey joked. 'I'm sure you'll manage. I really did like your owl story. One day you should write a book about your life with the hawks.'

I travelled home with my head spinning. The publisher had offered me an advance of nine hundred pounds. To me, this was a huge sum of money but I knew that to earn it I was going to have to work extremely hard. The paperback I had to start immediately. When that was finished, it was going to be a struggle to find time for a longer, more technical book in between sitting my 'A' levels and starting in the autumn at Gardner and Croft.

As the outskirts of London yielded to the Kent countryside, I stared out of the train window at the passing scenery, which was bathed in the pink glow of dusk. Life had been so busy recently that I had not had much time just to sit and think. Since Steve and I had first met, it was as if we were being pulled by an invisible string, woven from golden threads of opportunity, towards a distant goal which we had not yet identified. The publication of these books could open new avenues for us. The last manual on falconry to be written by a woman was Dame Juliana Berners' *Book of St Albans*, from which I quoted during the medieval banquets. Was I destined to follow in her footsteps seven centuries later, only to spend the rest of my life suffocating in airless legal chambers? Steve did not want me to read law, and it was a relief to know he sided with me on this. We worked as a team at the Bird of Prey Centre and we both knew that the business would suffer if I had to direct my energies elsewhere.

As the train rumbled inexorably on towards Chilham, I felt as though I too was set on tracks – tracks I was desperate to get off. Soon I would finish at college. Once at Gardner and Croft, I was embarking on a career which was scheduled to take me to retirement age. I had seen my father trapped on the self-same tracks. While I pursued my legal career, everything that was most important in my life – Steve, the hawks, the countryside – I would glimpse only in snapshots. As the train headed towards my destination, I felt under mounting pressure to think clearly and quickly. I had to reconcile this dilemma which was tormenting me. I flashed back nine years. I was sitting with Wally by the lake, feeling again the burning certainty that there was nothing I wanted more than to spend the rest of my life with hawks.

As the train drew in to Chilham station it jolted me into a decision. It was my life, my future. I was going to make falconry my career.

172

19

'I THOUGHT YOU'D KNOW what to do with this.' The woman's tone was apologetic as she passed me the familiar cardboard box.

The Bird of Prey Centre was now receiving over one hundred injured birds a year. Occasionally people tried to give us other types of birds too. The general public were far from infallible when differentiating between hawks and other species. I received boxes at the front door containing everything from seagulls to swifts: 'But it must be a hawk, look, it's got a little hooked beak.' The majority of such cases Steve and I transferred to a Canterbury couple who specialized in caring for other types of injured birds.

I peered into the box. To my surprise, a little pink nose greeted me. Pulling open the lid, I revealed a polecat ferret. I looked questioningly at the woman.

'I live in Mountain Street. I found it running round my garden,' she said. 'I was nervous of picking it up, but it seemed quite friendly.'

'We don't normally accept animals,' I said, 'but we can actually use ferrets. We put them down holes to chase out rabbits for the hawks when we're hunting, so if it's not claimed, we'll keep it.'

The woman thanked me and left. I lifted the ferret out of its box and inspected it. It was a hob – a male – in very good condition. He was brown, with a cream face and a dark Lone Ranger mask. His bright black eyes shone with vitality and his long whiskers twitched inquisitively. He made no attempt to bite me and I could see that he had been well handled. Although it is not unusual to lose a working ferret, I was slightly puzzled as I did not know anyone in the area who went ferreting. I named him Ferdinand.

That evening, Ferdinand kept Steve and me entertained with his antics in North Lodge. Generally ferrets are great characters and, if well handled, they are very friendly and playful. Ferdi was quite the most animated and likeable ferret I had ever come across. He humped his back and bounded from side to side, disappearing under the sofa, then emerging to mug me as I looked for him on all fours. Steve produced one of the rabbit lures which we used to train the hawks and towed it round the room with Ferdi in hot pursuit. When he was tired, Ferdi relaxed flat on his back beside me, his eyes half closed as I tickled his tummy.

The next day, Steve and I took Ferdi to some rabbit holes in the wapiti paddock. Although we had heard about working hawks in conjunction with ferrets, we had never had the opportunity to try it. For our first outing though, we decided that it would be better to try Ferdi on his own, until we got the hang of it.

To my disappointment, far from wanting to wage war on rabbits, Ferdi showed a distinct reluctance to go down holes.

After several fruitless attempts, Steve shoved him into a hole and put his boot over the top of it. When he removed his foot a minute later, Ferdi had disappeared. We retreated and sat patiently for fifteen minutes, watching the hole for signs of emerging rabbits. Nothing moved. Then I felt something at my elbow. Ferdi was standing beside me, peering short-sightedly in the direction of the hole. I had no idea how long he had been there, but clearly this was unproductive. Investigations revealed a bolt hole just behind me, a rabbit 'back door' from whence Ferdi had emerged.

I picked him up and we found another hole. This time as I dropped Ferdi at the entrance he scuttled underground imme-diately. We barely had time to back off a few paces before a rabbit emerged from a connecting hole and shot off across the field.

This was much more encouraging. Ferdi reappeared looking smug and I scooped him up.

'Maybe he can smell if there's a rabbit down the hole?' I sug-gested. 'Maybe that's why he was willing to go straight down this time.'

We tested the theory and it appeared to be correct. Glowing with success, I carried Ferdi home in my pocket. The following day, Ebony joined the team.

Ebony was an experienced rabbit hunter. That spring, rabbits had been plentiful and, on most outings, she had caught one. Recently, though, the rabbit population had thinned out and catching them had become harder. Sometimes I had walked through cover all evening without managing to flush a single rabbit for Ebony to chase. I was hopeful that Ferdi would give us the edge we needed.

I was worried, however, that Ebony would mistake Ferdi for a rabbit, so I held on tightly to her jesses as Steve dropped Ferdi in the mouth of a hole. He disappeared, then there was a long wait. I was so worried about accidentally releasing Ebony at Ferdi that, when a rabbit finally burst into view, I failed to release my grip on her jesses quickly enough. She shot off in pursuit, but the rabbit reached the safety of another hole before Ebony could catch up.

On our next attempt, Ferdi managed to conjure up two rabbits from their burrow and I released Ebony smartly. As the rabbits sped across the turf, she closed in behind the second one, extending her feet for the kill. Within inches of another burrow, she grasped the rabbit firmly in her talons and spun round with the momentum of the impact. Flushed with excitement, I ran over to her. With her wings mantled over her prize she started to eat.

Each evening thereafter, Steve and I armed ourselves with Ebony and Ferdi and headed off into the centre of the estate on rabbiting expeditions. It was August and the weather was at its best. Perfect, cloudless days were followed by long summer evenings. The meadow beside the heronry yielded rich pickings and quickly became our favourite spot for ferreting. The heronry comprised a stand of elm trees, still free of Dutch Elm disease, where herons perched like grey sentinels. The trees were faced by a broad sweep of grassland, rich in wild flowers.

Large, untidy bundles of sticks formed the herons' nests in the tree tops, vulnerable to the March winds which could rattle a nest to the ground. In the late spring the heronry echoed to the raucous voices of the herons as they reared their chicks and squabbled for territory. At this time of year, though, the tree tops were peaceful and the silence was broken only by the dulcet cooing of wood-pigeons and the drone of bumblebees. The heronry backed on to woods, dissected by broad, grassy rides which ran between thick-trunked horse chestnut trees and ancient oaks. Dense conifer plantations lay further within the woodland, providing sanctuary for fallow and roe deer.

Beneath the elms, the meadow sloped gently to form a shallow bowl. Around the edges of the bowl lay a cluster of rabbit holes, spaced in such a way that a fleeing rabbit would cross the centre of the bowl to seek sanctuary in a hole on the far side, or in the long bracken which fringed the meadow.

176

As Ferdi performed his duties diligently, rabbit after rabbit scurried through the long, clover-laden grass, with Ebony in hot pursuit. As I watched ferret and hawk working together, I felt a powerful sense of timelessness, of history coming full circle. Here in the heronry, I was hawking in the footsteps of Henry VIII.

One evening we carried kindling and some matches with us. I wanted to catch a young rabbit to barbecue. Since Ferdi's arrival, rabbit had featured heavily on the menu for both the hawks and us. Seduced by the balmy warmth of the evening, Steve and I determined to cook our catch outdoors.

Rooting around the edges of the bowl, Steve came across a large hole, partially obscured by bracken. I fished Ferdi out of my pocket and Steve sent Ebony up into an overhanging tree. Ebony was no longer a risk to Ferdi. Although she had bated off the glove towards him at first, she quickly seemed to grasp the fact that Ferdi was there to help, not to catch. This was useful because Ebony could now hunt loose from trees, giving her the advantage of a speedy descent.

Ferdi disappeared into the large hole with alacrity. Tense with anticipation, we waited. I could hear a faint scurrying noise coming from underground. My heart beat quickened. Suddenly from the mouth of the hole a fox burst into view. His summer coat burnished by the evening sun, he saw me and paused. No more than six feet separated us. Time seemed to stand still for a moment as he transfixed me with his chestnut eyes. Then he ran off across the meadow, loping into a distant patch of bracken.

Fortunately, Ebony stayed at her post. Had it been Sam accompanying us, he might have been tempted to give chase, but Ebony wisely realized that this prey was too large for her. Ferdi emerged.

'He could have been snapped in two,' I said with concern, recovering slightly from my surprise as I lifted the ferret up and scratched gently behind his ears.

'He must have disturbed it while it was sleeping,' Steve said.

'You're very brave, Ferdi, but we need some supper, so could you please concentrate on the job in hand?'

The next hole we tried yielded a monster rabbit, which scampered across the bowl with Ebony at full stretch behind it. She caught up with it and connected briefly, but it shrugged her off and, jinxing sharply, ran into the bracken.

'I wouldn't have wanted to cook that rabbit anyway,' Steve said. 'I reckon it was the grandad of this rabbit warren – I bet it would have been tough as old boots.'

We were finally rewarded when Ebony caught a couple of plump young rabbits, one after the other. I paunched them and skinned them, while Steve gathered wood, scraped a hollow with his knife and made a stick spit over a fire. Later, in the soft glow of dusk, we ate smoky rabbit with our fingers. When we had eaten our fill, Steve picked up Ebony, who was secured to a fallen tree nearby. With her crop bulging with rabbit, she sat loose feathered and relaxed on his glove. Ferdi lay curled up asleep in my pocket. After throwing earth on the red embers of the fire, Steve and I strolled home across the park, hand in hand.

Sadly, our pleasure in these outings was destined to be short-lived. On the fifth night, in the wapiti paddock, we lost Ferdi.

'He may have killed underground,' Steve said after we had waited for over half an hour. 'We'll have to come back to look for him first thing tomorrow.'

I was upset to lose Ferdi, not only because he worked well, but also because I had become attached to him. When above ground, he would come to my call and even walk short distances at my heels. Although I knew he could fend for himself, it was a wrench to lose him. In the middle of the night, we went out with a spotlight to see if we could spot him. As Steve swung the light slowly round, distant eyes glittered like sequins in the darkness. My hopes were raised, but as we walked towards the eyes they melted away, as a dozen rabbits sped off into the night.

There was no sign of Ferdi the following morning either. Steve lay with his ear to the hole, while I squeaked like a rabbit

178

in distress, a noise which usually brought Ferdi scampering towards me. Depressed, I returned home without the familiar furry bulge in my pocket.

Terry Wilde was waiting on the doorstep. Terry had first come to Chilham as a tourist. The owner of a flourishing pet shop in Chatham, he had been keen to expand into exotic animals. He had recently negotiated with Lord Massereene to open a pet park at the castle, called Petland.

Since embarking on the Petland project, Terry had exchanged his car for a long-wheel-base, zebra-striped Land Rover, with a huge roof rack and jerry cans strapped to the sides. When he was on duty he wore a camouflage bushman's outfit, complete with safari hat – the sort with a wide brim pinned up on one side – and gold-framed aviator's sunglasses. The bottoms of his camouflage trousers were tucked into German paratrooper boots laced to the knee, presumably to keep out snakes. Strapped to his waist there was a machete.

From the roof of his Land Rover, Terry directed the construction of the wire-mesh equivalent of the Great Wall of China around the area which lay to one side of the wapiti paddock, gesticulating with his machete in an Edgar Rice Burrows fashion.

A month after construction had started, the park was ready, complete with immaculate gravel paths and steps leading down the slope from the park field. Terry had purchased animals to stock Petland from a well-known zoological supplier which had a reputation for being extremely expensive. We were agog to see the new inhabitants arrive. They emerged from the back of a huge horse box like Noah's Ark. A rhesus monkey came out first, in a stout cage, followed by a llama, a dwarf Brahmin bull, a couple of raccoons, some wallabies, a fox cub, half a dozen muntjak deer and a short-legged, chunky creature which I could not identify. It looked like a cross between a gigantic guinea-pig and a rat. Overall, the collection struck me as more suited to a serious zoo than a children's pet park.

The large rodent, I was informed, was a capybara, a sort of

giant water rat from South America. As it was released into its compound, which was bordered by a shallow canal for it to swim in, I noticed that it had a raw spot on the end of its nose. Looking carefully at the other animals, I spotted other defects too. The monkey had a ragged stump of a tail and the llama was missing an ear. I asked Terry about these injuries.

'That animal supplier was shockingly expensive,' he told me, shaking his head ruefully. 'So I said to the geezer, "Look mate, I'm not made of the folding stuff. 'Aven't you got any cheap animals out the back?" And 'e had,' he continued cheerfully. 'They was a bargain. I don't mind tellin' you. I took the lot. Cleared 'im out, I did – and 'ere they are.'

He gestured in the manner of one pointing towards a vast herd of wildebeest crossing the plains of Africa.

After the zebra-striped Land Rover had disgorged the smaller fry such as parakeets, guinea-pigs and budgerigars from Terry's pet shop, Petland was ready to open its gates to the public. The *Kentish Gazette* was invited to cover the opening and a journalist interviewed Terry at length. The resulting article was not as helpful as it could have been.

'How can a hundred pound rodent possibly be described as a cuddly children's pet?' the feature enquired. Like me, the journalist had probably been expecting a children's pet park to contain lambs and bunny rabbits.

The bushman's outfit notwithstanding, I had already decided that Terry was no George Adamson. I was not surprised, therefore, to hear that he had come to seek help with another animal problem that morning.

'Some ferret's broken into Petland!'

Visions of Ferdi armed with a pair of wire-cutters flashed through my brain. As I opened my mouth to explain how delighted I was that Terry had found him, Terry cut me off.

'It's murdered 'alf me small stock!' he blustered. 'Do you want the bloody thing? Otherwise I'll kill it.'

Looking at Terry's livid face, I cowardly decided against telling him that it was my ferret that had caused the furore, but I said that I would come and get it. When we reached Petland, I was devastated to see the carnage which Ferdi had wreaked. Four guinea-pigs and a Reeves pheasant were lying dead. Tired after his busy night, Ferdi was relaxing in the corner of the guinea-pig enclosure, sunning himself with his back legs stretched out behind him.

'I didn't pick 'im up in case 'e bit me,' Terry said nervously.

I scooped up Ferdi – who overnight had grown into the fattest ferret I had ever seen – and, to my surprise, he bit me savagely. In less than twenty-four hours, he had turned from a sweet-natured pet into the ferret from hell. I took him back to North Lodge, wondering what on earth I was going to do with him and feeling guilty as sin.

That weekend Jim came down to see us.

'I don't suppose you want a ferret?' I asked hopefully. Showing Ferdi to him, I told Jim the awful tale. I had no option but to find Ferdi a new home. I could not risk working him on the estate again and, although he had calmed down a lot since I had retrieved him from Petland, I was wounded, literally and psy-chologically, by his new tendency towards biting.

To my great relief, Jim readily agreed to take Ferdi off my hands. When the Camaro left on Sunday evening, with the usual tuneful blast from its air horns, I heaved a huge sigh of relief. I had been honest with Jim: he knew that, potentially, Ferdi was trouble and I was very grateful to him for taking the animal off my hands.

A week later, Jim was eating supper with us in North Lodge.

'How's the ferret?' Steve enquired.

'Well, I've got something to tell you,' Jim said, looking edgy. 'Bout three weeks ago, I went poaching for rabbits down on the verges of Mountain Street. It was blazing 'ot, so when me ferret went down an 'ole, I opened a few cans of beer. I 'ave to confess, I dozed off, and when I woke up, there was no sign of the ferret. I 'ad to leave him.'

I could guess what was coming.

'The thing is, see, he was my ferret originally. Now 'e's broken into Petland and done all that damage.' His face was a picture of guilt. 'An 'e bites something awful too, the little terror. I don't know what to do with 'im.'

'You could always turn him into a Davy Crockett hat,' Steve suggested, 'and give it to Terry as a peace offering. It'd set off the camouflage gear a treat.'

20

THE BOX WAS a sight to behold. Three feet square, it was constructed from heavy ply and bound every six inches by thick bands of steel. What terror could be lurking within it?

With some difficulty, I prised open the lid and a pair of large, brown eyes looked up at me, fringed by extremely long and angelic-looking eyelashes. I inserted my gloved hand carefully. There was a raucous yell from the interior and something slashed at my arm. Hastily I withdrew, but I had an appendage. Hanging from my sleeve by its beak was the most extraordinary bird I had ever seen.

Its beak was white and its face was bare red skin, giving it the appearance of a clown. It had a glossy black crest, below which lay ivory feathers, finely banded with black. This variegated mantle extended down over the bird's shoulders, blending into black feathering on the lower back and wings. The tail and wing feathers were white, finely barred with black. A pair of long, bright yellow legs swung beneath it. This exotic creature rejoiced in an equally exotic name. It was an Audubon's caracara.

A friend in Yorkshire had sent it, telling me that in contrast to those of other birds of prey, its large yellow feet were as harmless as a chicken's but, he had warned, its beak was like a chainsaw, hence the reinforced box. Stupidly, I had decided that this was probably an exaggeration. The bird was a female but, her sex notwithstanding, I determined to call her Cuthbert.

I had genned up on our latest acquisition. Audubon's caracaras live on savannahs and pampas from Florida to the Argentine. They have wide-ranging tastes, feeding on live and dead fish, mammals, rotting meat, eggs, young or wounded birds, insect larvae, live shellfish and iguanas. They frequent newly ploughed fields, clean up roadways and slaughter pens and pick up floating carrion from the rivers. Their propensity also to attack young livestock makes them unpopular. Nowhere, however, did my reference book mention a penchant for human flesh.

As I lowered my appendage gently on to the kitchen floor, she reared back and slashed into my upper arm with a vicious blow, removing a piece of flesh. Pausing briefly, a thoughtful expression on her face, Cuthbert proceeded to swallow the bloody morsel, smacking her beak like an epicurean relishing a particularly fine mouthful of fillet steak.

I leapt back in shock, clasping my wounded arm, and eyed Cuthbert balefully. Cuthbert eyed me in turn. I got the uncomfortable feeling that she was trying to work out which portion of my anatomy would yield the most tender snacks. Edging my way round her to the door, I left the room, returning armed with a thick bath towel. As I circled her, towel at the ready, it was hard to determine who was stalking whom. Her crest raised, she padded menacingly round the floor on her stubby yellow feet. The boiler murmured behind her and, momentarily distracted, she glanced over her shoulder. Seizing my opportunity I threw the towel over her head and rugby tackled her.

Despite the thickness of the material, several splits appeared in the towel as her razor-sharp beak stabbed away blindly. I lowered the bundle on to the table and passed a few extra turns of the material around it. Temporarily subdued while I attached jesses to her feet, Cuthbert contented herself by issuing a volley of ear-splitting yells.

Contrary to my expectations, she proved exceptionally quick to train, but I gained scars at a rate to match the progress. She used her beak indiscriminately, removing her first set of jesses within hours and reducing her thick nylon leash to a pile of threads. Her jesses I replaced with the thickest leather I could find and, after chewing fruitlessly at them for an hour or so, she turned her attention to gardening, hacking up the turf around her perch in search of leather jackets and worms. She could raise or lower her crest at will, leaving me in no doubt whatsoever about her mood at any given time. When she was annoyed, her red face would flush yellow and her strident voice expressed her displeasure in unmistakable terms. In the early days of manning, she frequently threw what can only be described as tantrums, throwing herself off the glove and spinning upside down, snapping and bellyaching as she rotated. Despite the warmth of the spring weather, it was not safe to handle her without long sleeves. Soon the left arms of most of my shirts were torn to shreds.

Cuthbert's saving grace was that, in common with many extroverted individuals, she could be charming company when the spirit moved her. When at peace with herself and me, she would plant her feet widely on the glove and gaze trustingly into my eyes with an expression of benign bonhomie. I quickly came to realize that she was not really belligerent, she just could not resist sampling different tastes and putting her best asset, her redoubtable beak, to work whenever possible.

She flew with a grace belied by her comical appearance, but spoilt it by dropping on to the ground half way to my fist and covering the remaining distance on foot. Visitors adored watching her – she had quite a turn of speed on the flat, but invariably she would get her long legs in a tangle and trip over. Picking herself up, she would raise her crest and glare at the spectators before trotting over to me and hopping up for her reward. Sometimes, she would stop *en route* to snip the head off a daffodil or rummage through the handbag of a tourist, picking out vanity mirrors and handkerchiefs. Discovering to her dis-appointment that the objects were not edible, she would discard them on the ground and continue on her way, leaving the crowd convulsed with laughter.

In the spring of 1979, Cuthbert's popularity with visitors to the castle was temporarily overshadowed by a crèche of young Tawny Owls – three half-feathered orphans. Our breeding aviaries were fully occupied and space was at a premium, so at night I kept them in a huge cardboard box in the kitchen, taking them up to the display ground with me each day to get some fresh air. Un-jessed, the three of them were an awkward armful to carry across the lawn, as they abandoned their perch on my forearms whenever the spirit took them. Once one went, they all went, so in the end I resorted to carrying them in their unwieldy cardboard box.

Still too young to fly, the owlets moved about in a series of leaps and bounds, snapping their beaks and parachuting off the kitchen table on velvet-soft wings. One of them, who I called Snuffles because he had a mild respiratory infection, developed a novel way of increasing his mobility. As Rebel passed beneath him, he leapt off the table on to the dog's back.

Fortunately, Rebel's response was typically good-natured. He made no move to dislodge Snuffles, who gripped into his thick, creamy fur as he continued on his way. This gave me an idea. I placed the other owlets on to Rebel's back behind Snuffles and, to my delight, Rebel seemed content for them to travel in this manner all the way up to the display ground. Concentrating on keeping their balance, the owls showed no desire to leap off mid-way and thus Rebel relieved me of a daily chore.

The weathering ground was overhung by a yew tree. Lifting the owls off Rebel's back, I released them into the lower branches of the yew, where they could clamber about or doze, shutting their pink eyelids against the sunlight. Visitors were entranced to spot them amongst the branches. The only disad-vantage with this system was that sometimes the owls clambered upwards out of my reach, and at the end of the afternoon I had to climb the tree to retrieve them for their dog-ride back to North Lodge.

It was pretty typical that the visitors were more enthusiastic about three baby owls than the rest of our burgeoning collection put together. Only one occupant of the weathering ground could successfully divert attention away from the owls. Cuthbert hated being ignored. When a good crowd had gathered, oohing and aahing at the antics of the owlets, she would perform a spectacular party piece.

Some of the other birds would bathe regularly when the weather was fine. Hopping off their perches on to the ground, they approached their shallow bathing pans cautiously, stepping on to the lip of the bath first, then gingerly lowering themselves into the water. However, most of them would refuse to bathe if they were being watched.

Cuthbert suffered from no such modesty. From her favourite vantage point, on the apex of the shelter behind her perch, she dived straight into the water with a tremendous splosh, commanding instant attention and soaking any visitors within range. As she was clearly not satisfied with the depth of the usual bath pans, I managed to find an old tin washing tub in one of the greenhouses. This held ten inches of water, enabling Cuthbert to immerse herself up to her neck. She bathed as she did everything else in life, noisily and with great gusto.

Cuthbert also had an annoying ability to find carrion. Taking off from my glove with such enthusiasm that I was fooled into believing that she had spotted a live victim, she would drop on to the ground and consume the festering carcass of a rabbit or a wind-blown heron chick, picking out maggots and eating these too with relish. Attempts to part her from these smelly prizes were met with ugly scenes and bellicose protests. When she finally returned to the glove, her feet were covered with putrid slime and her breath was repugnant.

During the spring and early summer of that year, the Bird of

187

Prey Centre got some good publicity. Steve and I were invited to appear with Sam and Ebony on a Saturday morning television show which was being broadcast live that week from Canterbury. After the broadcast, several newspaper reporters got in touch and printed stories on the birds. 'Snuffles makes a happy landing,' said the *Kentish Express* alongside a picture of Snuffles on Rebel's back. Not to be outdone, the *Kentish Gazette* responded with, 'A question of sex – should it be Cuthberta?' and a photo of Cuthbert and me sitting in the daffodils.

We also received a telephone call from Eagle Breweries, asking if we could supply an eagle for a television commercial. Steve, Sam and I travelled to a pub in Bedford, where the commercial was being filmed. On our arrival the director told us that he wanted Sam to perch on a lager dispenser, while the voice-over said, 'Discover where the eagle lands'. In front of the dispenser, the set designer had meticulously positioned a couple of bottles of lager, a ploughman's lunch and a frothy pint of the said beverage. Unfortunately, Sam found the pint too tempting and started to take little sips out of it.

The director was not impressed. The hygiene laws, he said, would not allow footage of an eagle drinking from a pint glass to be shown on television, lest a potential consumer thought they might be given the same glass. I thought this was utterly ridiculous, but meanwhile Steve and I were becoming concerned about Sam. His little sips appeared to be having a cumulative affect on him: he was becoming noticeably truculent. During the next shot, to our alarm he picked up the glass in his beak, waved it briefly at the camera then, with a toss of his head, threw it at the ploughman's lunch, spilling the contents over the bar and breaking the plate. Someone in the crew suggested that we give him a cup of Mellow Bird's coffee to sober him up.

The day after we returned from filming, Steve had a serious argument with Cuthbert. Like all the birds we were flying, Cuthbert needed to be weighed every day so that we could determine how much food to give her. Weighing Cuthbert was a task which Steve and I fought each other not to have to carry out. She was a real nuisance on the scales, continually jigging about, making it extremely difficult to get an accurate weight.

On the day in question, we were running late for getting the birds up to the display ground. With mounting impatience, I was waiting to weigh Ebony while Steve attempted to weigh Cuthbert.

'Will you sit *still*,' Steve said in frustration, as Cuthbert bounced from foot to foot.

Cuthbert responded by delivering a deep and vicious blow to Steve's face with her beak. I rushed to his aid and was horrified to see a large V-shaped wound on his left cheek well with blood. Later, as we inspected the full extent of the damage, we realized that Steve would be scarred for life.

'Thank heavens she didn't manage to tear the flesh away,' I said ruefully. 'You'd have had a hole the size of a pencil sharpener.'

'I think it may be a good time to retire Cuthbert from active service,' Steve said. 'I can't believe she got me.'

As a child, I had been bitten and scratched by hawks more times than I cared to remember, but working with birds of prey on a full-time basis, I had begun to believe that it was quite possible to avoid 'being had', as we termed it, by dint of developing quick reactions. I knew Steve's reactions were if anything quicker than mine, but Cuthbert's were obviously far superior. Sadly, therefore, despite her popularity during flying displays, I was forced to agree that it would be safer to put her into an aviary and try to find her a mate.

We started work on an aviary for her that evening. While Steve furnished the interior with care, arranging rocks, fixing stout branches for her to perch on and sinking a plastic bath tray into the ground, I worked on a nest box. Diligently applying my extremely amateurish carpentry skills, I went to great pains to construct a carefully thought-out box. Although I sliced open my hand with the saw and blackened a thumb-nail with the hammer, I had to admit I was extremely proud of the box when it was finished. I waterproofed it with roofing felt and placed a layer of earth and soft grasses on the inside. Steve helped me to fix the box securely in the back corner and we stood back to survey the result of our labours. The aviary looked very smart indeed.

I collected Cuthbert from the mews and took her into her new home, where I cut off her jesses and placed her on a perch. To my delight, she flew immediately to the nest box and inspected it minutely. We left her that night perched in the entrance. I spent most of that evening on the telephone and, to my delight, managed to locate a male caracara, which I arranged to buy.

The following day, as I did the morning feeding-round in the breeding centre, I could not believe my eyes when I reached Cuthbert's aviary. Overnight, she had eaten her nest box. Starting at the front of the box, she had chewed her way steadily backwards through the roof. The top of the box now had a semi-circular hole in it.

Cuthbert, perched in the remains of my ruined handiwork, looked immensely satisfied with herself. As I stood looking at the box with mounting annoyance, she flew down and grabbed her bath. Wrenching it from its depression, she towed it round the aviary in her beak.

Watching her gloomily as she started to demolish the perches, I began to feel sorry for her forthcoming mate. Life closeted with Cuthbert was an unenviable prospect. On the other hand, he might not last long enough to experience it – with her track record she would probably eat him.

21

'DOUGLAS! THE SHEEP bloody are all over the gardens.' Lord Massereene appeared never to have mastered the art of swearing. Much to our amusement, he invariably inserted his expletives in all the wrong places. With resignation, Dougie collected his sheep dogs from the kennels at the rear of South Lodge and headed off to gather the sheep from the terraces and deposit them back into the park.

As sheep dogs went, Dougie's were pretty good. I put it down to the fact that they got plenty of practice: when money was tight, holes in the rickety park fences were inadequately repaired with baler twine. Dougie, however, claimed it was due to his visionary training methods. Once a week he ushered his dogs into South Lodge and sat them in front of the television to watch *One Man and his Dog*.

The sheep themselves were a motley crew. In the main, they were purchased from the sale ring in the Ashford livestock market. Due to Dougie's tight budget it tended to be the under-sized, wormy or otherwise disadvantaged that came back to the estate in the rear of his rusty pick-up. The lambing average of the ewes was deplorable and the lambs, consistent with their lineage, were a sickly bunch. They emerged each spring complete with a death-wish of alarming proportions.

The sheep were supposed to stay in the agricultural part of the estate, beyond the ha-ha. However, a number of them managed to find their way into the gardens by tagging along behind visitors who had parked in the park field. A small footbridge spanned the ha-ha, affording access to the top lawn. By cunningly picking their moment, a band of sheep would barge across the bridge behind a visitor and career into the gardens before the surprised individual could shut the gate at the far end. One in particular had another peculiar talent, which it revealed for the first time on a busy May Bank Holiday afternoon, in the middle of one of our demonstrations.

Steve used the bottom lawn below the terraces for the bulk of his demonstrations. The long bank at one end and the two terraces above it formed a natural amphitheatre for spectators and the topiaries which punctuated the terraces provided ideal perching points for the hawks in-between flights.

There had already been a little excitement that day. In an earlier demonstration, I had flown a ferruginous buzzard called Schmuck, whom I had only recently completed training. Like the majority of her species, which spends much of its time on the ground in its native North America, Schmuck was not keen on perching in trees. I had trained her on the lawns in the quiet of the evening. During these sessions, she had learned to make full use of the terrace walls as perching points, preferring those to the topiaries.

For the first demonstration of the day, three thousand people had packed themselves around the display area. They sat in the sun on the bank, on the crumbling brick steps which linked the terraces and along the terrace walls, their legs dangling over the edge.

Cast off the glove for her maiden flight for the public, Schmuck circled briefly before heading as usual for the terrace wall above the bottom lawn. To our consternation, she appeared

192

undaunted by the fact that a line of people were sitting on it. As she came in to land, two people flung themselves sideways to make space for her to alight between them. Throwing out their arms to balance themselves, they knocked the people sitting on either side of them.

Like a row of dominoes, one by one the spectators sitting along the entire length of the wall toppled over backwards. All we could see was a row of legs waving in the air. For a second there was a stunned silence. Then a row of heads emerged from behind the wall. Although the drop in front was about eight feet, the path behind was only a foot below them. When they saw nobody was hurt, the rest of the audience roared with laughter appreciatively.

The crowd had not diminished for the last display of the day. We were flying a different set of hawks and Steve's lively commentary was in full flow, when he realized that he did not have the spectators' full attention. They were staring behind him towards the far edge of the bottom lawn, where a line of well-spaced topiaries backed on to a wall. On the far side there was a drop of fifteen feet to the paddocks below. Following the crowd's gaze, Steve glanced over his shoulder. There was nothing there.

He continued with the display, but a few seconds later he lost the crowd's attention again. He looked behind him, but still he could not see what was distracting them. Confused he pressed on. The next time ripples of laughter from the spectators alerted him. He swung round quickly in time to see a sheep emerging from behind a topiary, balanced nonchalantly on the rounded coving stones of the wall. The sheep trotted another twelve feet or so, before being lost from view behind another topiary.

Steve was a good showman, but he could not compete with a tightrope-walking sheep. With the undivided attention of the audience, it proceeded down the full length of the wall, appearing and disappearing behind the topiaries, until it was finally obscured by a yew hedge at the far end. Thereafter, it performed its curious walk spasmodically throughout the summer, always during demonstrations and generally only if there was a good crowd. It easily evaded Dougie's sheep dogs and became a permanent fixture in the gardens.

It was not the only sheep to cause a stir that spring. The price of ewes had increased dramatically. To combat this, Lord Massereene came up with the bright idea of shipping a transporter full of black-faced sheep down from his other estate on the Isle of Mull. Why should he buy sheep at an extortionate rate from the market, he declared to Dougie, when he could get plenty of them for free simply by rounding up the wild hill flock on his own land? In due course, a fully laden livestock transporter arrived in the park field.

We went to watch the unloading. Dougie was already waiting, his two dogs all rapt attention. Even Lord Massereene himself turned up for the occasion. Dougie and the driver unlatched the back of the lorry and lowered the ramp to the top deck, while Lord Massereene expounded enthusiastically on the virtues of black-faced sheep, renowned for their hardiness. Before the men could get the ramp gates open more than a couple of feet, the first of the sheep emerged at the gallop. It leapt off the top ramp and burst across the field like a thing possessed. It was closely followed by several more.

As the gates were fully opened, the entire lorry erupted. Sheep exploded from the transporter, sailing through the air, touching down and racing across the park like woolly tornadoes. As they reached the boundary of the field they rampaged straight through the fence without breaking stride. Strands of baler twine fluttered forlornly in their wake.

The majority of them were never seen on the estate again. As they scattered to the four winds – for all we knew heading back north of the border – Lord Massereene hunched his shoulders and muttered miserably to himself and the assembled company.

'Damn, damn sheep. Don't just stand there, Douglas, send your dogs bloody to get them back!'

For months to come, we spotted their black faces on our travels – as far afield as the outskirts of Ashford – lurking amongst flocks of native Romney Marsh sheep.

There were many incidents that summer which intensified my happiness at being free to pursue a future which was so rich with promise. I met my first deadline by writing *Birds of Prey* in six days. I then embarked with enthusiasm on the writing of *Falconry in Mews and Field*. Writing was a new discipline but one I found surprisingly easy. I set myself five hundred words a day and plugged away. Steve and Charles Jardine did the drawings.

I was teaching falconry too now, to students who attended our falconry courses. The courses we offered lasted a week and students lived as part of the family at North Lodge. I quickly found that I really enjoyed teaching, much more so than helping Steve with the displays. It helped me with the writing too: I spent so much of my time explaining falconry techniques to students, I soon became word perfect. In fact, the writing proved much less arduous than studying for my 'A' levels.

After my decision to pass up my chance to read law, I had told my mother of my change of heart with considerable trepidation. She had allowed me so much freedom with Steve; I was acutely conscious of the fact that I was repaying her by reneging on a bargain. To my relief, she was not angry, although I could see that she was disappointed. Her only stipulation was that I should sit my 'A' levels as planned. Later in the summer holidays she was mollified by the news that I had passed all my exams.

Nobly, she agreed to wrestle with my appalling hand-writing in order to type the manuscripts for the books. The first chapter I wrote for the hardback was on the kestrel. When the typed version came back to me, I did not have the heart to tell mum she had spelled kestrel 'kestral' throughout. She was not left in the dark for long. Telling Charlie that she now knew everything there was to know about kestrels, he could not resist retorting, 'Except how to spell them!'

That autumn, my mother fell in love. She met Tom Farr by chance when he came to the door of Carpenters looking for the sawmills which Alex had sold for development. Slim and distinguished-looking, Tommy was a chartered surveyor. Divorced with a grown-up family, he was the perfect match for my mother.

I was thrilled to see her so happy. I was also quietly relieved. I had felt a heavy burden of guilt when Steve and I moved out of Carpenters. My mother had never lived alone before and although I tried hard to include her in everything that was going on in my life, I knew it could never be the same as the three of us sharing Carpenters, with all the day-to-day interest of the hawks.

On a Monday morning in early September, a large chauffeur-driven Mercedes pulled up outside North Lodge. Two dark-suited gentlemen – one thin and one fat – climbed out.

I was expecting them. Recently, the *Daily Telegraph* had published a photograph of me with a buzzard and a caption outlining the work which I did at the castle. The following day, I had received a telephone call from a representative of the Bank of Credit and Commerce International. The caller, who told me that he was telephoning from the Arabian Gulf, asked if he could come and see me. He explained that he wanted to talk to me about falconry, as one of the bank's major clients was a sheikh who was himself a keen falconer. He arranged to fly in with a colleague on the following Monday.

I had no idea what to expect from this encounter. I knew that Arabs were interested only in falcons, rather than eagles or buzzards. The only falcons which Steve and I had at the time were a couple of lanner falcons, paired up for breeding in an aviary. If we were to spark any interest in our visitors, we would need to have some falcons on jesses. As it was not the breeding season, we took the decision to take the lanners out of the aviary. They had never been handled before, but we had three days to hood-train them and get them steady on the fist.

While Steve and I were manning the lanners, Lord Massereene had happened upon us. I recounted my curious conversation with the bank and, rather to my surprise, he took a keen interest. Five minutes after the Mercedes pulled up outside North Lodge the following Monday, Lord Massereene appeared on the doorstep.

To his obvious annoyance, I timidly asked him to remove his wellingtons before he came inside. He took his boots off, revealing holey socks, and strode into the drawing-room, introducing himself to our guests before I had a chance to.

'Jock Massereene. I, er, own the castle,' he said, waving an airy hand in the direction of the front drive.

Our guests greeted him politely. I poured coffee for everyone and waited with burning curiosity to find out why they had travelled so far to meet us. Rather to my irritation, Lord Massereene hardly let them get a word in edgeways, as he tucked in to chocolate biscuits and held forth about the estate. Our guests seemed as nonplussed as I was.

'What do you actually *do*?' one of them finally asked him.

'I sit in the House of Lords,' he told them importantly. 'But I suppose I would describe myself as a farmer. Are you looking for any investments in this country?'

Steve and I exchanged anxious glances. We had no idea what Lord Massereene was up to, but we did know that our two guests had come to talk about falconry, not to be treated to a rambling discourse on the investment potential of country estates in the South East of England. When everyone had finished their coffee, Steve rose to his feet and suggested that our guests might like to come and see the falcons. Outside, we parted company firmly from Lord Massereene, who looked rather disappointed.

Steve and I showed our guests all the hawks and, as I had suspected, they were only seriously interested in the lanners. They took a number of photographs of me handling the birds which, mercifully, were well behaved, despite the brevity of their introduction to falconry. Although the two gentlemen chatted enthusiastically about falconry in the Gulf States, to our frustration, they revealed nothing of the purpose behind their visit. In due course, we returned to North Lodge where we showed them photographs of Corky and Digit's chicks, explaining that we also bred falcons. They exclaimed over a picture of a tiny kestrel chick, lying like a frog on its back. The photograph seemed to impress them and, as they studied it, the plumper of the two, Mr Faisal, spoke.

'One of BCCI's main clients is His Royal Highness Sheikh Zaid,' he announced. 'As you probably know, Sheikh Zaid is the ruler of Abu Dhabi and the President of the United Arab Emirates.'

He raised an enquiring eyebrow and I felt obliged to nod knowingly, although I had barely heard of Abu Dhabi, let alone its ruler.

'His Royal Highness is a falconer without peer,' he continued. 'Like his father and his father before him, he is first and foremost a hunter. However, his Royal Highness now has a great sadness to bear: the young people in his country are no longer interested in the virtues of hunting with falcons and in the ways of the desert. The riches bestowed upon the Gulf by oil have turned the heads of its Bedouin youth. They are squandering their heritage, exchanging their passion for falcons, pure-blooded Arabian horses and thoroughbred riding camels for a passion for

198

fast cars and fast living.

'You are different,' he told us. 'We read of you, Emma, by chance in the *Daily Telegraph*, which was delivered to our offices in the Gulf.'

As he swelled with the air of one with portentous tidings, I knew he was finally coming to the point.

'BCCI would like to fly you both to Abu Dhabi to meet Sheikh Zaid,' he announced. 'We want to be able to show him that we empathize with his current predicament and that we respect the Bedouin heritage.' His dark eyes burned with intensity and he leaned forward in his seat. 'By taking you to meet him, we hope to show him that his ways – the ways of the hunter – are not to be relegated to the history books, that there are young people in the world who still share his passion.'

His speech over, he relaxed back on the sofa. His colleague Mr Ahmed then piped up with arrangements for the trip. They appeared to be in no doubt that we would want to go. They were right. The chance to see Arab falconry was not one which we would be likely to turn down. We jumped at the opportunity.

'When can you leave here to travel to the Gulf?' Mr Ahmed enquired.

'Not before November, when the grounds shut for the winter,' I replied.

'That is good,' the thin one told us. 'The falcon season will have started by then. We will make the arrangements and send you your tickets.'

'What sort of clothes should we bring?' I asked, my mind grappling with the practicalities.

'Abu Dhabi is the largest and the most sophisticated state in the United Arab Emirates,' Mr Faisal told me. 'You will be staying in a fine hotel and you will need suitable clothing. You will also need clothes for the desert, but please bear in mind that despite our Western influences, women are still expected to dress respectfully when in the presence of his Royal Highness. You will need long-sleeved dresses which come to below your knees.'

I thanked him for his advice and they prepared to leave shortly afterwards, telling us that their London office would be in touch.

'One last thing,' Mr Faisal added, as they rose to their feet. 'We will take you to see our bank. Please be sure to tell his Royal Highness when you meet him that you have seen our bank and it is very good.'

This struck a slightly jarring note, but I was too excited about the trip to worry about it. As the weeks passed though and we heard nothing further, I began to wonder if the whole thing had been a hoax. Then, at the end of October, as I had almost given up hope, two first-class British Airways tickets arrived for a flight to Abu Dhabi in mid-November. The trip was scheduled to last for a week.

A representative from the bank's London office also told me that Sheikh Zaid would present us with two saker falcons, warning that I would need to get the import permits arranged. Sometimes known as the desert falcon, the saker is a soft-feathered hawk with a tough constitution and a resilience to heat, making it the ideal partner for the Bedouin, hunting under the unyielding conditions of the desert. The thought of bringing sakers home compounded my excitement; they were comparatively rare in Britain and two imported birds would be prizes indeed. I could scarcely believe that we were really going to the Middle East to return with falcons from a sheikh: it was the stuff that dreams are made of.

We did not have much time to prepare for the trip. We had few suitable clothes and no money, but to our relief and gratitude, friends and family came to the rescue. My mother bought me two smart dresses and I borrowed some cocktail dresses from a friend. We dared not travel without some cash so, with great reluctance, we sold one of our three European buzzards to another falconer for a hundred pounds.

When the day of our flight dawned and we took off from Heathrow, I felt as though I was travelling on a magic carpet to a romantic land of mystery and adventure.

22

As we headed away from the green verges and flowering
plants of Abu Dhabi, so the surrounding scenery changed.
Sand as far as the eye could see gave way to dunes, glowing red
and gold in the last rays of the evening sun. The wind had
formed rippling wave patterns in the sand, whipping the crests
of the dunes into sharp ridges. It was starkly beautiful.

'To the south lies Rub al Khali,' our guide said. 'The "Empty
Quarter". It is one of the largest and most forbidding of all the
hot deserts in the world. In the past it isolated the coastal
sheikhdoms from their more powerful neighbours.'

'Sheikh Zaid does not speak any English.' He had kept up a
running commentary since we left the hotel. He seemed more
excited than we were.

It had been a whirlwind couple of days since we had arrived
in Abu Dhabi. We were given a palatial hotel suite in the Hilton;
a chauffeur-driven limousine had been placed at our disposal; we
had drunk champagne and dined on mouth-watering food; and
we had explored the town and swum in the turquoise waters of
the Arabian Gulf.

Our driver, Aziz, had taken us to the souk in the centre of
Abu Dhabi. It had been milling with people, men in robes and
colourful head-dresses and women shrouded in black, their faces

completely covered apart from their eyes. There was an atmosphere of bustle and commotion. At some of the stalls, fierce arguments seemed to be in progress.

'This is haggling,' Aziz told us. 'Always the price starts at more than double what they hope to get. You offer less than half and go up a little. Sometimes if you want something, you have to walk away and they run after you.'

Reedy music came from the open door of one of the flat-topped buildings behind the market stalls. Sweet smells of vanilla and cinnamon drifted out of another.

'This Lebanese sweetmeat shop,' Aziz said. 'They make cakes – very small, with nuts and honey – very good.'

We passed stalls laden with shiny, waisted brass jugs with curved handles and spouts and ornate lids, like the domes on mosques.

'These are jugs for *ghah'wah* – coffee,' Aziz explained. 'It is served in little cups like these.' He indicated some ornate cups, not much bigger than egg cups, with no handles.

'When you have had enough, you shake your cup like this,' he flicked his wrist from side to side. 'And it will not be refilled.'

There were stalls strewn with bales of silken fabric in brilliant colours. Some were shot with gold and silver threads. I fingered them longingly. We had been told that silk was very cheap in the United Arab Emirates, as was gold. The gold souks sold gold chain by length, the price dependent upon weight and carat.

There were piles of exquisite, finely stitched silken rugs, stacked neatly one on top of the other. We came to a stall selling postcards and started to look through them, picking out any that depicted falcons. Aziz was at our elbow. When the price was totalled he shouted vehemently at the stall holder. They argued for at least five minutes before Aziz would allow us to hand over any money.

'You will address your conversation to His Highness, but your comments will be translated by an interpreter,' our guide inter-

202

rupted my thoughts, as the limousine turned off the main road towards a pair of gates in the distance.

'You,' he said, turning to me, 'must be an honorary man in order to enter the palace. You will be the first white woman to enter the palace after your Queen.

'Sheikh Zaid will receive you in the Majlis. When food and drink are offered to you, please remember that it is impolite to refuse.'

As the car pulled up at the palace gates, armed guards peered inside, inspecting us closely. When they were satisfied, the driver was permitted to continue. We were followed down the drive by an open-topped jeep with a large machine gun mounted in the back. The car wound its way through beautiful gardens and came to a halt outside a structure which resembled a Greek temple, its roof supported by ornate white columns.

We stepped out into air that was perfumed with jasmine and orange blossom. Following our guide like children in a dream, we descended into a marble-floored room. We were surrounded on all sides by Arabs in white robes holding falcons.

There must have been one hundred men in the room in total. I could feel their eyes on me as I walked nervously behind Steve. The floor was covered in the centre by a bright-green carpet. Huge silk cushions were piled on the wide marble steps around the edges of the room. Four television sets playing scenes of falcons hunting were arranged so that everyone in the room could see a screen. In the centre of the room, a slight man was sitting cross-legged on pale blue and silver cushions. He had nut-brown skin, a dark moustache and beard – shaved under his lower lip so that the moustache met his beard in a fine line – a pronounced, aquiline nose and deeply hooded eyes. He was hard to age, but I judged him to be in his early sixties. He wore black robes piped with gold.

As we approached him, he stood up. Some words were exchanged in Arabic and our guide bowed his head. He turned to address us.

'I would like to present His Royal Highness Sheikh Zaid bin Sultan al-Nahayan.'

I bowed my head and extended my hand, as we had been instructed. Sheikh Zaid grasped our hands lightly in turn, his face unsmiling. He indicated the cushions beside him and we sat down. I gave him some gifts which we had brought for him: falcon hoods and a tiny but exquisite enamelled brooch of a falcon. My mother had been given the brooch originally, but she had felt it would serve a better purpose if we gave it to Sheikh Zaid.

Sheikh Zaid accepted the gifts graciously. While he was studying them, I could not take my eyes off the falcons. The falconers were not wearing gloves, as we would have done, but were holding their birds on cuffs of carpet or canvas covering their left fists. These cuffs, I later learnt, were called *magalahs*. The Arab falconers in the Gulf States used them in preference to gloves, as they were cooler to wear in the heat of the desert. Beside each falconer lay a box of tissues. If a falcon muted on the marble floor, the falconer wiped it up instantly.

The falcons themselves were mainly immature saker falcons and a few peregrines. Most of the falcons were hooded, but some were unhooded, resting peacefully on the *magalah* as the falconers stroked their chests. I had never seen so many beautiful falcons in one place before. It was hard to tear my eyes away and concentrate on our host.

A servant appeared with a *ghah'wah* pot and poured thick black coffee into little cups like the ones we had seen in the market. I sipped the steaming liquid cautiously. It was piping hot and very strong. On the floor lay a metal tub, about two feet in diameter, containing a green, gelatinous substance dotted with little brown nodules. My stomach churned as I was reminded of the ordeal of eating brawn at the Reece Webb's and Lionel's grisly tales of Middle Eastern potentates and sheep's eyes.

To my dismay, Sheikh Zaid nudged the bowl in my direction, nodding towards it with his head. I had no idea how to tackle the contents and he must have seen the concern in my eyes, for he dug into the bowl himself with his fingers. Lifting out a chunk of the glutinous jelly and eating it, he pushed the bowl towards me once more.

To my relief, there was nothing sinister lurking in the green jelly. I followed his lead, lifting out a small portion and tasting it. It was Turkish Delight. A closer inspection revealed that the little nodules covering the surface were peanuts. As Steve and I helped ourselves, nodding appreciatively at Sheikh Zaid, he whipped all the nuts off the top and ate them.

Sheikh Zaid then said something in Arabic to a man sitting on his right. The man moved round to sit in front of us.

'Sheikh Zaid would like to know how many birds you have in England?'

'We have fifty-three,' Steve answered. 'We have brought some photographs with us, if His Royal Highness would like to see them.'

I handed over a small photograph album which I had compiled. Sheikh Zaid took it and flicked through it. He paused briefly to inspect photographs of the lanners, then flicked quickly past shots of eagles and hawks until he reached the end of the album, where he came across the photograph of the baby kestrel lying on its back in Steve's palm. He spoke again to the interpreter, eyeing us quizzically from beneath his hooded brows.

'Is this a young falcon?' the interpreter asked.

'Yes,' I replied. 'It's one which we bred last year.'

This information was relayed and Sheikh Zaid nodded his head slowly. More questions followed. He asked about the husbandry of falcons and falcon diseases and ailments. Steve and I answered the questions in detail, sharing the knowledge which we had gained in caring for our own hawks. Sheikh Zaid seemed keenly interested. After we had talked for half an hour, he leaned back on his cushion and looked at us for a moment without speaking. Then he turned to the interpreter and spoke rapidly.

'Sheikh Zaid would like you to work for him here in Abu

Dhabi,' the interpreter said. 'He would like you to breed falcons for him.'

It took a moment to sink in. Steve and I looked at one another. We both knew we had just been offered the opportunity of a lifetime.

'Please tell Sheikh Zaid that we would be honoured to work for him,' Steve replied. We did not need to discuss it.

Our acceptance was relayed and Sheikh Zaid nodded his head, looking satisfied. He spoke again to the interpreter.

'BCCI will make all the arrangements,' the interpreter translated. The matter appeared to be settled.

'His Highness wishes to know if you have been shopping since you have been here?'

'We have been to the souk,' I said.

'And what did you buy?'

'Only some postcards of falcons.'

Sheikh Zaid's face betrayed the glimmer of a smile before this information had been relayed to him. I got the feeling that he understood more English than he was prepared to let on.

'Sheikh Zaid says why do you go to the souk if you don't buy anything?'

Before either of us had time to respond, the interpreter continued. 'He will send you some money tomorrow morning so that you can go shopping. In the evening, he would like you to come to see his falcons being exercised.'

Sheikh Zaid rose to his feet and we scrambled to ours. He extended his hand to us and for the first time he smiled. We thanked him and left, weaving our way through the televisions and more tubs of Turkish Delight. Outside, our guide was waiting by the car.

'You were with him a long time,' he greeted us. 'Much longer than I expected.'

'He's offered us a job,' I explained to him in awed tones.

'No, this cannot be,' our guide said, looking perplexed. 'I will go to check.'

206

With disbelief on his face, he turned on his heel and left. We waited for him in the dusk, drinking in the heady perfume of the gardens.

'I don't really believe it,' Steve was the first to break the silence.

'Well, we're not dreaming,' I said. 'But I feel as though I need to pinch myself.'

Our guide returned after a short interval. 'It is true,' he said. 'Sheikh Zaid has offered you a job. You are to go home, tell your employer that you will no longer be working for him and you must get married. You must be man and wife before you return to Abu Dhabi next March, when Sheikh Zaid will have returned from his hunting trips. He told me that he will give you a house, a house boy and a salary equivalent to forty-eight thousand pounds per annum. You are to breed falcons for him and he will provide you with a helicopter and pilot to travel between your house and the site in the mountains where the breeding station will be constructed. A contract will be forwarded to you on your return to Britain.

'He wants to see you again tomorrow evening,' he added. 'And he has asked me to inform you that every evening before the news, he will arrange for the Abu Dhabi Television Company to screen half an hour of hunting with falcons for you personally to watch.'

We travelled back to the hotel in stunned silence. When Steve and I were finally alone in our room, we sat on our bed and talked into the small hours of the morning. It was almost too much to take in. In the course of a single evening, our entire future had changed. Mainly I was excited, but I was also a little anxious. What about my mother? I would miss her terribly. What about our hawks and dogs at home? Could we bring them with us? Would they stand the heat? When it came to it, would I be happy to exchange the countryside I loved so much for the desert?

Despite our late night, we were awake early the next morning. At nine o'clock, the telephone rang.

'Good morning, Miss Braham.' It was our guide. 'I wonder if I may come to your room please? Sheikh Zaid has sent some money for you to go shopping.'

Sheikh Zaid had sent over five thousand dirham – about £750 – for our morning's shopping. Feeling rich beyond words, I telephoned Aziz to pick us up and we headed for the souk. We had no intention of spending all the money – to us it represented over four months' salary – but there was something special which we wanted to buy.

Aziz drove us to the gold souk where a row of glass-fronted shops lined the pavement. Their windows gleamed with their wares. We picked a shop at random and went inside. Everywhere, gold chain was wound on huge reels, in thicknesses varying from chain finer than cotton thread to chain with links so large it could have been used to tether a camel. Steve asked to see plain gold rings and box after box was produced from under the counter. Inside the boxes, the rings were loose, so we picked our way through them, trying them on for size. After ten minutes or so we decided on two plain gold bands. The rings were weighed and, with Aziz's help, we negotiated a price. We left the shop with our wedding rings and a pair of beautifully crafted gold earrings for my mother.

At four o'clock that afternoon we were driven to another palace on the outskirts of the city. We were led to an area to one side of the palace, which resembled a sandy football pitch on the edge of the desert, bounded on the far side by a castellated wall. All the falconers who we had seen the previous evening appeared to be there with their hawks. They had exchanged their white robes for heavier ones, mainly in shades of beige, fawn, brown and grey. More falcons were sitting hooded on Arabic perches, dotted across the sand. To our surprise, there appeared to be an equal number of bodyguards dressed in uniform and carrying automatic weapons. We joined Sheikh Zaid, who was sitting on the ground cross-legged. In place of his black and gold robes, he was wearing an undistinguished heavy cotton robe in tan. He

208

greeted us and shook our hands and we settled in the sand beside him. I felt a little more relaxed in his company this time and I plucked up the courage to ask the interpreter a few questions.

'How many falcons does Sheikh Zaid have?' I enquired.

'This season, His Highness has approximately one hundred and fifty falcons,' the interpreter answered smoothly.

Two particularly large and glossy sakers were brought forward on a double perch and placed in the sand near us. Steve nudged me.

'Do you reckon those are for us?' he whispered.

I nervously asked the interpreter the question which had been burning in me since the previous evening.

'When we come to Abu Dhabi to live, may we bring our dogs and our own falcons from home?'

'Of course you may,' we were told after a short consultation. 'But there is no need to bring your falcons unless you really want to. Sheikh Zaid will give falcons to you.'

I was relieved that we had been allowed that freedom. We could not possibly leave Sam, Ebony and the dogs behind: they were part of our lives.

An old man came forward carrying a massive silver platter bearing three raw legs of lamb. He placed this in front of Sheikh Zaid. One after another, the falconers brought their hawks to him, presenting them for him to hold on flattened *magalahs*, rather as one would pass a slice of cake on a plate. I watched in awe as Sheikh Zaid felt the breast bone of each falcon and the muscle on its wings and legs, before handing it back to the falconer.

To keep our hawks at the correct weight for flying, we weighed them each day and we weighed their meat too, yet Sheikh Zaid had the skill to make these calculations accurately by feel and by eye. With 150 falcons in training, this was no mean feat. I began to appreciate what a wealth of experience Sheikh Zaid had amassed in his years as a falconer.

Those falconers who had received their ration of meat started

to exercise their hawks. Three at a time, they went to one end of the training ground and released their falcons to callers at the far end. As one falcon approached the lure, the next was unhooded and released. It was a slick operation – rather like watching the Red Arrows in formation flight – and it was accompanied by whooping and yelling. Sheikh Zaid watched intently.

With very few exceptions, the falconers appeared to be in their late forties or older. Some could have been eighty, with their sun-hardened skin baked into heavy lines. There were a couple of young boys of around my own age. One of these managed to wrap the lure line round his neck as he called his falcon and everyone, including Sheikh Zaid, roared with laughter as the falcon landed on his head.

As the last falcon was called, a bell chimed in the distance. Sheikh Zaid climbed to his feet and, followed by a small entourage, walked across the training area to the far side, where he prostrated himself in prayer. We remained where we were. Quite suddenly, all the falconers and bodyguards formed a circle around us and sat down cross-legged. The guards propped their weapons on their knees.

I became frightened. Dusk was falling and it was eerie sitting in this silent circle. After a few minutes had passed, though, I relaxed. The circle seemed more protective than threatening. I longed to be able to communicate with the falconers to break the silence. I turned to one of them and indicated that I would like to stroke his falcon, which was bareheaded. She was a striking pale-blonde saker, with the huge, dark, liquid eyes typical of the species. The falconer turned his shoulder slightly, shielding his falcon in a gesture of possessiveness.

I persisted, pleading with him with my eyes. I wanted him to understand that I was a falconer too. Grudgingly, he held his falcon out towards me so that I could stroke her. As I put my hand up to the falcon's chest, I was aware again that every eye was fixed on me. As I touched her chest, the falcon sunk her beak into my finger and all the falconers laughed.

The one thing you must not do when a falcon bites you is to try to remove your finger. If you do this, they know they can hurt you and their biting will become worse. Sakers have beaks like sharpened nut-crackers and it hurt like hell, but I resisted the temptation to yell and snatch back my finger, leaving it in her beak for her to chew on. After about ten seconds, she gave up and allowed me to stroke her chest. The atmosphere around us changed palpably. In those ten seconds, the sheikh's men realized that I too was a falconer. Their bearded faces broke into smiles as they nodded their approval. Honorary man or not, I had been accepted.

Sheikh Zaid eventually rose in the distance and left the training ground. All the remaining men then turned in the direction he had been facing and knelt low in the sand. The falconers removed their *magalahs* and placed their falcons on the ground in front of them. The guards laid down their weapons.

211

Horizontally they bent in prayer, their foreheads almost touching their falcons. As the setting sun coloured the desert pink and
red, I was bewitched by the scene in front of me. It had a quite
unearthly quality, like an image from a dream that would melt
away as I awoke.

After the prayers were over, we were beckoned to follow. The
falconers led us to the Majlis to sit with Sheikh Zaid once more,
who had changed into his black and gold robes. A falcon was
brought over to him and unhooded. I could see from her eyes,
which were slightly pointed at the corners instead of round and
full, that she was sick and weak. Sheikh Zaid felt her breast bone
and asked the falconer some questions.

A man in a western suit then entered the Majlis. He looked
as if he might be Egyptian. He greeted Sheikh Zaid and sat down
on my left, introducing himself in perfect English as Sheikh
Zaid's physician.

A short while later, a young Arab appeared holding two
pigeons. They were no more than squabs, little plump, pink
objects with wisps of yellowish down. Sheikh Zaid stroked them
briefly and handed them back to the young man, who took
them away. Five minutes later the young man was back, carrying the squabs – which had been killed and dressed – on a silver
platter. Sheikh Zaid accepted the platter and picked up a squab,
turning it over and over in his fingers. After a few seconds, he
replaced the carcass and pushed the platter towards me.

My insides curled up in a knot. Surely he did not expect me
to eat a raw squab? I knew it would be the height of bad manners
to refuse anything we were offered, but if I ate one I would be
sick for sure.

'You have to eat it,' Steve breathed in my ear, confirming my
fears. I returned a desperate glance.

Sheikh Zaid was watching me intently. He reached forward
and, picking up a squab with the hint of a smile, he fed it to the
sick falcon. I suddenly felt embarrassed by my foolish naïvety. I
got the uncomfortable feeling that Sheikh Zaid knew perfectly

well what I had been thinking. Had he been teasing me? I kicked myself for harbouring such irrational fears.

Four Arab men dressed in robes as lavish as Sheikh Zaid's suddenly swept into the Majlis. Everyone scrambled to their feet and, as I followed suit, the physician gestured to me to remain sitting.

'You should not stand when a sheikh enters the Majlis,' he hissed. 'They do not recognize women; it is for the men only to stand.'

I felt at once rebuked, yet at the same time impolite as the new arrivals greeted Sheikh Zaid, kissing him on the cheeks. Before I came to work in this country, I clearly had a lot to learn about a western woman's place in Arab culture.

'They are Sheikh Zaid's cousins,' the physician told me when the greetings were completed and he sat down once more. 'You can always recognize members of the royal family from their robes.'

Shortly afterwards, we took our leave of Sheikh Zaid, who parted from us with great courtesy, telling us that he looked forward to our return in March. The following day we were scheduled to fly back home. On the morning of our departure, our guide from BCCI telephoned us in our room.

'Can you come down to the lobby?' he enquired. 'I have gifts for you from Sheikh Zaid.'

My heart was pounding, as we hurried from our room, to take the lift to the lobby. Would this be the two beautiful sakers we had seen the previous afternoon? I was disappointed to see our guide holding two tiny carrier bags. He must have seen my face fall.

'Sheikh Zaid told me that although he was intending to give you falcons to take home, there is no point now, as he will give you many falcons when you return.'

Reluctantly, I had to admit that this made sense. After the problems we had experienced in acquiring import licences from the British government at short notice before we left, there was no point in exporting the falcons, only to import them again three months hence.

'He has asked me to give you these.'

We were each handed presentation boxes containing matching gold watches of a type we could only have dreamed about owning in the past. Asking our guide to relay our sincere thanks to His Highness, we returned to our packing, feeling overwhelmed at the prospect of returning to live amongst these unfamiliar, opulent surroundings.

As our plane took off from the airport some hours later, I felt as if I had lived another lifetime during the past week. My head spinning with images of sleek falcons and desert scenery, I drifted off into a deep sleep until we landed at Heathrow. We had come down to earth with a bump.

23

I CRACKED MY SPONGE off the edge of the bath and ran it under the hot tap to thaw it out. It wilted in the steaming water and I washed my face, grateful for the warmth as I hopped from foot to foot in the freezing bathroom. Abu Dhabi seemed a long way away.

We had decided not to tell anyone beyond our immediate family about Sheikh Zaid's offer. It had been tough breaking the news to my mother that Steve and I were emigrating. We planned that she would come and stay with us in the Gulf and that we would come home for holidays, but it was a big step from moving half a mile away and it had come about so soon after I had first left home.

I was thrilled – and in some respects relieved – when my mother and Tommy announced their engagement in early December. They fixed a date for their wedding just before we were scheduled to leave for the Gulf in March. We had fixed a date for our wedding too. We had originally planned to get married the following September but, because of the new job, we had brought the wedding forward to early February, just before my eighteenth birthday. It seemed ironic that my mother and I should marry within a month of each other.

With the castle grounds shut to the public in the winter, our time was pretty much our own. Steve helped out on the estate when he was needed and both of us continued to work those hawks which we were hunting. In the evenings, North Lodge was so cold that we sat under duvets in front of the fire. The BBC showed *O Lucky Man* shortly after our return from the Gulf and I was at long last able to understand why I had not been allowed inside Challock church all those years ago. Steve was highly amused to see what I looked like at the age of ten. Seeing myself on the screen suddenly made me conscious of what a lot had happened to me in the intervening seven years; I had been a little girl then. Now I had written two books, I was engaged to be married and about to emigrate to the Arabian Gulf.

One of the lowlights of the winter calendar at Chilham was Lord Massereene's shoot. He accepted a number of invitations to shoot on other estates and, consequently, he was obliged to reciprocate. Unlike the estates he was invited to, he did not put any pheasant down for shooting. The invitation, therefore, was for a walked-up day of rough shooting, where the guns walked in line with beaters, taking pot shots at any game which was flushed out in front of them.

On the Saturday before Christmas, Steve and I, Dougie, the Smurfs and Trevor from the White Horse, gathered in front of the castle at Lord Massereene's behest to act as beaters. There were five guns, including Lord Massereene himself and his son, John Skeffington, who communicated in the same half sentences as his father. The guns had a glass of sherry before heading off across the estate, accompanied by the beaters and a handful of dogs, including Barra, Lord Massereene's labrador who was too long in the tooth for picking up pheasants, and Jack, Trevor's Jack Russell terrier.

While there might be a few ducks on the lake later in the day, I reflected as I stomped along beside Lord Massereene that morning, we were unlikely to see many pheasant. Nobody who knew the estate well held particularly high expectations for the

216

day's shooting. The guests, however, were in a mood of high anticipation. An invitation to shoot at Chilham was a rare opportunity and, sadly misguided, they appeared optimistic. After walking for half an hour without seeing any game whatsoever, their enthusiasm waned a little. Suddenly, a rabbit broke fifteen feet ahead and ran down the line.

'Rabbit!' Steve yelled.

Lord Massereene swung his gun right across me and pulled the trigger as the rabbit hopped on to a rotten tree stump. The tree stump exploded and the rabbit ran on, unscathed. Shaken by the gun going off inches from me, I dropped back a little, feeling twitchy.

The next rabbit that broke was coursed by Jack. Displaying more courage than sense, he caught it in front of the guns and paraded down the line with his prize, shaking it vigorously.

'Damn! Damn unsporting,' Lord Massereene shook his head with disapproval. 'Trevor . . . keep dog damn away from rabbits.'

Trevor pointed out acidly that if it had not been for Jack flushing it in the first place, the line would have walked straight past the rabbit. As the morning wore on, Jack did rather better than the guns. By this time Lord Massereene was clearly beginning to feel glimmers of embarrassment about the paucity of the sport.

By lunchtime, the bag was eight rabbits – five of which had been accounted for by Jack – and, surprisingly, one pheasant. The only member of the party still in good spirits was the Jack Russell who had enjoyed an excellent morning. Nobody seemed particularly excited when Lord Massereene announced that, after lunch, they would shoot duck.

As we set off towards the lake that afternoon, Lord Massereene turned to Trevor.

'Put damn dog on leash,' he instructed peevishly.

One of the guests was dispatched in his car to drive down Mountain Street and come in on the far side of the lake, to take full advantage of any duck which flushed in that direction. The lake was completely iced over, but the four remaining guns were cheered to see a dozen or so mallard sitting on the ice, about twenty feet out from the edge. Lord Massereene told the beaters to stay back and the guns approached surreptitiously, taking advantage of any natural cover. Rather to their surprise, they managed to reach the edge of the lake without the duck lifting. As they waited, fingers poised on triggers, Lord Massereene gave a cautious shout.

'Oush! Oush!'

Nothing happened.

'Damn duck. *Oush*!'

Attracted by Lord Massereene's shouts, the duck began to make their way on foot across the ice. All summer long they were fed by tourists. They lined up, quacking expectantly, at the guns' feet.

'Would you like us to throw stones at them?' Trevor suggested brightly, with Jack straining at the end of his leash. Lord Massereene shot him a withering look. As the assembled company walked back to the castle empty-handed, he muttered confidingly to his guests: 'Dog bloody spoilt day! Won't invite it next year.'

It was not long after this non-event that the pair of wild boar escaped. Their pen had not been upgraded since Allan had first built it and the mesh buried around the perimeter of the run had begun to perish. The boars had merely to lean against it and it gave way. All hands were called to try and round them up. The sow was eventually recaptured, but as most of us were scared of the boar, our efforts to find him were cautious. He disappeared into the depths of the estate.

It went very quiet for a few weeks. After my earlier experiences with the same animal, I fervently wished that he had left the estate and disappeared across Kent. One afternoon, however, Steve and I were hunting with Ebony below the heronry when the boar emerged from the undergrowth like an express train. We were scared out of our wits, but we knew we could not outrun him, so we stood our ground. He stopped short and eyed us beadily, before trotting back into the bracken. I felt weak with relief.

The following day, Lord Massereene received a call from a local pig breeder who kept pedigree sows. He was incensed. The boar had broken in to his pedigree sows and mated with them. It had then run amok through his yard, creating havoc. He demanded compensation.

Lord Massereene asked how the farmer could be sure that it was his boar which had caused the damage. He pointed out that the local zoo park kept a small overflow facility in some old army huts on the boundary of the estate. Could the culprit not equally well be a boar which had escaped from this facility, he enquired?

In truth, both the zoo itself and the overflow facility did have more than their fair share of escapees. Although everyone on the estate knew it was Lord Massereene's boar which had done the dastardly deed, there was enough plausibility in his argument for the pig farmer not to be able to disprove it. As the escapee could not be pinned down to either establishment, the farmer's claims were never met, despite the fact that in due course his prize sows gave birth to hairy, rampaging little half-breeds.

After these two sightings, it was impossible to walk on the estate without fearing that you were going to be molested by the boar. Everyone was nervous: the Smurfs again worked back to back, armed at all times with rakes. The following week, the front page of the *Kentish Gazette* reported the story of a boy who had been out riding his new motorbike. A wild boar had run across his path on the road to Challock. He had hit the boar, killing it outright, and in the process written off his new bike. The boy was shaken and bruised but otherwise unhurt. Not since the death of the pharaoh hound had there been such joy at the news of a road traffic accident.

January was a dismal month. Chilham was shrouded in a murky fog which did not clear for days. It made me look forward to Abu Dhabi all the more. I imagined the bliss of working in sunshine all year round: recurring images of white sandy beaches, turquoise sea and pink and gold dunes lingered seductively in my mind. BCCI's London office had been in touch and reassured me that they were in contact with the Gulf. We were eagerly awaiting the arrival of the contract.

It was during this period of murky weather that we were woken early one morning by the milkman hammering on Dougie's door opposite. Steve stuck his head out of the window in time to hear the milkman explaining to Dougie that one of the estate's cows was out on the main road.

'Do you want a hand?' Steve called across sleepily.

'Naw,' said Dougie. 'It'll be that old bitch I got from the market last week. She's already got through two fences.' He collected a shepherd's crook and headed for his pick-up truck.

We were drinking coffee downstairs twenty minutes later when Dougie appeared on the doorstep, looking shaken.

'You look like you could do with a coffee,' I said.

Dougie sat down heavily on the sofa. I gave him a cup of coffee and he cradled it, without drinking.

'What's up?' Steve prompted.

Dougie's eyes had a hunted look as he launched into his tale.

'When I got down to the main road, the mist was so thick, I could hardly see to drive,' he said. 'So I parked up on the edge of the road and walked. I hadn't got more than fifteen feet before I saw the backside of the cow, so I hit it smartly with my crook and said, "Get on there you awd bitch!"'

Dougie's normally pallid complexion was grey and his eyes were bulging as he recalled the scene.

'This bleedin' great head turned and I realized it wasn't my cow at all, it was the zoo's bull water-buffalo.'

I gasped. I had seen this massive beast inside its pen. It had a set of horns on it which must have been over four feet wide.

'It turned to face me and pawed the ground with its horns weavin' from side to side. I had a friggin' fit. I turned and legged it. I've never run so fast in my life. I could 'ear it behind me as I reached the pick-up. I thought I'd never see Moll and Trace and little Trev again,' he said. 'Moll'll have a bleedin' fit when I tell 'er.'

When North Lodge got too cold to bear in the evenings, we went over to the White Horse to warm up. It was during one of these evenings that we missed a television programme which caused a sensation in the press the next day. *The Death of a Princess* told the true story of a Saudi princess who was publicly executed in her own country. The showing of the programme was highly controversial and the press warned that governments in the Middle East were very aggrieved it had been shown on British television.

The upshot of the incident was that many British contracts with the Middle East were lost over the coming months. From that day we heard nothing further from BCCI. Eventually, with time ticking away, I telephoned the London office. The executive we had been dealing with came on the line, sounding wary.

'I'm afraid it isn't going to happen,' he told me. 'It was one of those ideas which never gained momentum. I'm very sorry.'

This was a body blow from which it was hard to recover. The golden future we had been promised had slipped through our fingers like a handful of sand trickling back into the desert. Thoughts of what might have been plagued my every waking moment and my dreams too. Steve and I had been given a glimpse of an exciting new world. Now it had been replaced by the stark reality of North Lodge, a paltry wage packet and the long, hard summer season ahead of us at the castle. My only consolation was that we had not announced we were leaving.

In addition to my overwhelming disappointment at losing the job, I also began to feel that we had been manipulated. BCCI had flown us out to meet Sheikh Zaid for purely commercial reasons. I had taken their motive at face value before but, in retrospect, I felt they had not been entirely happy when we were

221

offered the job. I strongly suspected that it was not Sheikh Zaid who had dropped the idea, but that BCCI were using the documentary as a convenient excuse to let things slide. Maybe they had told Sheikh Zaid that we had changed our minds?

When we had been offered the job in Abu Dhabi, I had felt vindicated in my decision not to read law. Now I felt that I had to prove more than ever before that our work with the birds could offer us a glowing future. For better or worse, the Gulf excursion had opened my eyes. A lifestyle which had seemed ideal to me before we left for the trip had palled considerably since our return.

I began to question our future. I knew we could not spend the rest of our days at Chilham giving demonstrations for the general public. I voiced these thoughts to Steve and within a week we had resolved to look for a new future. We would continue working full time with the birds, but find a place where our dreams could come to fruition. I had no idea where or what this future would be, but our resolve helped me to cope with the crushing disappointment.

One plan which was not altered by the bad news was our wedding. Steve and I were married in a local parish church on a warm, springlike day in February. My mother and father were both there, together with Steve's parents, Lord and Lady Massereene and all our friends. We left the following day for a honeymoon in Tunisia, a wedding present from Tommy.

On our return, Steve prised a pay rise out of Lord Massereene and we took the decision to sell our gold watches. We had enjoyed wearing them, but it now seemed ridiculous to be adorned with a pair of hugely expensive watches. In addition, every time we looked at them, they were a painful reminder of what might have been. With the money from their sale we bought our first peregrine falcon, whom we named Shadow. Had he known, I felt sure Sheikh Zaid would have approved.

24

IT WAS HARD to get past those teddy-bear eyes. Mesmerizing orbs of bright orange stared up at us, set in a feathered head the size of a soup plate topped with two feathery ear tufts. There was something wrong though. She was lying down in a far corner of the cage when I first saw her but, as I approached, she stood up awkwardly, shifting her weight until she was propped against the mesh.

'She's beautiful,' my mother whispered to me.

I shot her an anxious glance. Why was the owl not up on a perch? Something was definitely amiss.

The zoo owner held the cage door open for me to go inside. I walked right up to the owl and, although she hissed and clicked her beak at me, she made no attempt to fly away. I scooped her feathery bulk gently up into my arms and looked her over. The condition of her streaked, tawny-brown feathers was fair, her wings flexed normally and those huge eyes looked clear and healthy. It was when I examined her feet that I got to the nub of the problem. The undersides were rotten and putrid.

If the talons of a bird of prey become overgrown, they can puncture the bottom of the foot, causing septic swellings. Falconers term this 'bumblefoot'. This bird's talons were far too long and were clearly responsible for the terrible condition of her feet. They should have been clipped long before she reached this state. I had never seen bumblefoot this severe before.

If bumblefoot is noticed early, it is fairly simple to treat. The feet of this owl, however, had been left untreated and were now grossly deformed. They were massively swollen, with scabs bigger than ten pence pieces oozing pus. The skin between the toes had been pushed outwards by the infection, which formed cheesy clods held in place by ridges of skin, giving the feet a webbed appearance. The burning pain of standing on these feet must have been indescribable. I turned to the zoo owner, feeling upset and angry.

'I haven't had her more than three days,' he told me apologetically. 'She belongs to a local man who couldn't keep her any longer, so I offered to keep her here until I found a buyer.'

'She needs urgent treatment,' I said. 'She's in an awful state. I can't possibly pay a hundred pounds for her.'

This had been the price we had agreed over the telephone. For a perfect Eagle Owl it was a fair deal, but not for this wretched creature.

'He won't let her go for much less,' the zoo owner told me. 'If *you* don't buy her, he'll try to find someone else who will.'

I looked down at the owl. She was lying passively in my arms, but seeing my gaze on her she snapped her beak again in defiance. Despite the pain she must be suffering, she still had spirit. I could not turn her back into the cage and walk away. My mother said nothing, but she had her heart in her eyes.

'Could you telephone her owner and tell him how bad her feet are?' I asked. 'See what he has to say.'

The zoo owner left to make the call. When he returned five minutes later, I could see from his face that he was not happy.

'The lowest offer he's prepared to accept is sixty pounds,' he said.

My mother and I looked at each other. I knew I should not

buy her. Never mind the purchase price, the vet's bills were going to be extortionate.

'OK,' I said. 'I'll take her.'

I placed the owl gently into a large cardboard box with carpet on the base. She sunk on to her chest as she was lowered inside. I wondered what Steve would say when we arrived home with the invalid, and how long it would be before she was well enough to breed from.

Our collection of over fifty hawks now included a number of eagles. In addition to Sam, we had Idi, a Bateleur Eagle. The word *bateleur* is taken from medieval French, meaning acrobat or tumbler. Bateleurs have long wings but very short tails. Aerodynamically Idi was – in common with the rest of his species – highly specialized, resembling a design for the original flying wing. In repose he was a comical looking bird, with a black chest and fan-shaped black crest, offset by a yellow face which could flush vivid scarlet when he was annoyed. His short, stubby toes were the colour and texture of raspberries. Most of these unusual anatomical features reflected the fact that, in their natural state, Bateleurs hunt snakes. Idi could give a remarkable threat display, puffing himself up to twice his normal size and spreading his wings to reveal brilliant white patches. When lit by the sun of his native Africa, these could dazzle a victim. Idi had a sunny disposition. Between strutting his stuff on the ground with his ungainly, rolling gait and his stylish aerial displays, he was a huge favourite with the crowds.

Steve and I had also purchased a pair of Pallas's Sea Eagles. There were only two of these birds in the country and they came to us from different sources. We got the male first, from a zoo in Norfolk. We then contacted a zoo near Manchester and per-suaded them – with some difficulty – to part with their female. Jezebel, as we named her, dwarfed Schooner the male, being a full three pounds heavier than him. Such size differences are not unusual between male and female eagles, the females always being the larger birds. It was a big disappointment that spring

225

when Schooner laid an egg. Plans to breed from them were abandoned and we started to train the two eagles for use in flying demonstrations.

Since the breeding centre had been established, I had been very keen to acquire a pair of European Eagle Owls. I had first fallen in love with these owls, which can weigh as much as eight pounds, when I met Mozart, Phillip Glasier's Eagle Owl at the Falconry Centre. So when a zoo in Essex telephoned me to say that they had a female European Eagle Owl which was surplus to requirements, I leapt at the chance to buy her. Now, instead of taking the owl home we drove straight on to our vet in Dover.

I first met the Smith brothers when David handed over to us a kestrel and a Tawny Owl some years earlier. He and his brother Patrick were both vets. Together they ran a thriving practice in Dover. David had said that any injured wild birds which were handed in to the Bird of Prey Centre, they would treat free of charge. Over the years, this generous gesture had proved a godsend. Naturally, Steve and I also used the practice for veterinary work on our own birds and, in the process, both brothers had accumulated a rare degree of expertize in raptor medicine. I did not expect this owl to qualify for free veterinary treatment, but I knew Patrick and David would do their best to restore her to health, if it was at all possible.

We just caught the end of evening surgery. David ushered us in to the consultation room and I lifted Mrs Potter – as I had decided to call her – out of the box.

'My God!' David exclaimed. 'I've never seen worse bumble-foot. What sort of cretin let her get into this state?'

David was never one to mince words. Tall, slim and sandy-haired, he had an impatient energy at all times except when he was in the operating theatre, when his long, skilful fingers moved with painstaking care.

'Can you treat it?' I asked anxiously.

'I can have a go, but who knows what's happened to the tendons under all that muck? You'd better bring her downstairs.'

In the operating theatre, David injected Mrs Potter with anaesthetic. Within a minute, her head was lolling on to the table.

'Right, she's under! Let's get on with it.'

He sprung into action, snatching up a tray of instruments. He was a brilliant surgeon and it was thrilling to watch him at work. Whenever I went down to the surgery, he invited me in to the theatre to watch him operate on a few cases. In the past, I had seen him remove from the intestines of dogs items ranging from a pair of surgical stockings to a child's metal tractor – which showed up beautifully on the X-ray. I had also seen him descale the teeth of a Yorkshire terrier, squeeze ninety-six huge black-heads – 'a record' – from the body of an anaesthetized Alsatian and patiently rebuild from tiny fragments of splintered bone the rear legs of a cat which had been run over. I had great faith in him.

David tied tourniquets around Mrs Potter's ankles to restrict the flow of blood and started to open up the feet. As the scabs were removed, pus trickled down Mrs Potter's toes and on to the operating table. David mopped out the feet with swabs soaked in alcohol and carefully scooped out as much of the cheesy substance as possible. He jabbed the clods of infection between her toes and they popped out like Stilton marbles. Cutting away the useless ribs of skin which remained, he started to scrape away carefully at the centre of each foot.

'The trick with grade three bumblefoot like this,' he said, without raising his head as he worked away. 'Is to try to remove every fragment of the lining of the bumble itself. It's similar in structure to a grape,' he elaborated. 'You need to scoop out the soft centre, but you also need to remove the skin which cases it, or the foot will re-infect. What concerns me here is to get it all out without accidentally severing a tendon. There's a tendon, look. At least it's not been rotted through by the infection.'

I peered into the wound on the bottom of one of Mrs Potter's feet. Despite the tourniquets, the blood was oozing thickly, making it difficult to differentiate between infected and healthy tissue. My mother retreated to sit down on a cat cage against the wall of the theatre. As David swabbed away the blood, I could see one of the tendons, gleaming like a piece of white thread.

'I reckon she's lost the tendon to this outside toe,' he said, nudging a toe which flopped uselessly. 'But if that's all the permanent damage she's suffered, she's got off lightly.'

He finished cleaning up the hollows inside the feet, packed them with antibiotic cream and stretched the remaining skin back as best he could, stitching it into place. Then he cropped the talons short to prevent them from interfering with the healing. Just as he finished bandaging the feet, one of Mrs Potter's eyes blinked and she started to come round.

'You've got a lot of work ahead of you,' David informed me. 'It's essential to keep the feet clean. You must change the dressing twice a day. Where are you going to keep her?'

I had not even thought this far ahead. It was a problem. Because of her sore feet, she could not be put on jesses and there was nowhere at home where I could guarantee to keep the bandaged feet scrupulously clean.

'I can lend you a quarantine kennel,' David volunteered. 'It's about four feet long by three feet high, but it breaks down into sections, so you'll be able to get in into the car. You'll need to tape dressing sheets over the base and up the walls and change them each time you change her bandages. I'll give you some rolls of the stuff.'

Loaded to the gunnels, we headed back to Chilham with a woozy Mrs Potter back in her box. After a long and guilty explanation to Steve he reassured me: 'I'd have done the same thing if I were you,' he said.

We constructed the quarantine box in the kitchen next to the warmth of the boiler. I crawled inside to line it, as David had instructed, armed with the dressing sheets and a roll of Sellotape. The job completed, I lifted Mrs Potter out of her cardboard box into the kennel and propped her on her chest against some soft towels. Although I knew her feet would hurt dreadfully when she came round fully from the anaesthetic, I desperately hoped that somehow she would know she was being helped.

The following morning Mrs Potter was still lying down. She looked quite bright though, considering her ordeal. I reached in and lifted her out of her box. Wrapping her in a bath towel, I sat down on a kitchen stool and unravelled her bandages. As I progressed down through the layers, I was alarmed to see that they were soaked in blood. I squeezed antibiotic cream down the lines of the stitches, sprinkled the feet with wound powder and applied a layer of lint followed by a layer of gauze, as David had shown me. I then re-bandaged her feet. It did not look nearly as good as David's bandaging, but I hoped it would suffice.

Steve held Mrs Potter while I clambered inside the box to replace the dressing sheets. The entire operation, which we would have to repeat each morning and evening, took forty-five minutes from start to finish. I began to appreciate what David had meant when he warned me that there was a lot of work ahead.

During the week that followed, Mrs Potter spent nearly all her time lying down, except when she was feeding, when she climbed gingerly on to her feet. I concealed her oral antibiotics inside her food. Despite the fact that she was eating, I was concerned. Her feet were swollen and very hot – a sign that the infection had not abated. I had arranged with David to take her back to the surgery after two weeks but, changing her dressings eight days after the operation, I was upset to see fresh pus oozing through the stitches. We rushed straight back to the surgery, where David took off the bandages.

'Damn! There's still a lot of rubbish in there,' he said. 'You'd better bring her down to theatre.'

He anaesthetized Mrs Potter once again and cut open the stitches. 'I'm going to try something different this time,' he told us. 'We've just got a new toy for the theatre, a diathermy unit. Basically, it generates an electrical current which burns out infection. One of its advantages is that it simultaneously cauterizes any bleeding, so you can see what you're doing.'

David's eyes gleamed as he set up the diathermy unit. The well-equipped practice was a testament to his admiration for new technology and he never let an opportunity pass to put a new development into use. I held Mrs Potter's ankles as he tentatively started to burn the infected tissue with the metal conducting prod.

My nostrils filled with the acrid smell of burning flesh. The interior of the wound smoked as the prod touched it but, despite the unpleasant physical effects, it was an impressive instrument to watch. As a seam of blood appeared, it was instantly sealed by the prod, rather like doing up a zip. Being careful to avoid the tendons, David worked away delicately for about fifteen minutes before finally straightening up.

'That ought to do it,' he said cheerfully. 'She'll have a lot of scar tissue, but we can't help that. Take her home and keep up with the regime of changing the dressings. Bring her back in three weeks – or earlier if you're worried.'

'That stench was awful,' I said in the car on the way home. 'It smelled like burning fingernails.'

'Let's hope it does the trick,' Steve said. Then, after a pause, 'Do you think we're right to put her through this?'

'I hate causing her more pain, she's been through so much already. But David seems optimistic, so we've got to give her every chance.'

I had grown exceptionally fond of Mrs Potter. It was impossible to handle the big owl on a daily basis without being smitten by her feline beauty and her gentle tolerance at being man-handled morning and night. Like many sick birds I had cared for in the past, she seemed to know I was trying to help her. Now she would lie in my lap as I bandaged her feet without even bothering to struggle. Of course, the unmistakable sign that a sick bird is getting better is when it starts to misbehave and becomes awkward to handle – as if to let you know that it does not need you any longer. I longed to see this change occur in Mrs Potter.

In the days immediately after the second operation, Mrs Potter started to stand up for short intervals. I was thrilled when I saw her pull down the dressing sheets on one side of her box. I had to admit that the endless re-bandaging and scrubbing out of the kennel was beginning to get me down and the pungent stench of owl droppings had pervaded the house, but if Mrs Potter was improving, that was more than sufficient reward. The following week, however, she stopped standing up. She even began to eat lying down. Suspicious that the infection had returned, I gently pushed the bottom of one foot and a fine trickle of pus emerged through the stitches.

David next attempted to cure the problem with cryosurgery. The opposite to diathermy, this treatment involved quick freezing the bottoms of the feet. If this did not work, he told me, he was running out of ideas.

It did not work. Despite all David's endeavours and my unstintingly attentive nursing, the bacteria causing the infection refused to be shifted. I despaired when I unravelled the bandages one morning and found them running with pus yet again. Looking at Mrs Potter, lying on her chest in the box, I noticed that her brilliant orange eyes were dull with pain. I turned to Steve, who was cutting jesses from a hide of leather on the kitchen sideboard.

'I don't think we can put her through any more,' I said.

'You should telephone David,' he said. 'He's worked so hard on her. Consult him before making a decision.'

The upshot of my conversation with David was that Mrs Potter should be taken to the surgery the next morning to be put down.

'We've given it our best shot,' he told me. 'She's a fighter, but this staphylococcus bug can be a devil to shift. If I go any deeper to try and clear it, she's not going to have any feet left; I've been dangerously close to nicking the tendons as it is.'

I could not look at Mrs Potter as I moved around the kitchen that morning. I felt as if I had committed the ultimate betrayal. She even tried to stand up briefly at one point, when I put food in front of her, but slumped back down after tottering uncomfortably. Tears welled in my eyes. I knew I had made the only ecision possible in the circumstances, but that did not make it any easier.

I tried to keep my mind off Mrs Potter as much as possible as I helped Steve with the demonstrations that afternoon, but the image of her lying in her box haunted me. I returned to North Lodge at the end of the afternoon with a heavy heart. There was a package lying on the mat outside. I picked it up, absently tearing open the envelope as I went inside. It was a book I had ordered some months earlier.

Steve and I had built up a reasonable library in the last few years, avidly collecting any new titles on falconry and birds of prey. It was so long since I had sent off for this book, I had forgotten I had ordered it. Its title, *Care and Rehabilitation of Injured Owls*, immediately caught my attention. It seemed a strange quirk of fate that it should arrive on this particular day. Immediately I turned to the entry for bumblefoot. There was a photograph of the feet of a large owl with bumblefoot every bit as severe as Mrs Potter's. In the picture, one foot had yet to be treated and the other, curiously, was totally encased in plaster of Paris. With my heart pounding, I started to read.

The book's description of surgery on bumblefoot mirrored David's technique, but it was the sentence at the end of the second paragraph that caught my attention: 'The whole area is then encased in plaster with the terminal joints and talons protruding.' I telephoned David.

'There is a logical reason why the plaster may help,' he mused, after I had read the relevant section to him. '*Staphylococcus aureus* is aerobic – it needs air to live. If the plaster effectively cuts off the air supply, it could kill the bacteria.'

'Do you think it's worth a go?' I asked him anxiously.

232

'We've got nothing to lose,' he said. 'Bring the book when you come down tomorrow.'

At the eleventh hour, Mrs Potter had been reprieved. The next day David studied the book, then anaesthetized her yet again and, with his usual patient dedication, did his best to clean out the infection from the feet. After the operation he applied a light bandage, as directed by our new bible, while I cut strips of plaster and soaked them in a dish of water.

'I'm going to make a bridge under her feet with the hollow casing of a large syringe tube,' David announced. 'When the plaster hardens, this will leave a small gap between her foot and the plaster casing. If it works, she'll be able to stand without putting any pressure on the bottoms of her feet.'

Just before the plaster set, David wriggled each of Mrs Potter's digits so that when it hardened, the plaster did not cut off the circulation to her toes. When the job was finished, her feet were

completely encased in balls of plaster, with just the last joints of the toes and the talons protruding. The book advised leaving the casts in place for four to six weeks.

Back at North Lodge, the change in Mrs Potter when she came round from the anaesthetic was dramatic. For the first time she could stand without pain. With her feet encased in plaster bovver boots, she was a little unsteady, but she rapidly got the hang of it. Standing up, she immediately looked much happier. A sick bird of prey which is lying down looks – and probably feels – particularly vulnerable. Standing up seemed to restore much of Mrs Potter's dignity. She even snapped her beak at me when I put some food in the kennel.

The best part of all was that David said she could go outside into an aviary. With her wounds covered in an impermeable layer, no infection could get inside. The next day, I carried her round to the breeding centre and turned her loose into the largest of the aviaries. Steve had covered the aviary floor with a thick layer of wood shavings. Our book, which was written in Canada, advised a carpet of pine needles, but this was the closest we could get. As I turned Mrs Potter loose, she flew once round the aviary, landing easily on the ground, apparently without any discomfort. It must have been wonderful for her to get out of the stuffy kennel into fresh air where she could stretch her wings for the first time in weeks.

It was wonderful for me too, I admitted to myself later while dismantling the quarantine kennel, to be free from the twice-daily chore of cleaning up after her and changing her dressings. It was now nearly six weeks since I had first brought Mrs Potter home from the zoo. I was ready for a break and the atmosphere in North Lodge needed to be de-owled.

During the weeks which followed, Mrs Potter went from strength to strength. Although I had no way of assessing her feet under the plaster, I could see that she was vastly improved in herself. Her feathers, which had turned dull in the kennel, regained their healthy sheen, her appetite was excellent and she even managed to perch. Rocking precariously on her plaster boots, with a glint of satisfaction in her eyes, she learned to balance on the highest perches in the aviary.

Eagle Owls nest on the ground, so when we had prepared the aviary originally for Mrs Potter's arrival, Steve had constructed a small hut in one corner with a sloping roof. We could frequently hear Mrs Potter clumping about noisily on the wooden roof in her boots. Observing her exploring every inch of the aviary, I was optimistic that I was watching an owl on the road to recovery.

When the casts were removed six weeks later, there was a marked improvement beneath them. David was delighted by the progress. 'The feet appear to have stewed in their own juices,' he said. 'The infection is greatly reduced. It's clearly working, so we'll do more of the same.'

It took thirty-six more weeks for the feet to heal completely. Six plaster casts later, healthy skin had grown back over the bottom of the feet and all traces of infection had been eradicated. The skin was still a little pink, so David applied light bandages, but a few days later Mrs Potter tore them off.

'Leave them off,' David told me over the telephone. 'The feet have to harden up at some stage.'

I went into the breeding centre and sat quietly in the grass at a distance to watch her. Now that she had no casts to get wet, I had been able to put a bath in for her, for the first time since she had been loose in the aviary. As I watched, she flew down from her perch in the sun at the top corner of the aviary. Landing beside the bath, she stepped in. She did not bathe properly, she just stood in the shallow water with her feathers fluffed out and her eyes half closed. It was like watching a fat lady paddling on Brighton beach with her skirts hitched up.

For my eighteenth birthday, Steve bought me a male European Eagle Owl. Potter was introduced to Mrs Potter in late February. Right from the outset, the two owls got on well. Potter was very vocal. His sonorous calls reverberated around the breeding centre – '*Oohoo, Oohoo*' – with the emphasis on the first syllable.

'*Oohoo*,' I mimicked him. To my amusement, he half closed his eyes, fluffed out his white throat and answered me back. Then he sidled up to Mrs Potter, leapt on her back and started to mate with her. Thereafter, any time I was in the breeding centre, I would call to him and stimulate him to mate with her. By the middle of March, Mrs Potter had a clutch of eggs. The weather, which had been uncharacteristically warm, had turned bitterly cold again. To our concern, she had unwisely chosen to lay her eggs not in the hut, but out in the open. Despite her cosy, feather-lined scrape in the ground and her devoted incubation, I feared for the eggs.

A week later, I awoke to a fine layer of snow. Dressing quickly, I slipped outside and ran round to the breeding centre. Mrs Potter was still incubating, but she was completely obscured by Potter, who was draped over the top of her like a duvet, his soft wings outstretched. The 'stack-an-owl' technique clearly worked. A few weeks after that the eggs hatched. The Potters were a family.

25

THE THREE OF them came across the top lawn like the Ovaltinies: Steve followed by the two teenagers in descending order of height. It was not the fact that the boys came to see us virtually every weekend that bothered me, nor the fact that they both dressed like Steve, in dark-brown corduroy trousers, checked country shirts and green army jackets. What really worried me was that, like Steve, they had started to roll their own cigarettes from Old Holborn tobacco.

The two of them were aged thirteen and fifteen and they had attended one of our falconry courses together. These had grown increasingly popular. At intervals during the summer, North Lodge resembled a small hotel, with new students checking in to the two spare bedrooms just hours after the previous occupants had checked out. Being chief cook and general dogsbody on top of my other chores was hard work, but I was delighted by the success of this side of the Bird of Prey Centre.

The students came from all walks of life. Most of them read about the courses in newspaper articles. As well as teenage boys, we taught people from a wide range of professions including a plastic surgeon, a debt collector, a male model, a university professor, several car workers from Dagenham, a trainee vet, a young producer from film school, and two housewives from Derbyshire, one of whom insisted on sleeping in the car with her Yorkshire terrier each night, until it had given birth to a litter of puppies mid-way through the week.

During the courses the mornings were spent in the drawing-room at North Lodge, tackling a variety of theoretical and practical studies such as imping and coping – mending broken feathers and filing back overgrown beaks and talons – or making hoods and jesses. Later, the students would help to carry the hawks up to the static display ground, a task which they enjoyed hugely and which we were grateful to share. In the afternoon, they were taught how to train and fly the hawks.

I was not at all surprised to see the two boys back at the castle most weekends. Over and above their hero worship of Steve, they were drawn by the same magnetic attraction which had first enticed me to climb over the Oswalds' wall eleven years ago. Luke, the elder of the two boys, was a tall, thoughtful lad who was rapidly becoming a great help. John, the younger boy, was something of a problem child. When his mother had booked him on the course, she had explained to me that John was encased in a plaster cast from the base of his neck to the tops of his legs. He had fallen out of a tree and broken his back while stealing apples. She and his father ran a pub on the south coast, the sort of pub, she told me, where even the ash trays had to be screwed down. John, she explained, had fallen in with a rough crowd in the local town and was heading for the juvenile courts unless something radical caused him to change tack. She and his father desperately hoped that this might be falconry. Aside from his various reprehensible activities, birds of prey were the only thing that John had ever shown any interest in.

Having witnessed before the effect that the hawks had on youngsters, I was fairly confident that John would not prove to be a problem. When he arrived at North Lodge, I liked him immediately. Short and dumpy, he was a cheerful, extrovert lad and, as an added bonus, he and Luke got on really well together.

238

It turned into a thoroughly good course. I enjoyed watching the blossoming of a passion for hawks in the two of them. For both of them this had first been germinated through reading books. Once they were in physical contact with the real thing, they were enraptured. Luke was clean cut, well mannered and disciplined in the theoretical side of the course, taking copious notes and studying diligently for the tests I set them at the end of each week. It was gratifying to watch Luke's approach gradually rub off on John: they were the first students I had ever had staying in North Lodge who helped with the washing up.

During the two weeks of their first stay, I was completing the training of Jezebel, the Pallas's Sea Eagle. Unwittingly, I had named her well: she was a nightmare to handle. Powerfully built, she was dark in colour, with cream head feathers which she would lift to form a crest when she was angry. In size alone, she was a handful. Her wingspan was nearly eight feet and she tipped the scales at over nine pounds. By adding a bad attitude to her bulk, she had the potential to be seriously troublesome.

I exercised her each day after the grounds were shut in the evening. Because of her temperament, I had abandoned all thoughts of using her for demonstrations in favour of trying to get her to hunt rabbits. Despite the fact that she was a sea eagle, this was not as incongruous as it sounded. As I explained to Luke and John, many sea or fish eagles also catch a variety of fish-eating birds and even mammals. Pallas's could take prey up to the size of pelicans. I could clearly see that Jezebel had the inclination to kill things; I needed to ensure that I was not on the menu.

When I called her to the fist for food, she came in like a Stuka bomber. When an eagle catches a rabbit, it accelerates towards it, then applies the brakes as it makes contact. When a sea eagle takes a fish from water, it makes contact and then accelerates by putting in a rowing wing beat to lift itself off the surface of the water. Jezebel used to hit my glove and – with my arm firmly in her clutches – put in an extra wing beat with the strength to throw me off balance. In one swift movement she would then grab my hair in her beak and attempt to tow my head close enough to enable her to foot me in the face. Steve urged me to stop flying her, but I was convinced that if I could only switch her aggression on to rabbits, she would make a most successful hunter. I had put a great deal of work into training her thus far and she had become a challenge.

Having heard a lot about Jezebel, Luke and John wanted to see her fly. I was wary, but they badgered me constantly for a few days and I finally capitulated. They were clearly enjoying the course so much that it seemed churlish to deny them any experience from which they could learn more. I had grown to love teaching: I relished sharing my own passion for falconry with people who were keen to learn.

Jezebel was on particularly evil form that evening. She snapped at me constantly as I carried her from the display ground to the ornate stone ball at the top of the terrace steps which we used to call off eagles in training. She was flying free now and at the stage where I was introducing her to the lure. It had turned into a beautiful summer's evening. The sun cast long shadows over the lawns. I checked to see that Luke and John had followed my instruction to tuck themselves well in at the base of the cedar tree on the back edge of the top lawn and was comforted that I could hardly see them in the shadows. With difficulty, I reversed Jezebel off my glove on to the ball and ran down the slope to the bottom lawn.

She was after me before I could get there. With blood in her eye, she stooped me from a height of fifteen feet, hitting my up-raised arm like a kamikaze. I grabbed her jesses and kept my head turned away while she snapped at my hair, until she eventually became more interested in the meat I was holding for her.

Her talons gripped my arm like steel as I climbed back up the bank with her. I was grateful for the leather police-dog handler's sleeve I was wearing. Extending from under my heavy eagle glove to the top of my left shoulder, it gave a welcome degree of added protection. To enable me to get a greater distance from Jezebel this time before she pursued me, I left some food with her on the stone ball. As I reached the far end of the bottom lawn, I glanced up the slope and was alarmed to see John edging forward to get a better view.

'Sit still!' I yelled.

It was too late. Jez had spotted them. Without hesitation she took off in the boys' direction. Luke and John saw her coming and – for a dreadful few seconds – froze to the spot. As I ran back across the bottom lawn, I could see from Jezebel's deep and purposeful wing beat that she meant business. Terrible thoughts crowded my mind. What was I thinking of, to allow the boys to watch such a dangerous, semi-trained bird? What was I doing flying her anyway when I knew she was a liability? If she got hold of one of the boys and hurt him, I would never forgive myself.

As Jezebel stormed towards them, the boys came to life. Leaping to their feet, they shot behind the thick trunk of the cedar tree. The eagle went after them. As I reached the slope with my lungs burning, I saw the boys reappear. With Jezebel hard on their heels, they started to circle the tree, John showing a surprising turn of speed considering the impediment of his plaster cast. Unable to sustain flight in such tight circles, Jezebel dropped to the ground and chased them on foot.

I arrived at the tree when the trio was on its fourth circuit. As the boys shot past me, I intercepted Jezebel and tripped her up. Turning her wrath on to me she bounced up at my legs. I hopped backwards and managed with difficulty to fend her off while I got a piece of food into my glove. She jumped up on to my fist, her crest raised in fury. The boys collapsed in a heap on the ground. To my relief, they were laughing. I stopped flying Jezebel after that.

Both John and Luke were desperately keen to get hawks of their own. For Luke, this was not a problem: his parents' house was detached with a large garden backing on to a park. His father was willing to help him build a weathering and mews in the garden and I knew that any hawk he owned would be flown regularly and well cared for. In contrast, John's home had no garden. The family lived in rooms over the pub. Despite the fact that both John's parents were keen for him to get a hawk of his own and immerse himself in falconry, and John himself was desperate for a buzzard, the problem of space seemed insurmountable. In the days leading up to John's departure, I questioned him in detail about his home surroundings.

'We do 'ave a flat roof over the pub kitchen,' John told me.

'How big is it?' I asked.

''Bout twelve feet by ten.'

I telephoned his father.

'Do you know, I never thought of that roof. I reckon I could build a shelter for the hawk out there,' his father told me. 'Only trouble is, John'd have to get in and out by climbing through the kitchen window.'

Two weeks after John returned home, his father telephoned me to report that he and John had completed the construction of a weathering on the flat roof.

'I've never seen John so dedicated to anything before,' he told me. 'He helped me every step of the way. We even hauled loads of pebbles for the base of the shelter from the beach in barrow loads and lugged them upstairs in buckets. It was 'ard work, but he really applied himself.'

Four weeks after that, during which time his father drove him to see us most weekends, John got a young buzzard from a breeder. He trained it on the sea front and telephoned me regularly to report on its progress. I was thrilled to hear the enthusiasm in his voice, but the best call of all came from his mother, six months later.

'I would never have believed the change in John if I wasn't seeing it on a daily basis,' she told me. 'When I 'phoned you to ask if you'd take him on the course, it was just a dream that this might be the one thing that would turn him round, but it has.

242

He hasn't been in trouble since. This buzzard has made all the difference in the world to him. I'm calling to say thank you.'

That autumn, we attended a trade fair in London on behalf of the castle. The castle's stand at the exhibition was organized by Max. Previous rifts forgotten, Steve and Max had been back on good terms for some years now and Max was keen for us to ensure that we gave a good account of ourselves to the tour operators and travel specialists who attend the fair. To attract as much attention as possible, Max was going to wear full armour and we agreed to take Hampton, one of the Potters' offspring, and Sebastian, a young captive-bred Golden Eagle which we had recently acquired. Lord Massereene had taken an interest in the proceedings and was threatening to put in an appearance in the afternoon.

'I hope he keeps well away,' Max said with feeling. 'He'll be more trouble than he's worth. He's useless at promotion – nobody can understand a bleedin' word he says, which is probably just as well anyway. He should leave it to us – at least we know what we're doing.'

When we arrived at the exhibition, I was surprised by the number of stands. Most of the leading country houses, castles and wildlife parks in the country were represented. I was even more surprised to see how many of them were now offering falconry displays as an attraction. One of the wildlife parks had also thought to take along hawks, but their buzzard and small owl turned out to be no match for the pulling power of Hampton and Sebastian. During the morning, our stand was thronged by buyers and other exhibitors who wanted to get a closer view of the two of them. Holding Hampton on my fist and talking to buyers packed four deep around the stand, I heard Lord Massereene's voice from the rear.

'Trying to get through – I'm the owner, y'see – yes – thank you.'

243

He eased his way through the crowd and stepped over the barrier. Fresh from the House of Lords, he was wearing a pin-striped suit with a long split down one leg. His trousers gaping and the customary patch of loo paper stuck to his chin with blood, he proceeded to engage buyers in conversation.

'I'm Lord . . . actually own the castle . . . very nice – must come.'

Disjointed snippets of conversation floated back to me as I resumed my question and answer session with a dedicated circle of ardent Hampton fans.

'Why doesn't he eff of out of it?' Max whispered loudly in my ear. 'Look at the state of him – he's a bleedin' embarrassment.'

From the expressions on the faces of the assembled crowd, I felt that if only we could guarantee to have Lord Massereene skulking somewhere in the grounds, the tour operators would probably fly in groups of Americans just to see him.

Our stand was easily the busiest at the exhibition, but travelling home that evening, I felt strangely depressed. Although the response had been gratifying, I had to admit that I was taken aback by the prominence of falconry at other establishments. When we had opened at Chilham, you could count the number of other places boasting falconry on the fingers of one hand. Now, falconry displays seemed to be becoming commonplace.

The following week an American student in his early twenties flew in to attend a three-week falconry course with us. Bryant had worked a thousand man-hours in a hamburger joint to earn the cost of his tuition fees and his return air fare. Widely read on the subject of falconry, he was one of the keenest, most knowledgeable students we had ever had. He was also articulate and outspoken.

'Why are you guys doing these demonstrations?' he asked one day towards the end of his three weeks with us. 'You obviously don't enjoy doing them, so why don't you quit and teach falconry full time? You could open a school and call it the International School of Falconry.'

244

It was one of those ideas which is so blindingly obvious that you cannot believe it has not occurred to you. Steve and I looked at him, open mouthed. It was like a revelation. We knew without even needing to discuss it that this was the future we had been searching for. We could open the first school in the world dedicated to the teaching of falconry.

Whilst believing that we had now identified the end, we had difficulty identifying the means. As usual, my mother came to our aid. Even before we had discussed the idea with her, she came up to see us one evening with Tommy.

'I want to buy you a place of your own,' she told us. 'Tommy has bought a half share in Carpenters from me, so I have some spare money. Although it would come to you eventually, I feel it would be more use to you now.'

We calculated that if the school was to be viable, we needed to find a house with at least three spare bedrooms for students. We also needed a couple of acres of level ground on which to construct hawk aviaries and weatherings. After searching as far afield as Wales and Lincolnshire, we finally found the ideal place fifteen minutes from Chilham, in the village of Stelling Minnis. We settled on 'The British of School of Falconry' as the name of our new venture.

Together, Steve and I went to tell Lord Massereene that we were moving on. I knew he would not be happy.

'Where's the fire, where's the fire?' he greeted us, when we presented ourselves.

We must have looked totally blank.

'You said it was urgent,' he explained. 'I suppose you want a pay rise, Stephen?'

'No, we're leaving,' Steve said, without preamble.

'Damn,' said Lord Massereene sadly. 'Damn – could have told me sooner bloody.'

Shortly before we left Chilham in the February of 1982, Steve and I took the dogs for a walk down to the lake. With the bare branches of the trees glinting unadorned in the pale sunlight, the scene was beautiful. We followed the path round the lake and sat quietly on the bench at the far side, looking back towards the castle. As we sat there, I was transported back twelve years to my morning walks with Wally. As I gazed at the mirror image of the castle in the water, a pair of Canada geese half ran, half flew across the surface, blurring the reflection in their wake. Then they rose into the air. Buoyed up by my hopes for the future, I had the sensation of soaring upwards with them. I was fully fledged. It was time to spread my wings.

ACKNOWLEDGEMENTS

I would like to thank my darling Steve, my mother and Tommy
for their endless patience in checking the draft manuscript, and
Maher Al Tajir for keeping me straight on my Arabic spelling.
I am also deeply indebted to Caroline Knox of John Murray, for
having the courage to take me on to write this book in the first
place, and to both her and Kate Chenevix Trench for their
inspired editing. My grateful thanks, too, must as usual go to my
agent Patrick Walsh for alternately encouraging, bludgeoning
and comforting, as necessary.